PRAI

Living the

Rebecca Lawson truly captur
and unashamedly filled with
"the results of genuine, Spirit-filled living will produce revival." My prayer is that *Living the Christ Life* is one of the books that sparks another spiritual awakening—individually and corporately.

SHANE IDLEMAN

Lead pastor, Westside Christian Fellowship, Lancaster, California
Author, *Oh God, Would You Rend the Heavens?* and *If My People*

The center of our lives is our devotional life. So many times we don't need something new—we need to go back and learn from those who have met with God in the past. From Scripture to the saints of old, this devotional stirs us again to live a life worthy of God's name, fully surrendered to Him. Let it transform you to be fully and completely His so that the world may see again His grace and glory through His church.

JIMMY SIEBERT

Senior pastor, Antioch Community Church, Waco, Texas
Founder and senior leader, Antioch Ministries International
Author, *Passion and Purpose: Believing the Church Can Still Change the World*

Few realize the spiritual profundity that existed between the nineteenth and twentieth centuries at the Keswick Conventions. This collection of devotional readings introduces a new generation to the beauty, joy, and resurrection power that come from living in union with Jesus Christ. If you truly want to walk more closely with Jesus, these classic devotional readings will reinvigorate your faith, challenge your complacency, and refresh your soul.

KATHY MORALES, ED.D, M.DIV

Women's ministry director, Fervent (a Calvary Chapel), Las Vegas, Nevada
Author, *For Such a Time as This* and *Caught Up*

Living the Christ Life is a timeless collection of some of the most inspiring devotions ever written. This compilation is perfect for anyone desiring a deeper walk with Jesus.

DAN CARROLL

Senior pastor, Water of Life Community Church, Fontana, California
Author, *Into the Heart of God*, *Bound to the Heart of God*, and *Trusting the Heart of God*

Living the Christ Life is a resource/book that all Christians will want to read over and over again. Hearing from these spiritual giants of the past will ignite insights and perspectives that they uniquely and powerfully bring.

TOMMY WALKER

Worship leader, Christian Assembly, Eagle Rock, California
Producer and recording artist, *The Pursuit of God: Songs for a Thirsty Soul*, based on A. W. Tozer's celebrated devotional classic *The Pursuit of God*
Author, *He Knows My Name* and *Songs from Heaven*

I cannot think of anything more encouraging than to hear from those who've gone before us the ways the Lord taught them that "living the Christ life" is not only achievable but glorious. Thank you, Rebecca Lawson, for compiling such a wonderful collection of daily readings that will spur on believers to seek Him more and more!

DÁMARIS CARBAUGH

Recording artist, *Giving My Life Away* and *Damaris Live: Not Ashamed*
Sought-after conference speaker in the USA and Latin America
Former featured soloist with Day of Discovery and the Brooklyn Tabernacle Choir

The life-changing truth of Christ in the believer is beautifully highlighted in *Living the Christ Life*. Becky has woven together rich excerpts from classic authors in a thematic way that builds throughout the year's readings. If you desire to experience Jesus, *Living the Christ Life* will be used by the Spirit to nurture your faith and bring you into a greater experience of "not I, but Christ." Having read multiple daily devotionals, I believe that this one ranks with the timeless and the best.

JOHN VAN GELDEREN

President, Revival Focus Ministries, Ann Arbor, Michigan
Author, *The Revival Journey*, *The Liberating Life of Jesus*, and *Friendship with the Holy Spirit*

Living the Christ Life is a goldmine for the hungry-hearted Christian. When one finally discovers the futility of self-will and self-effort, he is ready to learn about the life of Christ within his redeemed soul. The Christ life is the only antidote for the self-life. These Christ-centered and cross-centered devotionals will feed your soul. The insights and liberating truths found here point to the only life worth living—the Christ life.

HAROLD VAUGHAN

President, Christ Life Ministries, Vinton, Virginia
Author, *Protocols for Prayer*, *Forgiveness: How to Get Along with Everybody All the Time*, and *Revival in Our Time*

It is imperative today for every believer in Jesus to nurture his or her roots to go deeper. We hear the phrase "supply line issues" and are tempted to fear. But our mission is far more than personal survival: abiding in Jesus allows us to distribute His love to a spiritually malnourished world. In *Living the Christ Life*, I love month 1, "Becoming Hungry for Christ." What a great launching point—right after the holidays, when everyone is bloated from too much of everything, Becky offers readers the opportunity to focus on what really counts: to be hungry for Christ!

PAUL CLARK

Singer, songwriter, recording artist
A founding father of the Jesus Movement

As a self-proclaimed devotional-holic, I can't wait to add *Living the Christ Life* to my rotation! The book contains some of my favorite authors as well as some who are new to me, so it's a perfect blend. There is a lot of wisdom and understanding to be gained from this "great cloud of witnesses," and anyone, regardless of the depth of his or her faith walk, will grow a deeper understanding of life with God by reading these selections.

JANE ALBRIGHT

Former women's head basketball coach, University of Nevada, Reno
Winner, Fellowship of Christian Athlete's annual Kay Yow Heart of a Coach Award, 2009
Owner, Things Above Christian bookstore, Graham, North Carolina

It is the duty of all who believe that the Lord Jesus Christ is the Savior of the world to follow Him as closely as possible. This means keeping your eyes fixed on Him—on who He is and what He has done. Both the daily reading of the Bible and of books like this will help. If you take your eyes off Christ, you will fall. Fixing your eyes on Jesus is your task! Do it well, and do it continuously!

RICHARD OWEN ROBERTS

One of the world's foremost experts on revival
Founder, International Awakening Ministries

Spiritual hunger for a deeper life in Christ is never out of date. The Keswick Convention may not be familiar to the current generation of believers, but the longing for spiritual power to live the Christian life and effectively serve God is inevitable when we find ourselves powerless and discouraged. To help us pursue a closer walk with God, this valuable book is being offered from the writings of men and women who knew God intimately and lived and preached the victorious life, or the Spirit-filled life, as it was variously called.

LEONA CHOY

Author, *Andrew Murray: The Authorized Biography*

LIVING THE *Christ Life*

LIVING THE *Christ Life*

366 DAILY READINGS BY CLASSIC DEEPER-LIFE AUTHORS

REBECCA ENGLISH LAWSON
GENERAL EDITOR

GLADBOOKS
PRESS

Deeper-Life Authors Featured

Paul Billheimer
William Boardman
Amy Carmichael
Samuel Chadwick
Charles Finney
Norman Grubb
Vance Havner
Roy Hession
Evan Hopkins
F. J. Huegel
J. H. Jowett
Guy King
William Law
J. C. Metcalfe
F. B. Meyer
H. C. G. Moule
Andrew Murray
Watchman Nee
Jessie Penn-Lewis
Hannah Whitall Smith
Corrie ten Boom
Charles Trumbull
Arthur Wallis

With Additional Testimonies of

J. H. Merle d'Aubigné
William Carvosso
Thomas Harford-Battersby
Rees Howells
"Mr. Paul"
Hudson Taylor
C. T. Studd
Hanmer Webb-Peploe

Published by GladBooks Press
Riverside, California
http://gladbooks.net
Printed in the USA

Italics in Scripture quotations are the emphasis of the author.

First edition published 2009

This edition published by special arrangement with CLC Ministries International, Fort Washington, Pennsylvania, USA

ISBN: 979-8-9867175-0-0

Cover and interior design: InsideOut CreativeArts

Cover photo of Derwent Water at the village of Keswick with the mountain Skiddaw in the background, Lake District, Cumbria, UK

Author photo by Greg Schneider

For additional information or to order bulk quantities of this book, please visit http://gladbooks.net or write to 6185 Magnolia Avenue #76, Riverside, CA 92506.

Thus says the L*ORD:*
"Stand in the ways and see,
and ask for the old paths, where the good way is,
and walk in it;
then you will find rest for your souls."

JEREMIAH 6:16

CONTENTS

FOREWORD

Jim Cymbala

The Christian life can only be lived out on a day-by-day basis. Even as Jesus taught us to ask for *daily* bread, so it is with the grace that God grants each new day to those who look to Him in faith. The primary calling that Jesus gave His disciples was simply to "be with Him" (Mark 3:14). That kind of spiritual fellowship can only be experienced one day at a time.

Living the Christ Life, compiled by Rebecca Lawson, has been a great help to me in my attempts to walk with Christ each day. The authors she has chosen and the excerpts selected from their writings provide excellent food for the soul.

I am thankful to God that *Living the Christ Life* is being republished and made available to Christians who feel their need of daily inspiration from God's Word.

PREFACE TO THE 2022 EDITION

I like to read. Some of the books I've read over the years have been interesting or helpful or informative, and I have appreciated them; but my favorite books are the ones that have spoken deeply to my heart.

The authors represented in this book have done just that. Thirteen years ago, when I was asked by CLC Publications to choose excerpts from their classic books for a one-year devotional, I spent several months with authors like Andrew Murray, F. B. Meyer, and Amy Carmichael, among others. The testimonies and teaching of these people who had walked closely with the Lord drove home powerful truths to my spirit day after day. All these authors had one topic in common: abiding in Christ, or living the Christ life. In essence, this is the idea that we must lay aside self and depend on Christ for holiness, service, and victory (see a helpful explanation of this in the April 5 entry by Evan Hopkins). When we do, we will serve in God's power, not our own, and the results will be eternal.

This concept wasn't a generic biblical idea to these authors—it was the basis of their entire lives. Abiding in Christ led Amy Carmichael to give up her life in Ireland and England and devote herself to ministering the gospel to children she rescued from sexual slavery (known more tastefully in her day as temple service). It brought about the powerful outbreaks of revival that Andrew Murray experienced as a pastor in South Africa and led to his prolific teaching and writing ministry that still strengthens and challenges believers today. It gave Corrie ten Boom the power to hold fast to her faith as a prisoner in Ravensbrück concentration camp, forgive her betrayer and captors, and spend the rest of her life taking the message of forgiveness around the world as a "tramp for the Lord." And it enabled Vance Havner, when he was emotionally devastated at the loss of his beloved wife, to write,

> When before the throne we stand in Him complete, all the riddles that puzzle us here will fall into place and we shall know in fulfillment what we now believe in faith—that all things

work together for good in His eternal purpose. No longer will we cry "My God, why?" Instead, "alas" will become "Alleluia," all question marks will be straightened into exclamation points, sorrow will change to singing, and pain will be lost in praise.[1]

Don't we need this kind of overcoming life ourselves? So much today distracts us from the deep things of God, divides us into camps, and discourages us from the work of ministry, but God wants His church to be full of His life and power. In light of His promise that we are more than conquerors, why should we lose time living in our own strength or fall prey to the enemy's schemes that drag us down? As Pastor Jim Cymbala wrote in his book *Storm: Hearing Jesus for the Times We Live In*, "Our time is fixed and much shorter than most of us think."[2] Regardless of our denominational affiliations or views on secondary matters, as we put off self and humbly ask God to fill us afresh, He will surely revive us, individually and corporately, and work through us in our day as He did through others in days past.

When the first edition of *Living the Christ Life* recently went out of print, I was thankful to be given the opportunity to update its look and release a new version. Several people have helped with this process. Thank you, Dave Fessenden and Jim Pitman of CLC Publications, for allowing me to produce a new edition of this book; I am grateful for our years of partnership in publishing books that make Christ known. Thank you to Greg Schneider for your outstanding photography—you are a true professional and a generous giver. Thank you, Jennifer Cullis, for your exacting attention to detail in proofreading; I can always count on you to be thorough. And to Rob Williams of InsideOut CreativeArts, thank you for the beautiful cover and interior design and for going above and beyond in contributing to this project. Thank you as well to each endorser of this volume and especially to Pastor Jim Cymbala of the Brooklyn Tabernacle for writing the foreword. Finally, thank you to my husband, Steve, whose constant encouragement and support have been a huge blessing to me in the shaping of this book.

May this new edition of teachings on the Christ life, which the authors in this devotional so helpfully unfold for us, be used of God to speak deeply to your hearts, as it has to mine, and to revive His people once again.

PREFACE TO THE 2009 EDITION

The compilation of this book fulfills a long-held desire of the publishing team at CLC Publications. For many years CLC has produced books by deeper-life authors such as Amy Carmichael, Andrew Murray, F. B. Meyer, and Roy Hession, to name a few, many of whom were closely associated with the well-known Keswick Convention in the nineteenth and twentieth centuries. Authors from varying backgrounds such as Corrie ten Boom, Vance Havner, and Samuel Chadwick proclaimed the same message of power and victory found in walking closely with Christ. The CLC team felt that a collection of these writings on living the Christ life would make a valuable contribution to the church today.

Some of the authors featured in this book are not well known in our day. Because of that, CLC decided that a compilation of selections from their works would provide a simple and accessible format to those who may be reading them for the first time. We are excited to reintroduce these men and women whose message is as vital today as when it was first written.

We chose excerpts from approximately 120 CLC titles to form a clear presentation of what some call "the deeper Christian life"—essentially living in union with Christ rather than depending on ourselves. We then arranged the entries to build a progressive picture of finding that life: wanting more of Him; trying to be holy and useful; then discovering God's provision through our identification with Christ in His death and resurrection. The results of that identification—increasing rest, an effectual prayer life, and a revived and fruitful church—are seen in the book's later entries.

We edited punctuation and capitalization slightly throughout the book for consistency of style. Very occasionally we adjusted a word or transition for the sake of clarity. Otherwise, the text is unabridged from CLC's most recent editions of these books (as of 2009) and faithful to the authors' original writings.

Many thanks to John Van Gelderen of Revival Focus for allowing us to quote from his article "Keswick: A Good Word or a Bad One?" in the introduction. Thanks go also to Isaac Lemon for his careful proofreading of the manuscript and his helpful observations. Acknowledgement is particularly due to Grace Palmer, who gave many hours helping choose excerpts and offering invaluable feedback on the organization and spiritual content of this book, and to Dick Brodhag, whose amazing patience through many revisions of layout and composition and whose kind, encouraging words have been much appreciated.

INTRODUCTION

One of the greatest tendencies of Christians is to try to live for Christ in our own wisdom and strength. We know that in ourselves we are hopelessly flawed, yet almost without realizing it, we continually strive to do and to become what God requires of us.

This leads to two problems: In our personal lives, we can become discouraged by the ongoing struggle—trying to be holy but continually falling short. And second, in our service for the Lord, we can easily start programs and hold events that fail to produce real spiritual change. Like Moses, we set out to help others, only to realize that the methods we thought so useful may not be producing eternal fruit.

Because this is so common, it's easy to be unaware that we are working in the flesh rather than the Spirit—keeping so busy with meetings and plans that we completely overlook the fact that we lack something deeper. But the fact is that only Christ can live the abundant, victorious life He wants us to have. If it's God's life we want and God's work we want to do, we need to operate in a different way.

This is what Jesus taught. He told us that He came so we could have abundant life (John 10:10)—His life. The apostle Paul later expounded on this, writing repeatedly in his letters about the fullness of life and how to live it. The sixth, seventh, and eighth chapters of Romans especially focus on the fact that we cannot live this life in our own strength but that the Holy Spirit can—and will—live through us, if by faith we receive Him and walk with Him.

The following statement summarizes it well:

> The "Higher Life," the "Deeper Life," the "Victorious Life," the "Spirit-filled Life," the "Christ-Life" is not a new line of teaching. It is not a mere set of doctrines; it is not a set of motions; it is not a conference, a convention, or a movement—it is a Life. That Life is a Person, and His name is Jesus! Jesus is the "Higher Life." Jesus is the "Deeper Life." Jesus is the "Victorious Life." How can it be otherwise?

> Sanctification or holiness by faith is simply accessing the "Holy Life" by faith. It is "I live, yet not I, but Christ liveth in me . . . by faith" (Gal. 2:20). Holiness by faith is accessing the Holy Life of Jesus to empower holy living and serving. It is becoming "partakers of His holiness" (Heb. 12:10), not imitators.
>
> The focus . . . is not that you cannot sin, but that you are able not to sin because of the indwelling Christ. . . . The focus should not be on being defeated, but rather on victory in Christ by faith.[1]

Seekers of a fuller life in Christ became prominent in mid-nineteenth-century Britain and America as a growing dissatisfaction with traditional Christianity was emerging in the church. The 1859 revival in Ireland and meetings held by D. L. Moody in Britain and Ireland in the 1870s, among other events, brought impetus to this increasing desire and sparked the gathering of Christians in Britain and America for focused teaching. Many conventions were founded in the mid to late nineteenth century to propagate the message of living the Christ life.

As a result of this growth of spiritual hunger and appropriation of biblical truths, evangelism and missions exploded from Britain and America. And it's not far-fetched to say that the various revivals that occurred between 1904 and 1910 around the world were fed by this increased spiritual enthusiasm.

Throughout church history men and women have hungered for a deeper walk with Christ. From the Galatians in the early church whom Paul rebuked ("Are you so foolish?") to Martin Luther to George Whitefield to D. L. Moody to the Keswick founders to A. W. Tozer to Corrie ten Boom, the answer has been the same: "Christ in you, the hope of glory" (Col. 1:27).

The results of genuine, Spirit-filled living will produce revival. Abandoning our own efforts in exchange for the powerful work of Christ living in and through us will result in life, joy, rest, increasing spiritual maturity, prayer, a desire for service, and a love for people.

CLC Publications began publishing deeper-life books in 1945, seeking to keep in print these classic teachings on living "the life that is Christ." For nearly a century these books have blessed countless numbers, and it is our prayer that the truths collected from them in this devotional will have the same effect on individuals today.

January

Becoming Hungry for Christ

The Testimony of William Carvosso

William Carvosso became an orphan at age ten and was apprenticed to a farmer. He had little education and knew nothing of the art of writing until he was sixty-five years old. In his youth he was inducted into the mysteries of cock-fighting, wrestling, card-playing, and other pursuits.

At twenty-one years of age, he was brought to Christ. "The moment this resolution was formed in my heart," he says, "Christ appeared within, and God pardoned all my sins and set my soul at liberty. The Spirit Himself now bore witness with my spirit that I was a child of God."

For a time life was peaceful, joyous, and happy, but he soon discovered a deeper need. He described it this way: "My heart appeared to me as a small garden with a large stump in it, which had been recently cut down level with the ground and a little loose dirt spread over it. Seeing something shooting up I did not like, I attempted to pluck it up and discovered the deadly remains of the carnal mind. What I wanted was inward holiness."

One night, about a year after his conversion, he returned from a meeting greatly distressed with a sense of his unholiness and turned aside into a lonely barn to wrestle with God. While kneeling there on the threshing floor, he gained a little light but not enough to burst his bonds and set him free. Shortly afterward, however, in a prayer meeting, his eyes were opened to see clearly. "I felt," he says, "that I was nothing, and Christ was All in All. I now cheerfully received Him in all His roles: my Prophet to teach me, my Priest to atone for me, my King to reign over me. Oh, what boundless, boundless happiness there is in Christ!"

William Boardman, *The Higher Christian Life*

January 1

Lo, I am with you all the days.

Matthew 28:20, YLT

As real and complete and certain as His suretyship was when He bore sin and gave His life for you, so real and certain is the fellowship which He holds out to you when He says, "I am *with you* all the days."

Too often it appears as if it were not true, as if it could not possibly be true. At other times you could not live long if you felt yourself to be so sinful and miserable as you are. And yet it is true that *Jesus is with you*. Only you do not know it, you do not enjoy it, because you do not believe it. But as soon as you learn to rely not upon your own feelings or on your own experience but on what He has promised and to direct your expectations according to faith in that which He has said—namely, that He will be with you—it will become your blessedness. "I am with you." Jesus Himself abides with His own. Oh, the blessed certainty of His presence and love which will not abandon us! He—the Living, the Loving, the Almighty One—He Himself is with us and in a position to make Himself known to us.

"With you all the days"—all the days without one single exception. And thus also all the day. Whether I think of it or not, there He is the whole day—near me, with me. Not on my own faithfulness but in that faithfulness of Yours which awakens my confidence and bestows on me Your own nearness, I have the assurance of an unbroken fellowship with You, my beloved Lord.

Andrew Murray, *The Lord's Table*

JANUARY 2

If when we were enemies we were reconciled to God through the death of His Son, much more, having been reconciled, we shall be saved by His life.

ROMANS 5:10

God makes it quite clear in His Word that to every human need He has but one answer: His Son, Jesus Christ. In all His dealings with us, He works by taking us out of the way and substituting Christ in our place.

The Son of God died instead of us for our forgiveness; He lives instead of us for our deliverance. So we can speak of two substitutions: a Substitute on the cross who secures our forgiveness and a Substitute within who secures our victory. It will help us greatly and save us from much confusion if we keep constantly before us this fact: that God will answer all our questions in one way only, namely, by showing us more of His Son.

WATCHMAN NEE, *A TABLE IN THE WILDERNESS*

January 3

He is the head of the body, the church, who is the beginning, the firstborn from the dead, that in all things He may have preeminence.

Colossians 1:18

In the gospel of God, of Christ, of the apostles, of the prophets, Christ is *all*. No surer test, according to the holy Scriptures, can be applied to anything claiming to be Christian teaching than this: Where does it put Jesus Christ? What does it make of Jesus Christ? Is He something in it, or is He all? Is He the Sun of the true solar system so that every planet gets its place and its light from Him?

Such is Jesus Christ that He cannot but claim to be "all things in all things" to us if we would be Christians indeed. The program of our personal religion must be nothing short of this if we would find in it not merely a law for external performance but an inward joy and force. Christ for us, Christ in us—this is religion at its heart, at its vitals.

It is Christ, glorious and personal; not Christ as a mere formula for certain ideas but the divine-human Lord, "in all things preeminent"—in nature, in grace, in the church, in the soul—for pardon through His cross, for life through His life, for glory through His appearing. To have Him and make use of Him is peace and power and purity. To do without Him is impossible—it is death. To use Him only partially is perpetual unrest and disappointment. He must be "all things in all things"; then there shall be a great calm within, and a great strength and great holiness with it, and at last an "appearing with Him in glory" to crown the process and give it its development forever.

H. C. G. Moule, *Colossian and Philemon Studies*

January 4

I will be like the dew to Israel; he shall grow like the lily,
and lengthen his roots like Lebanon.

HOSEA 14:5

These words [of Hosea 14:5] describe the beginning of everything in the experience of God's children. Dewfall is altogether vital to the life and growth of trees and flowers, and to us the Lord Himself promises to be as the dew. Everything in our lives as Christians comes down to us from Christ as source. He is made unto us wisdom, righteousness, holiness—yes, everything—and there is no human need that we shall find unmet as we receive Him, nor indeed will anything be given to us as a separate gift apart from Him.

"I will be as the dew," He affirms, and in the next half of the verse, Hosea shows how life with this as its foundation takes on a mysterious dual character. In it the blossom of the lily is wonderfully linked with the roots of the cedar—frail beauty and massive strength united in a single plant. Such miracles are wrought by heaven's dewfall alone.

WATCHMAN NEE, *A TABLE IN THE WILDERNESS*

January 5

All the saints in Christ Jesus . . .

PHILIPPIANS 1:1

The description of the Christians is given in terms of their relationship to the Lord Jesus Christ—and that must, of course, ever be remembered to be the true starting point of all Christian experience and all Christian instruction. We do well, in taking up the study of any of the epistles, to inquire carefully into that matter of where we stand in reference to Him.

In a fundamental sense, the epistles are the property of *believers*; they have, except incidentally, nothing to say to the people of the world. Their message is addressed to the church, the members of Christ's body; their teaching is to be grasped and enjoyed only by those who have been truly "born again" by the same Spirit who inspired the writing of the epistles. We are therefore not wasting time if we pause to ask ourselves about our relationship to Christ. Have we indeed received Him into our hearts and lives as our own personal Savior?

Only so do we have legitimate entrance to this treasure house; but if so, we have undisputed access to all its treasure trove. Our relationship to Him then determines both how we get into it and what we get out of it. Note what is said here concerning that relationship, for the terms employed are applicable to all believers—both to Paul and Timothy, who sent forth the epistle, and to the original and all subsequent readers of it, you and me among them.

GUY KING, *PHILIPPIANS: JOY WAY*

January 6

If anyone is in Christ, he is a new creation;
old things have passed away; behold, all things have become new.

2 Corinthians 5:17

I had been living in the fear of death, and I saw Him taking that death for me. My parents loved me very much, and up to that time, to me there were no people like them; but they never suffered death for me. He *did* it. His love for me, as compared with theirs, was as high as the heavens above the earth, and He won my love—every bit of it. He broke me, and everything in me went right out to Him.

Then He spoke to me and said, "Behold, I stand at the door and knock. May I come in to you? Will you accept Me?" "Yes," I replied, and He came in, and that moment I changed. I was born into another world. I found myself in the kingdom of God, and the Creator became my Father.

When I went home, my friend who had accompanied me to the meeting but had seen nothing in it seemed so rough to me. Everyone who was not born again seemed rough. The Savior became everything to me. He was not only the fairest among ten thousand but fairest among millions! That love of His had always been there, but before I saw it, there was no response from me; but He had plenty of response after this. Everything of this world was rough, but everything about Him so holy, pure, and beautiful.

I changed altogether. None of my old friends could understand what had happened. I had no fellowship with natural things. It wasn't a point of doctrine I saw; no, it was Calvary. It wasn't giving a mental assent; no, the veil was taken back, my eyes were opened, and I *saw* Him. That night I saw this world as a cursed place, and the thought came to me that I would never touch it again.

Norman Grubb, *Rees Howells: Intercessor*

January 7

Of Him and through Him and to Him are all things, to whom be glory forever. Amen.

Romans 11:36

Lord God, You are without beginning and without end. For You are Yourself both the Beginning and the End. You are the Eternal, with whom there is no yesterday and no tomorrow. You are Yourself yesterday, today, and forever. With You there is no changeableness or shadow of turning.

Lord, in You alone Your believing people find their comfort and their security. Nothing that we have done or still desire to do, nothing that we are or shall be, can give us rest. But thanks be to Your name, You Yourself, the Eternal, with Your unchangeableness, You are our rest and strength. In You alone and in Your faithfulness does our life become free of all fear.

Father, give me to understand this. Make me to know You as the God who has begun a good work in me. Let Your Spirit seal to me the truth that You receive me as the possession which You have bought for Yourself, which is precious to You and which no one shall pluck out of Your hands. And then teach me, in the midst of all my own weakness and the power of sin within, always to trust and always to exclaim, "He who began a good work in me will complete it!"

Teach me to go forward on my way, full of joy, full of confidence and courage, full of thanksgiving and love. My God, become everything to me—the God who has done everything, the God who will do everything, the God to whom all is due.

Andrew Murray, *The Lord's Table*

JANUARY 8

He who looks into the perfect law of liberty and continues in it . . . will be blessed in what he does.

JAMES 1:25

God meant us to know Himself even as Jesus knew Him in His human life. Such knowledge, unattainable by our own endeavors, is brought within our reach by our blessed Lord. He gives us eternal life in order that we might know the only true God. He bids us stand on Calvary that we may behold the heart of the Father. He reveals God to us in His own life so that to know Him is to know God. And yet how little do we know the Father! We know little about Him, and less of Him by personal intimacy and fellowship.

To take the lowest test—our knowledge of God's Word. While some individual explorers have pressed on into unknown and untrodden lands, the large majority of professing Christians are content with a few familiar and well-trodden patches. They read and read again the same passages in the Gospels, the Psalms, or Isaiah, but they never venture into the unexplored territory beyond. And the saddest point of all is that they have no deeper perception of the words which have become so familiar to them than at the first.

There are many subjects which the bulk of Christian people, by a tacit understanding, refuse to enter. In this respect there is much land to be possessed. Well may we be rebuked by the example of the psalmist, who took days and nights to master his scanty and meager Bible! We have much to learn from Nehemiah and many other characters in Holy Writ, whose prayers and songs are little else than chains of scriptural quotations. Let us mend our ways, not always traverse the well-trodden paths but seek for a completer acquaintance with the entire range of truth as given in God's Word.

F. B. MEYER, *JOSHUA*

January 9

Open my eyes, that I may see wondrous things from Your law.

Psalm 119:18

When I was a schoolgirl, I read James Gall's *Primeval Man Unveiled.* One wonderful day I sat on a stool at the feet of the writer of that book and asked him to explain things I had not understood. I wondered, as I looked up into the face of that old man, at the loving joy I saw there.

I understand that joy better now. I know that there are few joys so great as to be asked, by one in earnest to understand, what the words one has written mean.

Is it not wonderful to think that we may give joy to the Writer of our Book by asking Him to open it to us? We do not think enough of the love of the Spirit of God. Here is a prayer for all who want to enter into the land whose wealth is prepared for us: *Let Thy loving Spirit lead me forth into the land of righteousness.*

May we all be led further and further into that land in this new year.

Amy Carmichael, *Whispers of His Power*

January 10

When He, the Spirit of truth, has come, He will guide you into all truth.

John 16:13

One thing is certain: revelation will always precede faith. Seeing and believing are two principles which govern Christian living. When we see something God has done in Christ, our spontaneous rejoinder is faith's "Thank You, Lord!"

Revelation is always the work of the Holy Spirit, who by coming alongside and opening to us the Scriptures guides us into all the truth. Count on Him, for He is here for this very thing. And when such difficulties as lack of understanding or lack of faith confront you, always address those difficulties directly to the Lord: "Lord, open my eyes. Make this thing clear to me. Help Thou my unbelief!" He will not let such prayers go unheeded.

Watchman Nee, *A Table in the Wilderness*

January 11

My sheep hear My voice, and I know them, and they follow Me.

John 10:27

The written Scriptures and the living human messenger—these two God-given gifts to every believer are among the most precious factors that contribute to our Christian life.

We dare not despise God's messengers. We need again and again the arresting challenge of a truly prophetic spoken word or the calm of mature spiritual instruction. Still less dare we despise God's written Word. The inspired Scriptures of truth are vital to our life and progress, and we would not—we dare not—be without them.

Truly the kingdom is more than these. It involves a recognition of the absolute authority of Christ and a repudiation of every authority but His as final. It demands a personal, firsthand intelligence of the will of God that embraces these other God-given aids but does not end with them.

Christianity is a revealed religion, and revelation is always inward, direct, and personal. That was the lesson Peter had to learn. In the kingdom there is only one Voice to be heard, through whatever medium it speaks. Christianity is not independent of men and books—far from it. But the way of the kingdom is that the "beloved Son" speaks to me personally and directly and that personally and directly I hear Him.

Watchman Nee, *What Shall This Man Do?*

January 12

The kingdom of heaven is like a merchant seeking beautiful pearls who, when he had found one pearl of great price, went and sold all that he had and bought it.

Matthew 13:45-46

A great many Christians delight to read about the Spirit-led life, but that is not enough. It now becomes a matter of the will. I must "buy" it. At what price? Give up *all*! You must sell all to buy the pearl of great price. Come with every hateful sin and every folly, all that temper—plus everything you *love*, your whole life—and place it in the possession of Christ. Die to everything, and be fully given up to God. The Holy Spirit can do His sanctifying work only in the vessel that is wholly yielded.

When a man gives up all, he may look up at the Lord Jesus to whom the Father has given the Holy Spirit, claim the promise, and know that he has received it. Bow before God, the Holy One, in deep humility and submission. Have faith in His promise, His power, His great love, His intimate providence. God, who is a Spirit and gives us the Spirit, will, in this fellowship with Himself, make you a spiritual person.

May God in His mercy open the eyes of all His people. May He bring many to the acceptance of the full Spirit-led life He has provided in Christ Jesus.

Andrew Murray, *The Spiritual Life*

JANUARY 13

Every place that the sole of your foot will tread upon I have given you.

JOSHUA 1:3

Before the children of Israel crossed the Jordan, they had a declaration from God that every place that the sole of their feet should tread upon *had been given them*; but they had to walk over it and take it foot by foot. God did not hand it over to them and say, "Now you have it," so that they had nothing further to do. He said, "I have given it. Now you must take it step by step."

But as we read on, we see how on Joshua's part it was necessary that he should be strong and courageous so as to cooperate with God for the fulfillment of these promises. How the words ring out in power: "Only be thou strong and very courageous, and then shalt thou cause this people to inherit the land." Joshua was responsible for the courage; this is what every child of God must take heed to in the battle of today. We are responsible not to get depressed or discouraged for a moment by yielding to the temptations of the enemy to look away from God.

Joshua is not left in any doubt as to how he is to become full of courage. He is bidden to turn to the commandments of God as written in the Law: "Observe to do according to all the law . . . : turn not from it to the right hand or to the left." Implicit, undeviating obedience to the Word of God. "This book of the law shall not depart out of thy mouth; but thou shalt meditate therein day and night" (Josh. 1:7–8, KJV).

The only way to be strong and very courageous is to be filled with the Word of God and to have the mind full of it by meditating upon it. Not simply reading a little and then putting the Book down but really meditating on God's Word until you know the heart truth of all that is written in the sacred Book.

JESSIE PENN-LEWIS, *THE CONQUEST OF CANAAN*

January 14

The Scriptures . . . testify of Me.

John 5:39

In my early ministry I found that great stress was laid on believing "the articles of faith," and it was held that faith consisted in believing with an unwavering conviction the doctrines about Christ. Hence an acceptance of the doctrines, the *doctrines*, the DOCTRINES of the gospel was very much insisted upon as constituting faith. But these doctrines I had been brought to accept intellectually and firmly before I was converted. And when told to believe, I replied that I did believe—and no argument or assertion could convince me that I did not believe the gospel. And up to the very moment of my conversion, I was not and could not be convinced of my error.

At the moment of my conversion, or when I first exercised faith, I saw my ruinous error. I found that faith consisted not in an intellectual conviction that the things affirmed in the Bible about Christ are true but in *the heart's trust in the person of Christ.* I learned that God's testimony concerning Christ was designed to lead me to trust Christ and that to stop short in merely believing about Christ was a fatal mistake that inevitably left me in my sins.

Now this illustrates the true nature of faith. It does not consist in any degree of intellectual knowledge or acceptance of the doctrines of the Bible. These truths and doctrines reveal God in Christ only so far as they point to God in Christ and teach the soul how to find Him by an act of trust in His person.

When we firmly trust in His person and commit our souls to Him by an unwavering act of confidence in Him for all that He is affirmed to be to us in the Bible, this is faith.

Charles Finney, *Power from On High*

JANUARY 15

Come to Me.

MATTHEW 11:28

From personal conversation with hundreds, and I may say thousands, of Christian people, I have been struck with the application of Christ's words as recorded in the fifth chapter of John to their experience. Christ said to the Jews, "Ye do search the scriptures [for so it should be rendered]; for in them ye think ye have eternal life, and they are they which testify of me. And ye will not come to me, that ye might have life" (John 5:39–40, KJV). They satisfied themselves with ascertaining what the Scriptures said about Christ but did not avail themselves of the light thus received to come to Him by an act of loving trust in His person.

I fear it is true in these days that multitudes stop short in the facts and doctrines of the Bible and do not by any act of trust in Christ's person come to Him concerning whom all this testimony is given. Thus the Bible is misunderstood and abused.

Many, understanding the confession of faith as summarizing the doctrines of the Bible, very much neglect the Bible and rest in a belief of the articles of faith. Others, more cautious and more in earnest, search the Scriptures to see what they say about Christ but stop short and rest in the formation of correct theological opinions. But others love the Scriptures intensely because they testify of Jesus. They search and devour the Scriptures because they tell them who Jesus is and what they may trust Him for. They do not stop short and rest in this testimony but by an act of loving trust go directly to Him—thus joining their souls to Him in a union that receives from Him, by a direct divine communication, the things for which they are led to trust Him. This is certainly Christian experience. This is receiving from Christ the eternal life which God has given us in Him. This is saving faith.

CHARLES FINNEY, *POWER FROM ON HIGH*

JANUARY 16

Lift your eyes now and look from the place where you are—
northward, southward, eastward, and westward; for all the land which you see
I give to you and your descendants forever.

GENESIS 13:14-15

It is difficult to read these glowing words—*northward, and southward, and eastward, and westward*—without being reminded of "the breadth, and length, and depth, and height of the love of Christ, which passeth knowledge." Much of the land of Canaan was hidden behind the ramparts of the hills, but enough was seen to ravish that faithful spirit. Similarly, we may not be able to comprehend the love of God in Christ, but the higher we climb, the more we behold. The upper cliffs of the separated life command the fullest view of that measureless expanse.

In some parts of Scotland's Western Highlands, the traveler's eye is delighted by the clear and sunlit waters of a loch—an arm of the sea running far up into the hills. But as he climbs over the heathery slopes and catches sight of the waters of the Atlantic, bathed in the light of the setting sun, he almost forgets the fair vision which had just arrested him. Thus do growing elevation and separation of character unfold ever richer conceptions of Christ's infinite love and character.

God's promises are ever on the ascending scale. One leads up to another, fuller and more blessed than itself. In Mesopotamia God said, "I will show thee the land"; at Bethel, "This is the land"; here, "I will give thee all the land, and children innumerable as the grains of sand." And we shall find even these eclipsed. It is thus that God allures us to saintliness. Not giving anything till we have dared to act—that He may test us. Not giving everything at first—that He may not overwhelm us. And always keeping in hand an infinite reserve of blessing. Oh, the unexplored remainders of God! Whoever saw His last star?

F. B. MEYER, *ABRAHAM*

January 17

This is the testimony: that God has given us eternal life, and this life is in His Son.

1 John 5:11

Many persons make the mistake of thinking that they can measure the certainty of their salvation by their feelings. It is the Word of God that is their foundation, and therefore it is essential for the Christian to have a practical knowledge of the Bible.

One of the enemy's favorite darts is, "It is not true that you are really saved." This must be met with Scripture, such as this in 1 John 5:12: "He that hath the Son hath life; and he that hath not the Son of God hath not life."

Another form of attack that Satan uses is to bring to the memory the weaknesses and sins of the past and then to suggest that because of them, we can never be called a faithful follower of Christ. No amount of reasoning or argument can overcome this temptation but only the Word of God. It says in 1 Corinthians 10:13 that "there hath no temptation taken you but such as is common to man: but God is faithful, who will not suffer you to be tempted above that ye are able; but will with the temptation also make a way to escape, that ye may be able to bear it."

The third attack is one that tries to rob the Christian of his assurance of forgiveness. The Bible answers this in 1 John 1:9, where we read, "If we confess our sins, he is faithful and just to forgive us our sins, and to cleanse us from all unrighteousness." What a gracious provision!

The Word of God is like a checkbook with all the promises made out in our names and signed by Jesus Christ at the very moment we are born again into the family of God. How can we learn to cash our checks? We must know the promises.

Corrie ten Boom, *Plenty for Everyone*

January 18

I have come that they may have life, and that they may have it more abundantly.

John 10:10

These two sons represent two classes of Christians: the prodigal—away backslidden; the elder son—out of full fellowship with God. They were alike poor, and the elder son needed as great a change as did the prodigal.

Ask yourself, "What is the reason I am not enjoying full blessing?" Come to God and say, "Why is it I never live the life You want me to live?"

You will find the answer in our story. The elder son had an unchildlike spirit and entertained wrong thoughts about his father; and if you had known the real character of your Father, your life would have been all right.

A dear minister told me once that an abundant life was not for everybody, that it was of God's sovereignty to give this to whomsoever He pleased. Friends, there is no doubt as to God's sovereignty. He dispenses His gifts as He will. We are not all Pauls or Peters; places at the right and left hand of God are prepared for whomsoever He will. But this is not a matter of divine sovereignty; it is a question of child's heritage. The Father's love offers to give to every child in actual experience His full salvation.

Oh, do believe in the love, the willingness, and the power of God to give you full salvation, and a change must surely come.

Andrew Murray, *Divine Healing*

January 19

Let us pursue the knowledge of the Lord.

Hosea 6:3

If we know comparatively little of the Bible, we know less of God. Some of us dwell on one trait of His character in complete ignorance of others. We magnify His mercy at the expense of His righteousness or His justice at the cost of His grace. Our knowledge of Him, moreover, is borrowed from hearsay evidence and from the reports of others. We do not hear and know Him for ourselves.

We are not content to know at secondhand the symphonies of Beethoven or the pictures of Murillo. And we ought not to rest content till we can say with the patriarch, "I have heard of thee by the hearing of the ear: but now mine eye seeth thee." Oh, to know God, to follow on to know Him, until He break on our hearts as the morning or as the early rain! There would be a new meaning in life if we began to explore the being of God. There is much land here to be possessed.

F. B. Meyer, *Joshua*

January 20

Jesus said to him, "Go your way; your son lives." So the man believed the word that Jesus spoke to him, and he went his way.

John 4:50

You cannot separate God from His Word. No goodness or power can be received separately from God, and if you want to get into this life of godliness, you must take time for fellowship with God.

People sometimes tell me, "My life is one of such scurry and bustle that I have no time for fellowship with God." A missionary said to me, "People do not know how we missionaries are tempted. I get up at five o'clock in the morning, and there are the natives waiting for their orders for work. Then I have to go to school and spend hours there; and then there is other work, and sixteen hours rush along, and I hardly get time to be alone with God." Ah, there is the snare!

Go to the God of omnipotence and the God of the Word. Deal with God as that nobleman dealt with the living Christ. Why was he able to believe the word that Christ spoke to him? Because in the very eyes and tones and voice of Jesus, the Son of God, he saw and heard something which made him feel that he could trust Him. And that is what Christ can do for you.

Do not try to stir and arouse faith from within. You cannot. Look into the face of Christ, and listen to what He tells you. Look up into the face of your loving Father, and take time every day with Him, and begin a new life with the deep emptiness and poverty of one who has nothing and who waits to receive everything from Him; with the deep restfulness of one who rests on the omnipotent Jehovah. And try God, and prove Him if He will not open the windows of heaven and pour out such a blessing that there shall not be room to receive it.

Andrew Murray, *Absolute Surrender*

January 21

He Himself often withdrew into the wilderness and prayed.

Luke 5:16

What we need so specially in these hurrying times is a deeper entrance of our souls into the secret of the presence of the Lord, which is the secret of His power on us.

We must live upon Jesus Christ. We must, in the rule and habit of our lives, watch over times of solemn, sacred, blessed intercourse with Him in secret. We must, despite all the influences of our day, make time for thoughtful prayer, for reverent search into His Word, for recollection of our treasures in Him—time to exercise the more deliberate acts of a living faith in His great promises and in the unseen realities of the things eternal.

It is fatally easy to think that we are living up to our creed when our creed is held without life—a thing far different from the creed of the glory and salvation of Christ so known by the soul that it holds the holder.

When we see *Him* in deed and in truth, what words can fully tell the gladness and the freedom? But in that same consciousness, as we behold Him, we are made aware in our inmost souls of our own unworthiness and of the progress to which we are always called in a perpetual repentance.

H. C. G. Moule, *The Second Epistle to the Corinthians*

JANUARY 22

You search the Scriptures, for in them you think you have eternal life; and these are they which testify of Me. But you are not willing to come to Me that you may have life.

JOHN 5:39–40

One may study the Bible in an academic way and never know its Christ. To be an expert in a biography is not to know the subject of the biography. And greater is the condemnation if we know the Bible and know not Christ. The heathen has not that condemnation. To read travel folders is not to travel! All roads in the book lead to Christ; but do you travel the road?

At the grave of Lazarus, Jesus said to Martha, "Thy brother shall rise again." She said, "I know that he shall rise again in the resurrection at the last day." Martha was orthodox; she was correct in her doctrine, a good fundamentalist. But our Lord changed the emphasis from the doctrine to the Person: "I am the resurrection, and the life: he that believeth in me, though he were dead, yet shall he live: and whosoever liveth and believeth in me shall never die. Believest thou this?" He made the resurrection not *something* to believe but *someone* to believe, and it brought personal confession from Martha: "I believe that thou art the Christ, the Son of God, which should come into the world." One may know doctrine and not know Him. It is not he that believes in the resurrection but he that believes in Him who rose who is saved.

Certainly one who comes to Him will read the Bible and believe doctrine. But back of all these stands Christ Himself. The devil will have men become theologically orthodox if only they do not touch Christ. And one may come *almost* to Christ! Jostle Him in the crowd but never touch Him and feel His virtue: this is *almost*. Be sure you get through to Jesus!

VANCE HAVNER, *REFLECTIONS ON THE GOSPELS*

JANUARY 23

They constrained Him, saying, "Abide with us. . . ." And He went in to stay with them. . . . Then their eyes were opened and they knew Him.

LUKE 24:29-31

When "Jesus himself drew near," their eyes were restrained, and they didn't recognize Him. How often Jesus comes near to show Himself to us, but we are so slow of heart to believe what the Word has declared.

But as the Lord spoke with them, their hearts began to burn within them, even though they never thought it might be Him. It is often the same today—the Word becomes precious to us in the fellowship of the saints; our hearts are stirred with a new vision of what Christ's presence may be; and yet our eyes are restrained, and we fail to see Him.

When the Lord acted as though He would have gone farther, their request, "Abide with us," constrained Him. What led our Lord to reveal Himself to these two men? Nothing less than this: their intense devotion to their Lord. Despite our ignorance and unbelief, if we have a burning desire that longs for Him above everything else, a desire that is fostered by the Word, we may count on Him to make Himself known to us. It is to strong desire and constraining prayer that Christ is certain to reveal Himself.

ANDREW MURRAY, *SECRETS OF INTERCESSION AND PRAYER*

January 24

From that time many of His disciples went back. . . . But Simon Peter answered Him, "Lord, to whom shall we go? You have the words of eternal life."

John 6:66–68

Jesus is the bread of God. Bread furnishes to our digestions what the wheat plant has absorbed from sun and earth. Similarly, our Lord brings to us the wealth of the eternal and infinite God in such a manner that His words of life and the living presence of the Spirit in our hearts convey to our receptive natures that eternal life which was with the Father before all worlds—that life which was manifested to Peter and the rest, and through them to the world. We know that bread nourishes us. So with our Lord. We know and are sure because we have handled, tasted, and felt.

Though there is mystery in His words which repels superficial followers, that very mystery is an additional reason for our faith. They go away because they do not understand; but we are attracted because, though we do not understand, we find that there is a fitness in the mystery of our own profound experience being met by an equal mystery in Him.

A Christ whom we could absolutely fathom, measure, diagnose, weigh, and analyze would be no Christ for us. We are sensible of desires for joy unspeakable, peace that passeth understanding, and love that passeth knowledge; and we find Him always before us. Deep calls unto deep and finds a response. He satisfies. He does better than we can ask or think. For brass He brings gold, and for iron silver, and for wood brass, and for stones iron. He is always leading to fresh fountains of water of life. Eye hath not seen nor heart conceived what He has in store for those that love Him.

Oh, my heart, with thy heights and depths and insatiable longings, thou hast found more than thy match in Jesus! To whom else canst thou go?

F. B. Meyer, *Peter*

January 25

When Moses came down from Mount Sinai, . . . his face shone.

Exodus 34:29

We are justified by the highest authority in deriving spiritual lessons from this incident in the life of the great lawgiver. The apostle expressly refers to it when he says that we all may, with unveiled face, behold the glory of the Lord and be transformed (2 Cor. 3:13–18). That blessed vision which of old was given only to the great leader of Israel is now within reach of each individual believer. The gospel has no fences to keep off the crowds from the mount of vision; the lowliest and most unworthy of its children may pass upward where the shining glory is to be seen.

"Oh that I knew where I might find him!" "My soul longeth, yea, even fainteth for the courts of the Lord; my heart and my flesh crieth out for the living God." "My soul thirsteth for thee." The very presence of these intense yearnings for Himself—for face-to-face fellowship and intercourse—are the herald symptoms, the premonitory signs, that within our reach there is the possibility of an intercourse with God which up till now our hearts have not conceived.

And if we garner every opportunity, cultivate every faculty, and keep our faces ever toward the mountain of communion, we shall infallibly find that the heart which yearns for the vision shall not be left without the vision for which it yearns and that the yearning is the unconscious awakening of the soul to the fact that it is standing on the threshold of the highest privilege possible to man.

F. B. Meyer, *Moses*

JANUARY 26

Your love is better than wine. . . . Your name is ointment poured forth.

SONG OF SOLOMON 1:2–3

We cannot tell how much time may elapse after receiving new life from the Lord before a believer begins to feel desires for fuller measures of love's relationship. But we know that such desires do arise in the redeemed ones after having been awakened to life by the Holy Spirit. Subsequently a condition begins to stir within which expresses itself in thoughts of pursuing Christ for a more realizing and satisfying sense of His love. This marks the starting point of real spiritual progress. It is an inward spiritual longing for the Lord Himself.

How is it, we may ask, that one is able to have such intense spiritual longing for the Lord Jesus Christ? The answer lies in spiritual vision. The Holy Spirit is able to give a vision of the glorious person of the Lord Jesus by which we love Him for Himself and are drawn to Him by virtue of the greatness of His person and the worth of His name.

When He was here on earth, men did not smell much of that sweet fragrance, but since His ascension to the throne, there are those who have done so enough to love Him reverently. Thus the revelation of the glorious person of the Lord Jesus is not only what causes *praise* to spring forth but what inspires men to really *love* Him.

WATCHMAN NEE, *SONG OF SONGS*

January 27

Delight yourself also in the Lord.

Psalm 37:4

True religion is a thing of the heart, an inward life. It is only as the desire of the heart is fixed upon God—the whole heart seeking *for* God, giving its love and finding its joy *in* God—that a man can draw near to God.

The heart of man was expressly planned and created and endowed with all its powers that it might be capable of receiving and enjoying God and His love. A man can have no more of religion or holiness or love or salvation or of God than he has in his heart. As much as a man has of the inward heart religion, so much has he of salvation, and no more. As far as Christ through His Spirit is within the heart making the thoughts and will like-minded with Himself, so far can a man's worship and service be acceptable to God.

God asks for the *heart*. Alas, how many Christians serve Him still with the service of the old covenant! There are seasons for Bible reading and praying and churchgoing. But when one notices how speedily and naturally and happily, as soon as it is freed from restraint, the heart turns to worldly things, one feels how little there is of the heart in it—it is not the worship of a true heart, of the *whole* heart. The heart, with its life and love and joy, has not yet found in God its highest good.

The true heart is nothing but true consecration—the spirit that longs to live wholly for God, that gladly gives up everything that it may live wholly for Him, and that above all yields up itself, as the key of the inner life, into His keeping and rule.

Andrew Murray, *Let Us Draw Near*

JANUARY 28

There is none upon earth that I desire besides You.

PSALM 73:25

The great lack of our spiritual life is that we need more of God. We have accepted salvation as His gift, but we have not comprehended that the object of our salvation—and its chief blessing—is to bring us into that close relationship with God for which we were created and in which our glory in eternity will be found.

All that God has done in making a covenant for His people is designed to teach them to trust in Him, to delight in Him, to be one with Him. It cannot be otherwise. If God is indeed the very fountain of goodness and glory, of beauty and blessedness, then the more we have of His presence, the more we conform to His will, the more we are engaged in His service, the more we have Him ruling and working in us, the more truly happy we shall be. If God is indeed the owner and author of life and strength, of holiness and happiness, and can alone give and work this in us, then the more we trust and depend on Him, the stronger and holier and happier we shall be.

The only *true* life is one that brings us every day nearer to God and makes us give up everything to have more of Him. No obedience can be too strict, no dependence too absolute, no confidence too implicit to a person who is learning to count God Himself his chief good, his exceeding joy.

ANDREW MURRAY, *THE TWO COVENANTS*

JANUARY 29

Do you not know yourselves, that Jesus Christ is in you?—
unless indeed you are disqualified.

2 CORINTHIANS 13:5

It was much for the apostle Paul to learn that Jesus of Nazareth was in very deed the Son of the Highest and that the Christ must suffer and be the first by His resurrection from the dead to proclaim light unto the people and the Gentiles; much to be taught that remission of sins and the heritage of a holy life were the gift of God to the open hand of faith; much to discover that there was no distinction between Jew and Greek but that the same God was Lord of all and rich to all. But more than all was the unveiling of the indwelling Christ, living literally within him by His Spirit, so that while he was in Christ, Christ was also in him, as the branch has its place in the vine and the vine lives through the branch.

O soul of man, has this revelation ever been your experience? Do you know that Christ is in you? If you truly believe in Him, there is no doubt of it. And yet you may be in ignorance of this transcendent possession. Ask God to reveal His Son in you, to make you know experientially the riches of the glory of this mystery. He will rend the veil of the inner life in twain from the top to the bottom and in the most holy place of your spirit disclose the Shekinah of His eternal presence. Two conditions only must be fulfilled: you must be prepared to yield your own will to the cross, and to wait before God in the silence and solitude of your spirit.

God was pleased to make this known to Saul of Tarsus. He will be equally pleased to make it known to you, because He lives to glorify His Son and afford the full measure of blessedness to His children.

F. B. MEYER, *PAUL*

January 30

Having boldness to enter the Holiest by the blood of Jesus, . . . let us draw near.

HEBREWS 10:19–22

God does in very deed mean that every child of His should always dwell in His presence.

Oh, the blessedness of a life in His holy presence! Here the Father's face is seen and His love tasted. Here His holiness is revealed and the soul made partaker of it. Here the sacrifice of love and worship and adoration, the incense of prayer and supplication, is offered in power.

Here the soul, in God's presence, grows into more complete oneness with Christ and into more entire conformity to His likeness. Here, in union with Christ in His unceasing intercession, we are emboldened to take our place as intercessors who can have power with God and prevail. Here the outpouring of the Spirit is known as an ever-streaming, overflowing river from under the throne of God and the Lamb. Here the soul mounts up as on eagles' wings, its strength is renewed, and imparted are the blessing and power and love with which God's priests can go forth to bless a dying world.

Here each day we may experience the fresh anointing with which we go forth to be the bearers and the witnesses and the channels of God's salvation to men—the living instruments through whom our blessed King works out His will and final triumph. Child of God, the Father opens unto you the Holiest of All and says, "Let this now be your home." What shall our answer be?

ANDREW MURRAY, *LET US DRAW NEAR*

January 31

I will put My law in their minds, and write it on their hearts; and I will be their God, and they shall be My people.

Jeremiah 31:33

Do not pass over these words [of Jeremiah 31:33] lightly. They express the very highest experience of the covenant relationship. It is only when God's people learn to love and obey His law, when their hearts and lives are together wholly devoted to Him and His will, that He can be to them the altogether inconceivable blessing that these words express: *"I will be your God."*

He is saying, "All I am and have as God shall be yours. All you can need or wish for in a God I will be to you. In the fullest meaning of the word, I, the Omnipresent, will be ever present with you in all My grace and love. I, the Almighty One, will each moment work all in you by My mighty power. I, the Thrice-Holy One, will reveal My sanctifying life within you. I will be your God. *And you shall be My people,* saved and blessed, ruled and guided and provided for by Me, known and seen to be indeed the people of the Holy One, the God of glory."

We need to give our hearts time to meditate and wait for the Holy Spirit to work in us all that these words mean.

Andrew Murray, *The Two Covenants*

February

Discovering Our Need for Christ

The Testimony of J. H. Merle d'Aubigné

J. H. Merle d'Aubigné, a noted author and church historian, was born into a French family in exile in Geneva, the home of Calvin and the stronghold of the Reformation.

While studying at the university in Geneva, he was converted through the ministry of the Scottish nobleman and evangelist Robert Haldane. Haldane had a reputation for talking about the Bible, which seemed very strange to d'Aubigné and his friends, who didn't think the Bible was relevant. The students met Mr. Haldane at a private home and heard him read from Romans about the sinfulness of man. D'Aubigné had never been taught this doctrine and was astonished to hear of men being sinful in nature, but he was clearly convinced by the passages read to him.

He said to Mr. Haldane, "Now I do indeed see this doctrine in the Bible."

"Yes," Haldane replied, "but do you see it in your own heart?"

It was a simple question, but it hit home, pricking his conscience sharply. He realized that his heart was corrupt and knew from the Word of God that he could be saved by faith alone in Jesus Christ.

After his conversion, d'Aubigné completed his course at the university at Geneva, was ordained, and went to Germany. There he pursued further academic achievements and spent four years as the pastor of a French church at Hamburg. Several years passed before he came to the point where the Lord gave him the final full knowledge of Jesus as All in All.

This occurred when d'Aubigné joined two former classmates and fellow converts at an inn in Kiel to begin a trip to Copenhagen. Steamboats were irregular, which meant they were detained at the hotel for a few days. While waiting for the steamboat, they devoted part of their time to reading the Word of God together.

D'Aubigné was at that time in the midst of a deep spiritual struggle. He had confided his doubts to a Bible professor at the university in Kiel. D'Aubigné says, "I asked him to explain several passages of Scripture for my satisfaction. The old doctor would not enter into any detailed solution of my difficulties. 'If I succeeded in ridding you of them,' he said to me, 'others would soon arise; there is a shorter, deeper, more complete way of annihilating them. Let Christ really be the Son of God to you, the Savior, the Author of eternal life! Be firmly settled in His grace, and then these difficulties of detail will never stop you! The light of Christ will chase away all your darkness.' The old doctor had shown me the way: I saw it was the right one, but to follow it was a hard task."

D'Aubigné and his friends began studying Ephesians at the inn at Kiel and eventually reached the end of the third chapter. As he read "Now to Him who is able to do exceedingly abundantly above all that we ask or think, according to the power that works in us" (Eph. 3:20), he realized that this was the truth he needed to claim.

"This expression fell on my soul as a revelation from God. 'He can do by His power,' I said to myself, 'above all we ask, above all that we even think—no, exceedingly abundantly above all!' A full trust in Christ for the work to be done in my poor heart now filled my soul.

"From that time forward," he concluded, "I understood that all my own efforts were of no use; that Christ was able to do all by His 'power that works in us'; and the habitual attitude of my soul was to lie at the foot of the cross, crying to Him, 'Here am I, tied hand and foot, unable to move, unable to do the least thing to get away from the enemy who oppresses me. Do all Yourself. I know that You will do it. . . .' I was not disappointed."

WILLIAM BOARDMAN, *THE HIGHER CHRISTIAN LIFE*

February 1

I find then a law, that evil is present with me, the one who wills to do good. . . .
O wretched man that I am! Who will deliver me from this body of death?

Romans 7:21-24

A study of Christian biography reveals the fact that the great saints of the church all have, with few exceptions, experienced a time when each panted after a fuller participation in the life of God. Some may speak of it as sanctification; others dwell upon the aspect of rest and speak of the "rest of faith." The modern emphasis seems to be upon its victorious aspects—it is the "victorious life." Or we might speak of it as the "abundant life."

Be that as it may, the fact remains that sooner or later the Christian is awakened to a sense of the sin of "selfhood." It is the Holy Spirit who works in the believer this conviction of the sin of a divided heart. He shows the believer how tragically self-will has thwarted Christ's purpose to bring him into utter union with Himself. He reveals the awful consequences of the self-life in its enmity to Christ and its power to choke the life of one's spirit. The believer sees that though he has been rooted into Christ, yet he has been drawing more from the old roots. He begins to understand Romans 7. The secret cry of his heart also becomes, "O wretched man that I am! Who will deliver me from this body of death?"

This marks a crisis. The hour has come for a fresh revelation of the scope and efficacy of Christ's redemptive work. The believer's eyes are now to be opened to the meaning of the deeper aspects of the cross of Christ.

F. J. Huegel, *Bone of His Bone*

February 2

The heart is deceitful above all things, and desperately wicked.

JEREMIAH 17:9

We do not think, we do not care to know, how much evil lies within. We read with listless interest the terrible description given by One who could not exaggerate (Mark 7:21–22) and attach a vague meaning to other words which characterize the human heart as "desperately wicked." And thus we do not feel so bad. We will not truly verify those words or realize how evil our nature is or what a dying need we have for God until we have been exposed to some searching test which shall reveal us to ourselves. Temptation is such a test.

God our Father permits us to be tempted, to lead us to see the hidden evils of our heart—to hold up a mirror before us in which we may behold what manner of people we are and to make us so sensible of our own worthlessness and deformity as to drive us to hand ourselves over to Him.

If you are truly desirous of ascending the higher reaches of Christian thought and life, you must not be astonished if, in answer to your prayer for more grace and life, your heavenly Lover should take some unexpected means of showing you what you are. To know oneself, and to despair of oneself, is to come within the sweep of that gracious power which can fashion a temple column out of a bruised reed, and a noble vessel out of a lump of clay, and an Israel out of a Jacob.

F. B. MEYER, *ISRAEL*

February 3

If we died with Christ, we believe that we shall also live with Him.

Romans 6:8

I belong to the race of Adam, and I have only Adam in me. Not only is my conduct bad, but I am bad. The man himself is wrong and not merely his actions.

As young Christians, we take a long time to learn this. Only after bitter experience does it dawn on us that it is no mere question of dropped goods but of the faultiness of the bag containing them. If we find one thing after another dropping out of our pockets, we eventually give up putting them back in there. We feel around instead to see if perchance the pocket has a hole in it! It is the unfailing recurrence of our sins of hasty speech, quick temper, avid self-seeking, and so on that, even when we know God's forgiveness, exposes the fact that the trouble is within ourselves.

God does not say, "The soul that sins must get his sins cleansed"; He says, "The soul that sins must die." "He who has died," says Paul, "has been freed [acquitted] from sin" (Rom. 6:7). There is no other remedy. In the sight of God we must die.

But what sort of salvation would be ours if we were to end there? We must not only *die* in God's eyes; we must *rise again*. But surely too there must be a new position. I must not only *live*, but I must live *for God*; and He is in heaven, so I must *ascend* there. Thus there must be a death, a resurrection, and an ascension before the trouble I have inherited from Adam is reversed.

How can this be? How can I die, and be raised, and ascend to where God is? The simple answer is that I cannot. There is only one solution. It is God's work that has placed me in Christ Jesus. It is nothing that I have done or could ever do. And everything for my salvation stems from the fact that God has done it.

Watchman Nee, *Changed into His Likeness*

FEBRUARY 4

He who does the truth comes to the light.

JOHN 3:21

One of the devil's greatest weapons has always been lying propaganda. It is the way by which he conditions men to disobedience. He wove a web of lies around man in the garden of Eden, and he has been doing so ever since.

The devil is still telling us that we are good people and devoted Christians and that there is nothing to be concerned about in our lives. And the tragedy is that we keep believing him. The result is that we have lost sight of things as they really are and are now living in a realm of complete illusion about ourselves.

Jesus says from the cross, "See here your own condition by the shame I had to undergo for you." If the moment the Holy One took our place and bore our sins He was condemned by the Father and left derelict in the hour of His sufferings, what must our true condition be to occasion so severe an act of judgment!

You and I may give one another the impression of being earnest, godly Christians, but before the cross we have to admit that we are not that sort of person at all. At Calvary the naked truth is staring down at us all the time, challenging us to drop the pose and own the truth.

In that place of humble truthfulness about ourselves, we shall find peace with God and man, for there we shall find Jesus afresh and lay hold as never before on His finished work for our sin upon the cross. Simple honesty, that is, "doing truth" about our sins, will put us right with God and man through the blood of Christ, where all the "doing good" in the world will not.

ROY HESSION, *WE WOULD SEE JESUS*

February 5

See if there is any wicked way in me.

Psalm 139:24

Anything that springs from self, however small it may be, is sin. Self-energy or self-complacency in service is sin. Self-pity in trials or difficulties; self-seeking in business or Christian work; self-indulgence in one's spare time; sensitiveness, touchiness, resentment, and self-defense when we are hurt or injured by others; self-consciousness, reserve, worry, fear—all spring from self and make our cups unclean.

Some may be inclined to question whether it is right to call such things as self-consciousness, reserve, and fear sins. "Call them infirmities, disabilities, temperamental weaknesses if you will," some have said, "but not sins. To do so would be to get us into bondage."

The reverse, however, is true. If these things are not sins, then we must put up with them for the rest of our lives—there is no difference. But if these and other things like them are indeed sins, then there is a Fountain for sin, and we may experience cleansing and deliverance from our sins if we put them immediately under His precious blood the moment we are conscious of them. And they *are* sins. Their source is unbelief and an inverted form of pride, and they have hindered and hidden Him times without number.

If we will allow Him to show us what is in our cups and then give it to Him, He will cleanse them in the precious blood that still flows for sin. That does not mean mere cleansing from the guilt of sin or even from the stain of sin—though thank God both of these are true—but from the sin itself, whatever it may be. And as He cleanses our cups, so He fills them to overflowing with His Holy Spirit.

Roy Hession, *The Calvary Road*

FEBRUARY 6

We have become partakers of Christ.

HEBREWS 3:14

One cannot make a study of the New Testament without experiencing something of the nature of a shock in view of the glaring difference between the Christian life as we customarily live it and the ideal set forth by the Master.

We are to walk as Jesus walked (1 John 2:6). We are to love our enemies (Matt. 5:44). We are to forgive as Jesus forgave—even as He, in the shame and anguish of the cross, looked down upon those who blasphemed while they murdered Him and forgave (Col. 3:13). We are to be aggressively kind toward those who hate us; yes, we are actually to pray for those who despitefully use us (Matt. 5:44). We are to be overcomers—*more* than conquerors (Rom. 8:37). Enough! We dare go no further. It would only increase our shame and our pain. We stand indicted.

Why does not the Savior, so tender and so understanding, so loving and so wise, make requirements more in keeping with human nature? Why does He not demand of us what we might *reasonably* attain? He bids us soar, yet we have no wings. Is there a way out? Yes, there is. Paul found it—we can all find it!

We have been proceeding upon a false basis. We have conceived of the Christian life as an imitation of Christ. It is not an *imitation* of Christ. It is a *participation* in Christ.

To proceed on the basis of imitation will plunge us into just the sort of "slough of despond" Paul found himself in when he wrote Romans 7. Only when Christ nullifies the force of my inherent "self-life" and communicates to me a divine life does Christian living in its true sense become at all possible for me. What is impossible to me as an imitator of Christ becomes perfectly natural as a participant of Christ.

F. J. HUEGEL, *BONE OF HIS BONE*

FEBRUARY 7

Without faith it is impossible to please Him.

HEBREWS 11:6

The great and fundamental sin which is at the foundation of all other sin is unbelief. The first thing is to give up that—to believe the Word of God. There is no breaking off from one sin without this. "Whatsoever is not of faith is sin."

Thus we see that the backslider and convicted sinner, when agonizing to overcome sin, will almost always betake themselves to works of law to obtain faith. They will fast and pray and read and struggle and outwardly reform and thus endeavor to obtain grace.

Now all this is vain and wrong. Do you ask, "Shall we not fast and pray and read and struggle? Shall we do nothing but sit down in antinomian security and inaction?" I answer, "You must do all that God commands you to do." But begin where He tells you to begin, and do it in the manner in which He commands you to do it—that is, in the exercise of faith that works by love.

Purify your hearts by faith. Believe in the Son of God. And say not in your heart, "Who shall ascend into heaven, that is, to bring Christ down from above; or who shall descend into the deep, that is, to bring up Christ again from the dead. But what saith it? The word is nigh thee, even in thy mouth, and in thy heart, that is, the word of faith which we preach."

CHARLES FINNEY, *SANCTIFICATION*

February 8

You must be born again.

John 3:7

God grant us the grace to be clear about one thing: Christ does not come into our lives to patch up the "old man." Here is where unnumbered multitudes of Christians have been hung up. They thought it was Christ's mission to "make them better." There is absolutely no biblical ground for any such idea. Jesus said that He had no intention of pouring His new wine into old pigskins. He said that He had not come to bring peace but a sword. He said that unless a man would renounce himself utterly, he could not be His disciple.

Christ does not come to us to simply straighten out the old life. He has never promised to make us better. His entire redemptive work, which was consummated upon the cross, rests upon the assumption (it is more than an assumption—God says it is a fact) that man's condition is such that only a dying and a being born again can possibly make any change in him. And He must impart to us an entirely new life. But we have the *new* upon the basis of our refusal of the *old*.

F. J. Huegel, *Bone of His Bone*

February 9

. . . that you may know what is the hope of His calling,
what are the riches of the glory of His inheritance in the saints,
and what is the exceeding greatness of His power toward us who believe.

EPHESIANS 1:18–19

Self cannot overcome self. We must be Christ-possessed to die to the flesh life. And to the degree in which we receive Christ, we die to self. Or, to state the matter conversely, to come more fully into Christ, we must more fully die to self.

In the first chapter of the Ephesian letter, Paul utters a marvelous prayer. He says to the Ephesians, "I do not cease to give thanks for you, making mention of you in my prayers: that the God of our Lord Jesus Christ, the Father of glory, may give to you the spirit of wisdom and revelation in the knowledge of Him, the eyes of your understanding being enlightened; that you may know . . . *what is the exceeding greatness of His power toward us who believe.*" And this power which is to us, for us, in us who believe—from where does it come? What actually is it? It is the "power which [God] worked in Christ when He *raised Him from the dead.*"

That is the matchless power which works in the believer—the power of Christ's resurrection!

F. J. HUEGEL, *BONE OF HIS BONE*

February 10

It is no longer I who live, but Christ lives in me.

Galatians 2:20

How can we be victorious, righteous, holy? First we must understand clearly that God has not constituted Christ our example to be copied. He is not giving us His strength to help us imitate Christ. He has not even planted Christ within us to help us to be Christlike. Galatians 2:20 is not our standard for record-breaking endeavor. It is not a high aim to be aspired to through long seeking and patient progress. No, it is not God's aim at all but God's *method.*

When Paul says, "It is no longer I who live, but Christ lives in me," he is showing us how only Christ satisfies God's heart. This is the life that gives God satisfaction in the believer, and there is no substitute. "No longer I but Christ" means Christ instead of me. When Paul uses these words, he is not claiming to have attained something his readers have not yet reached. He is defining the Christian life. The Christian life is the Christ life. Christ in me has become my life and is living my life instead of me. God gives Him to be my life.

It is just here that the second half of 1 Corinthians 1:30 is so splendid: "Christ Jesus . . . became for us wisdom from God—and righteousness and sanctification and redemption." This means that my righteousness and yours is not a quality or a virtue; indeed it is not a thing at all—but a living person. My holiness is not a condition of life but a person. My redemption is not a hope but "Christ in me, the hope of glory." Yes, Christ in me and Christ in you—this is all we need.

Watchman Nee, *Changed into His Likeness*

FEBRUARY 11

Of Him you are in Christ Jesus.

1 CORINTHIANS 1:30

When I was a young Christian, I was commended by various people for the Christlikeness of my life, but some years later I found to my consternation that my temper was often getting the better of me. Even when I managed to control it so that it did not actually flare up, it was seething inside; and to add to my distress and disillusionment, those kindly Christians who had commended me for the Christlike qualities that formerly impressed them were not slow to tell me how unfavorably my present life compared with my past. I used to be so humble and so patient, they said, so gentle and loving—but now . . . ! The worst of it was that their criticisms were not unfounded. I could have far outdone them with my own tales of failure. But how had this state of affairs developed? What was the trouble?

For two whole years I was groping in that kind of darkness, seeking to amass as personal possessions the virtues that I felt should make up the Christian life and getting nowhere in the effort. The trouble was that I had been accumulating things, spiritual things, and God had taken in hand to relieve me of them in order to make way for the life of His Son.

And then one day in 1933 light broke from heaven for me. Reading again 1 Corinthians 1:30, I suddenly *saw* that Christ was ordained of God to be made over to me in His fullness. What a difference! God is not seeking a display of our Christlikeness but a manifestation of His Christ. Once I saw this, it was the beginning of a new life for me. He Himself is the sum of divine things; and thus He was the answer in me to all God's demands. My daily life as a Christian would be summed up thereafter in the word "receive."

WATCHMAN NEE IN ANGUS KINNEAR,
AGAINST THE TIDE: THE STORY OF WATCHMAN NEE

FEBRUARY 12

Sin shall not have dominion over you,
for you are not under law but under grace.

ROMANS 6:14

In all my Christian life I have been pained to find so many Christians living in the legal bondage described in the seventh chapter of Romans—a life of sinning, resolving to reform, and falling again.

The directions that are generally given on this subject, I am sorry to say, amount to this: "Take your sins in detail, resolve to abstain from them, and fight against them, if need be with prayer and fasting, until you have overcome them. Set your will firmly against a relapse into sin, pray, and struggle, and resolve in this until you form the habit of obedience and break up all your sinful habits." To be sure, it is generally added, "In this conflict you must not depend upon your own strength but pray for the help of God." In a word, much of the teaching, both from the pulpit and the Christian press, really amounts to this: sanctification is by works and not by faith. In this way the outward act or habit may be overcome and avoided, but that which constitutes the sin is left untouched.

The fact is that it is simply by faith that we receive the Spirit of Christ to work in us to will and to do according to His good pleasure. He sheds abroad His own love in our hearts and thereby enkindles ours. Every victory over sin is by faith in Christ; and whenever the mind is diverted from Christ by resolving and fighting against sin, we are acting in our own strength, rejecting the help of Christ.

Nothing but the life and energy of the Spirit of Christ within us can save us from sin, and trust is the uniform and universal condition of the working of this saving energy within us.

CHARLES FINNEY, *POWER FROM ON HIGH*

FEBRUARY 13

Who will deliver me from this body of death? I thank God—through Jesus Christ our Lord!

ROMANS 7:24-25

There are two kinds of Christians in this world. Both may be familiar with the verse above [Romans 7:24-25], but they differ greatly in experience and understanding of it.

The first kind know the full and painful understanding of sin dwelling in them. They feel the bondage of sin, but they have not yet come to know the joy of deliverance, the sweet liberty of the children of God. Yet they see nothing better, so they cry out, "Who will deliver me from this body of death?" And there they stop.

The second kind of Christian also asks the question, "Who will deliver me from this body of death?" but answers it in the same breath with Paul's triumphant words: "I thank God—through Jesus Christ our Lord!" They have learned that there is deliverance now—in this life—through faith in Jesus. While others groan in their bondage as if there was no deliverance this side of the grave, they know from personal experience that Jesus Christ our Lord can deliver us now from the chains of sin.

As "Romans chapter seven" Christians, we thought of ourselves as mere servants in our own Father's house, living in fear before Him. But now, through faith in Christ, we recognize that we have been adopted and have become, in the fullest and happiest sense, sons and daughters of the Lord God Almighty. Our empty struggles have turned into sweet confidence in the strong arm and loving heart of Jesus.

WILLIAM BOARDMAN, *THE HIGHER CHRISTIAN LIFE*

FEBRUARY 14

. . . that I may gain Christ and be found in Him,
not having my own righteousness, which is from the law, but that which
is through faith in Christ, the righteousness which is from God by faith.

PHILIPPIANS 3:8-9

Jesus, you know, makes two offers to everyone. He offers to set us free from the *penalty* of our sin. And He offers to set us free from the *power* of our sin. Both these offers are made on exactly the same terms: we can accept them only by letting Him do it all.

Every Christian has accepted the first offer. Many Christians have not accepted the second offer. They mistakenly think, as I did, that they must have some part in overcoming the power of their sin; that their efforts, their will, their determination, strengthened and helped by the power of Christ, are the way to victory. And as long as they mistakenly believe this, they are doomed to defeat.

How did you accept Christ's offer of freedom from the penalty of your sins? You took it as an outright gift. By faith you let Him do it all. Will you not accept His offer of immediate and complete freedom from the power of your known sins on the same terms, and *do it now*? This is just as much a miracle as the miracle of regeneration. And it is just as exclusively the Lord's work.

Do not misunderstand me; I am not speaking of any mistaken idea of sinless perfection. It is not possible for anyone to have such a transaction with Christ as to enable him to say either "I am without sin" or "I can never sin again." This miracle is sustained and continued in our life only by our continuing, moment-by-moment faith in our Savior for His moment-by-moment victory over the power of our sin.

But He Himself will give us that faith and will continue that faith in us moment by moment.

CHARLES TRUMBULL, *VICTORY IN CHRIST*

February 15

God . . . made us sit together in the heavenly places in Christ Jesus.

Ephesians 2:4–6

Christianity is a queer business! If at the outset we try to do anything, we get nothing; if we seek to attain something, we miss everything. For Christianity begins not with a big *do* but with a big *done*. Thus Ephesians opens with the statement that God *has* "blessed us with every spiritual blessing in the heavenly places in Christ" (1:3), and we are invited at the very outset to sit down and enjoy what God has done for us—not to set out to try and attain it for ourselves.

God says that we are saved not by works but "by grace . . . through faith" (Eph. 2:8). We constantly speak of being "saved through faith," but what do we mean by it? We mean this: that we are saved by reposing in the Lord Jesus. We did nothing whatever to save ourselves; we simply laid upon Him the burden of our sin-sick souls. We began our Christian life by depending not upon our own doing but upon what He had done. Until a man does this, he is no Christian. For to say "I can do nothing to save myself, but by His grace God *has done* everything for me in Christ" is to take the first step in the life of faith.

The Christian life from start to finish is based upon this principle of utter dependence upon the Lord Jesus. There is no limit to the grace God is willing to bestow upon us. He will give us everything, but we can receive none of it except as we rest in Him. "Sitting" is an attitude of rest. Something has been finished, work stops, and we sit. It is paradoxical but true that we only advance in the Christian life as we learn first of all to sit down.

Watchman Nee, *Sit, Walk, Stand*

February 16

His divine power has given to us all things that pertain to life and godliness.

2 Peter 1:3

The elder son complained of the father's gracious reception of the prodigal, of all the feasting and rejoicing over his return, while he had never been given a kid that he might make merry with his friends. The father, in the tenderness of his love, answers him, "Son, you were always in my house; you had only to ask, and you would have got all you desired and required."

And that is what our Father says to all His children: "All I have is thine; for in Christ I have given it to you. All the Spirit's power and wisdom, all the riches of Christ, all the love of the Father—there is nothing that I have but is thine. I as God am God that I may love, keep, and bless thee."

If you are in spiritual poverty and there is no joy, no experience of victory over sin, temper, wandering, why is it so? "Oh," you say, "I'm too weak; I must fall." But does not the Scripture say that He is "able to keep you from falling"? A minister once told me that, although God is able, the verse does not say that He is willing to do it. God does not mock us, beloved. If He says that He is able, then it is a proof of His willingness to do it. Do let us believe God's Word and examine our own experience in the light of it.

Andrew Murray, *Divine Healing*

February 17

If you died with Christ . . . , why . . . do you subject yourselves to regulations?

Colossians 2:20

If you really and truly are Christians, why ever allow yourselves to be misled and tied up with rules and regulations, whether emanating from Judaism or from Gnosticism or from asceticism? "Stand fast therefore in the liberty by which Christ has made us free, and do not be entangled again with a yoke of bondage," the apostle would say, as in Galatians 5:1. In Colossians 2:19, he has put his finger on the reason why any such defection should ever take place: "not holding fast to the Head."

Perhaps our apostle has observed that some of these Colossian Christians are showing signs of developing into poor-hearted, small-minded, weak-kneed, flabby-muscled, thin-bodied, lame-limbed believers—all because, not holding to the Head, they have suffered their strength to be sapped by some insidious heresy. How different from the thrilling summons of Isaiah 35:3–4: "Strengthen the weak hands, and make firm the feeble knees. Say to those who are fearful-hearted, 'Be strong, do not fear! Behold, your God . . .'" Here is the fine, adventurous virility of the healthy, godly life.

Be it noted then that spiritual invalidism results from "not holding the Head" but that spiritual invigoration comes from "beholding your God." What a pity it is that any of us Christians should, through the enervating atmosphere of any heretical belief, allow ourselves to sink into spiritual mediocrity when we might be enjoying the vigor of God's full salvation.

Guy King, *Colossians: True Life in Christ*

FEBRUARY 18

She took him up with her . . . and brought him to the house of the LORD. . . . "As long as he lives he shall be lent to the LORD."

1 SAMUEL 1:24–28

Up to this moment, Samuel had lived largely in the energy and motive power of his mother's intense religious life. It was needful that he should *exchange the traditional for the experiential.* His faith must rest not on the assertions of another's testimony but because for himself he had seen and tasted and handled the Word of life. Not at second hand but at first the word of the Lord must come to him and be passed on to all Israel.

Probably this change comes to everyone who desires and seeks after the best and richest life. You may be the child of a pious home, where from boyhood or girlhood you were trained in the traditions of evangelical religion: you were expected to pray and to serve God. You have been borne along by a blessed momentum.

But suppose for a minute that momentum should fail you. Have you come to apprehend Christ as a living reality for yourself? It may be that God, out of mercy to you, will break up and destroy the traditions and forms on which you have been relying so that the eternal and divine may stand forth apparent to your spiritual perception and be apprehended by yourself for yourself, as though they were meant for you alone.

It is a great hour in the history of the soul when the traditional, to which it has become habituated by long habit and use, is suddenly exchanged for the open vision of God—when we say with Job, "I have heard of thee by the hearing of the ear: but now mine eye seeth thee"; when we say with the apostle, "Leaving the things that are behind and reaching forth to those that are before, I press toward the mark."

F. B. MEYER, *SAMUEL*

February 19

He said, "Let Me go, for the day breaks." But he said, "I will not let You go unless You bless me!"

Genesis 32:26

Whatever it is that enables a soul whom God designs to bless to stand out against Him, God will touch. It may be the pride of wealth or of influence or of affection, but it will not be spared—God will touch it. If it robs a man of spiritual blessing, God will touch it. It may be as small a thing as a sinew, but its influence in making a man strong in his resistance of blessing will be enough to condemn it—and God will touch it. And beneath that touch it will shrink and shrivel.

Then Jacob went from resisting to clinging. As the day broke, the Angel wished to be gone; but He could not, because Jacob clung to Him with a death grip. The request to be let go indicates how tenaciously the limping patriarch clung to Him for support. He had abandoned the posture of defense and resistance and had fastened himself onto the Angel—as a terrified child clasps its arms tightly around its father's neck.

That is a glad moment in the history of the human spirit when it throws both arms around the risen Savior and hangs on Him and will not let Him go. It is the attitude of blessing. It is the posture of power. It is the sublime condition in which Christ will whisper His own new name, which no man knoweth saving he that receiveth it. Have you ever come to this?

If not, ask God to show you what sinew it is that makes you too strong for Him to bless you; ask Him to touch it so that you shall be able to hold out no more. And then you will discover the blessing which is yours.

F. B. Meyer, *Israel*

February 20

The Lord *. . . said: . . . "I will not leave you until I have done what I have spoken to you."*

Genesis 28:13–15

God never once gave Jacob one word of rebuke or exhortation. But God worked. Without stopping to exhort or to explain, God disciplined him.

At Bethel God promised, "Behold, I am with you." And He was! He led him. And if God did not stay with us in delivering us from our natural strength, we would certainly never go through with it. Jacob never longed to make progress; he never wanted to be spiritual or to follow the example of Abraham and Isaac. God Himself sought him out and stayed with him and dealt with him over those long years, until at last at Peniel, when Jacob had produced his masterpiece of self-expression, God brought him to his knees, and he yielded the mastery. God did every bit of it! We can well afford to trust the discipline of the Spirit.

If we are His, the Spirit disciplines us all the time, just as He did Jacob. He prepares for us a host of different circumstances just with this one object. Everything in our lives is directed by Him to this end: to bring us to the place of Israel. God is an acting God. He will never let us go. The chastening we experience is for our profit.

If we are His, then, however bad material we are, God follows us. He is more tenacious than we are. We would need to be greater than God before we could prevent Him from doing His work. While we are only men, natural men, God will have His way. While Jacob is there, however bad, God will pursue His goal of an Israel. Trust His tenaciousness, count on His invincibility. Look to Him, and in His time and His way, He will finish the work.

Watchman Nee, *Changed into His Likeness*

FEBRUARY 21

Search me, O God, and know my heart . . .
and see if there is any wicked way in me.

PSALM 139:23-24

God is light. Silently, inexorably He shines on and in us, revealing things just as they are in His sight.

Sin is a revelation. It is God who graciously shows us sin, even as it is He who shows us the precious blood. Sin is only seen to be *sin*—against God—when He reveals it; otherwise sin may just be known as a wrong against a brother or an antisocial act or an inconvenience or a disability or some such thing. Indeed that is often the extent of the message of a "social gospel"—to be rid of sin as a hindrance to brotherhood, as an inconvenience to human progress; not as coming short of the glory of God.

God shows us sin. We do not need to keep looking inside ourselves. This is not a life of introspection or morbid self-examination. But as we walk in childlike faith and fellowship with Jesus step by step, moment by moment, then if the cups cease to run over, He who is light will clearly show us what the sin is which is hindering. God does not speak in terms of general condemnation; He speaks in simple, specific terms of any actual sin in the present which is hindering the inner witness of His Spirit.

What do we do then? Well, that is obvious. First John 1:9 says, "If we confess our sins . . ." Then where there is this confession, we all know there is the word of promise: "He is faithful and just to forgive us our sins and to cleanse us from all unrighteousness." Confession of sin does not deliver by itself. It is the *blood* that cleanses, and we must always pass on from confession to faith and praise for the blood, believing that the blood alone is what glorifies God and delivers us.

NORMAN GRUBB, *CONTINUOUS REVIVAL*

FEBRUARY 22

He made Him who knew no sin to be sin for us,
that we might become the righteousness of God in Him.

2 CORINTHIANS 5:21

Unless you know you are a sinner, you do not *want* a Savior. The knowledge that you are a captive to sin leads to the desire for a deliverer. It is only when the Holy Spirit shows you what sin is that you want a Savior.

A short time ago in an evangelistic campaign, the Spirit of God was working mightily. The speaker at the time was talking about sin and Calvary when a woman cried aloud with a piercing cry, across the mass of people, "You are speaking about me. What you are saying is true. I am a sinner; I am a sinner; God have mercy upon me!" She fell upon her knees. It seemed as though the speaker and the woman were the only people in the hall.

That is what the Holy Spirit does! He convicts of sin. When you are thus convicted, you want a Savior who bore your sins in His own body on the tree. It is because your sins were nailed to the cross in the person of Christ that God can forgive you and blot them out.

The blood of Jesus Christ does blot out sin. If you have fallen into the deepest, blackest sin, only the blood of Jesus Christ can remove it. This is what the Holy Spirit bears witness to, and there are thousands of souls who bear co-witness with the Holy Spirit that the blood of Jesus has washed away sin. A witness to such a fact is more effective than any mere teaching of the atonement. If all the theories of the atonement today were torn to shreds, you could not destroy the personal witness of millions to Calvary's power.

JESSIE PENN-LEWIS, *THE WORK OF THE HOLY SPIRIT*

February 23

In Him we live and move and have our being.

Acts 17:28

God, as Creator, formed man to be a vessel in which He could show forth His power and goodness. Man was not to have in himself a fountain of life or strength or happiness. The ever-living and only-living One was each moment to be the communicator to him of all that he needed. Man's glory and blessedness were not to be independent, or dependent upon himself, but to be dependent on a God of infinite riches and love. Man was to have the joy of receiving every moment out of the fullness of God. This was his original and blessed state as an unfallen creature.

When he turned from God, he became still more absolutely dependent on Him. There was not the slightest hope of his recovery from his state of death except in God—by His power and mercy. It is God alone who began the work of redemption. It is God alone who continues and carries it on each moment in each individual believer. Even in the regenerate man there is no power of goodness in oneself. He has and can have nothing that he does not each moment receive.

God unceasingly gives and works as His child unceasingly waits and receives. This is the blessed life.

Andrew Murray, *Waiting on God*

FEBRUARY 24

. . . that your faith should not be in the wisdom of men but in the power of God.

1 CORINTHIANS 2:5

Every deeper insight into what our daily life ought to be will lead us to the one deep conviction: Christianity is nothing unless it is supernatural. Our Christian life and work must fail unless we live deeply rooted in the power of God's inspired Word, in the supernatural power of the Holy Spirit, and in the importunate prayer to which the promise of the Father will most surely be given.

How inclined we are to listen to anything that calls for our activities! How ready we are to undertake the fulfillment of divine commands in our own strength! Unless we are very watchful, we may be deceived into putting our hope on what will turn out to be nothing but human devices.

Supernatural! Give that word its full force. Let us cultivate with our whole heart a sense of God's power at work in us. Let our attitude be one of dependence and prayer and waiting upon God with a deep consciousness that God will work in us, and the church around us, above what we can ask or think.

ANDREW MURRAY, *THE STATE OF THE CHURCH*

February 25

Learn from Me, for I am gentle and lowly in heart.

Matthew 11:29

In this statement [in Matthew 11:29] our Lord opens to us the inmost secret of His own inner life. He, the Teacher, meek and lowly of heart, wants to make you what He is. As a learner, you must come and study His disposition and seek to learn from Him how you can have it too.

Why is this so all-important? Because it is at the root of the true relationship of the creature to the Creator. Only God has life and goodness and happiness. As the God of love, He delights to give and work everything in us. Christ became the Son of Man in order to show us the kind of unceasing dependence upon God that we should have. That is the meaning of His being lowly in heart. In this spirit the angels veil their faces and cast their crowns before God. God is everything to them, and they delight to receive all from Him and to give all to Him.

What is the root of the true Christian life? To be nothing before God and men; to wait on God alone; to delight in, to imitate, to learn of Christ, the meek and lowly One. It is in this attitude that Christ comes to teach and only in this attitude that you can learn of Him.

What an insignificant place the church has given to the teaching of humility compared to its significance in the life of Christ and the teachings of God's Word. Only when we are meek and lowly in heart can Christ teach us by His Spirit what God has for us and what God will work in us.

Andrew Murray, *The Inner Chamber*

FEBRUARY 26

A man can receive nothing unless it has been given to him from heaven.

JOHN 3:27

The Spirit of the triune God, breathed into Adam at his creation, was that alone which made him a holy creature in the image and likeness of God. A new birth of this Spirit of God in man is as necessary to make fallen man alive again unto God as it was to make Adam at first in the image and likeness of God. And a constant flow of this divine life by the Spirit is as necessary to man's continuance in his redeemed state as light and moisture are to the continued life of a plant.

A religion that is not wholly built upon this supernatural ground but which stands to any degree upon human powers, reasonings, and conclusions has not so much as the shadow of truth in it. Such religion leaves man with mere empty forms and images that can no more restore divine life to his soul than an idol of clay or wood could create another Adam.

True Christianity is nothing but the continual dependence upon God through Christ for all life, light, and virtue; and the false religion of Satan is to seek that goodness from any other source. So the true child of God acknowledges that "no man can receive anything except it be given him from above."

WILLIAM LAW, *THE POWER OF THE SPIRIT*

FEBRUARY 27

You shall love the LORD your God with all your heart,
with all your soul, with all your mind, and with all your strength.

MARK 12:30

What is the purpose of life? This is a question to which many a professing Christian yet needs to find the answer as well as the man who has no knowledge of God. The Bible answer is to know and to love and to walk with God—that is, *to see God*. Today, however, we do not hear much about the need to see God.

Two emphases stand out today. First of all, instead of stressing holiness in order to *see* God, the emphasis is on service *for* God. We have come to think of the Christian life as consisting in serving God as fully and as efficiently as we can. Instead of a longing for God, our longing is for power to serve Him more effectively. Then there tends to be today an emphasis on the seeking of inner spiritual experiences. However, the concern arises not as much from a hunger for God as from a longing to have an inner experience of happiness, joy, and power, and we find ourselves looking for "it" rather than God Himself. Both these ends fall utterly short of the great end that God has designed for man—that of glorifying Him and enjoying Him forever.

This then is the purpose of life: to see God and to allow Him to bring us back to the old relationship of submission to Himself. Our highest good is achieved only in submitting.

If we will yield to this fact, some of us will have a new outlook on life. We will have a new zest for life, even in the dreariest surroundings. As soon as the emphasis is changed from *doing* to *being*, there is an easing of tension. The situations may not change, but we have changed. Gone will be the former striving, bondage, and frustration. We shall be at peace with our God and ourselves.

ROY HESSION, *WE WOULD SEE JESUS*

February 28

There remains therefore a rest for the people of God.

Hebrews 4:9

Canon Harford-Battersby read the open invitation to the Union Meeting for the Promotion of Scriptural Holiness at Oxford: "In every part of the country, the God of all grace has given to many of His children a feeling of deep dissatisfaction with their spiritual state." He could say amen to that.

Being an enquirer of crystal honesty, Harford-Battersby, on the spur of the moment, decided to go. As far as he could gather, they were saying that you could have intimate companionship with Christ all day long, that God's will and your happiness were one, that the Holy Spirit and not yourself overcame temptations; but you had to make a deliberate act of full surrender and enter a "rest of faith."

One address came from Evan Hopkins. Hopkins stressed that "seeking faith may be intensely earnest, importunate, and persevering but may exist with great distress, anxiety, and worry." And this, Hopkins pointed out, was the kind of faith common to a very large number of Christians.

Harford-Battersby stirred very slightly in his seat. "I said to myself, *Has not my faith been a seeking faith when it ought to have been a resting faith? And if so, why not exchange it for the latter?* And I thought of the sufficiency of Jesus and said, 'I *will rest* in Him'—and I did rest in Him. I found that a presence of Jesus was graciously manifested in a way that I knew not before and that I did *abide in Him.*"

John Charles Pollock, *The Keswick Story*

February 29

When I am weak, then I am strong.

2 Corinthians 12:10

Paul's discovery of his own weakness was related to the whole business of living a life that was pleasing to God. Some account of how he arrived there is given in the context of the latter part of Romans 7 and the beginning of chapter 8. Elsewhere he speaks of other experiences that brought home the same great principle, as when he prayed unsuccessfully for the removal of his "thorn in the flesh" and God said, "My power is made perfect in weakness" (2 Cor. 12:7–9). When the Holy Spirit brings home to us this truth of our insufficiency, we shall bow and accept it and prove with Paul that it is not *out of* weakness (that is, the thorn removed) but *in* weakness that God's power is made perfect.

Some know the *rest* of utter weakness, and others only know the *striving* of utter weakness. The one is a thing of faith, the other a thing of works; the one a thing of the Spirit, the other a thing of the flesh. It is, after all, only the pride of our own hearts that causes us to rebel against this innate weakness, to strive to escape from its clutches and attain a place of strength, of independence, of self-sufficiency. It seems to cut right across our efforts to achieve self-significance.

How wonderful it is when we discover, often through the discipline of repeated failure, that this weakness with which we seem to be permanently saddled is not the end but a new and wonderful beginning—the gateway to heaven's resources. "The Spirit helps us in our weakness." The weakness is perpetual only that we might be perpetually dependent on the Holy Spirit.

Arthur Wallis, *Pray in the Spirit*

March

Crucified with Christ

The Testimony of Watchman Nee

For years after my conversion, I had been taught that the way of deliverance was to reckon myself dead to sin and alive to God (Rom. 6:11). I reckoned from 1920 to 1927, and the trouble was that the more I did so, the more alive to sin I clearly was. I simply could not believe myself dead; sin was still defeating me. Whenever I sought help, I was sent back to Romans 6:11. I appreciated its teaching, but I could not make out why nothing resulted from it. No one, you see, had pointed out to me that knowing (Rom. 6:6) must precede reckoning (Rom. 6:11). For months I was troubled and prayed earnestly, reading the Scriptures and seeking light.

I remember one morning—how can I ever forget it!—I was sitting upstairs reading Romans, and I came to the words, "Knowing this, that our old man was crucified with him, that the body of sin might be done away, that so we should no longer be in bondage to sin." *Knowing* this! How could I know it? I prayed, "Lord, open my eyes!" and then in a flash I saw.

I had earlier been reading 1 Corinthians 1:30: "You are in Christ Jesus." I turned to it and looked at it again. If Christ had died, and that is certain fact, and if God had put me into Him, then I must have died too! All at once I *saw* my oneness with Christ—that I was in Him and that, when He had died, I had died. My death to sin was a matter of the past and not of the future. It was a divine fact that had dawned upon me.

Carried away with joy, I jumped from my chair and ran downstairs to the young man working in the kitchen. "Brother," I said, seizing him by the hands, "do you know that I have died?"

I must admit he looked puzzled. "What do you mean?" he exclaimed.

So I went on, "Do you not know that Christ has died? Do you not know that I died with Him? Do you not know that my death is no less truly a fact than His?" It was divine fact that had dawned upon me.

Oh, it was so real to me! I felt like shouting my discovery through the streets of Shanghai. From that day to this, I have never for one moment doubted the finality of that word: "I have been crucified with Christ; it is no longer I who live, but Christ lives in me."

WATCHMAN NEE IN ANGUS KINNEAR,
AGAINST THE TIDE: THE STORY OF WATCHMAN NEE

MARCH 1

I die daily.

1 CORINTHIANS 15:31

The apprehension of the fact that we were identified with Christ when He died on the cross unto sin often produces most sudden and decisive results in the experience and practical walk of the believer. It cuts us away abruptly from our former course of life, and we find a glorious emancipation from sin's power and service. But this effect, though sudden and immediate, is followed by a work which is progressive and continuous.

As oneness with the dying Christ becomes more and more an experienced reality, so the life increases: the living, risen Lord manifests His power and fills the soul with His fullness. The believer's true life—that is, the life of Christ in him—is a life, then, that is ever springing up out of death. "I die daily" is a declaration that is fraught with deep meaning, whatever may have been the sense in which the apostle used the words.

It is as we become practically identified with Christ in His death that all the hindrances to the manifestation of His life are removed. In no other way can they be set aside. Our own efforts cannot accomplish it; our resolutions will utterly fail in effecting it and leave us in despair.

We must submit to be conformed to that death, to be brought into actual sympathy with Him who died unto sin. Just as in the cross we find the power which sets us free from the authority of darkness and translates us into the kingdom of God's dear Son, so in that death also we possess the power that separates us from the self-life and keeps us in a condition of deliverance.

EVAN HOPKINS, *THE LAW OF LIBERTY IN THE SPIRITUAL LIFE*

March 2

I am the way, the truth, and the life.
No one comes to the Father except through Me.

John 14:6

The true and eternal life—which is the only worthwhile ideal of life—is not found in a philosophy or a principle but in a person: the Lord Jesus Christ. God is the one source of life, and Christ is the only way to God. He declared, "And this is life eternal, that they might know thee the only true God, and Jesus Christ, whom thou has sent" (John 17:3).

This means far more than that Jesus Christ preached eternal life or gave a philosophy or even lived it. It means that the very life of God was incarnate in Christ and, through Him, is communicable to us. "In him was life; and the life was the light of men" (John 1:4). If He were only a teacher of life, we would still be in our hopeless condition. But He *embodied* the life He taught, and we, through faith in Him, can share in it.

Even this is not enough. It was necessary for Him to die as a man that His life might be available to all men! Here lies a profound truth: sin has cursed the human race, and sin hinders men from knowing life so that the natural man cannot receive life or the truth about it. But the Lord Jesus Christ met the problem of sin for us, although He knew no sin. For as Moses lifted up the serpent that men might have life for a look, even so was Christ lifted up that whosoever believeth in Him might not perish but have eternal life (John 3:14–16).

Colossians 3:4 calls Christ "our life." When we believe in Him and yield ourselves to Him, God gives us a new and eternal life which is His own shared with us. It is not merely that we set out to live *like* Jesus. No, He becomes our very life, so that we can say, "To me to live is Christ." He is life itself. We are "partakers of the divine nature" (2 Pet. 1:4) and therefore of the divine life.

Vance Havner, *Reflections on the Gospels*

March 3

We were buried with Him through baptism into death, that . . .
we also should walk in newness of life.

Romans 6:4

It is clear that divine life can need nothing from man to increase its vitality. It does not need our efforts to make it live. Think what it is that we really possess if Christ is in us. It was no mere figure of speech that the apostle employed when he declared that Christ was living in him. And what was true of him may be equally true of us. What then is it that we possess?

We have *Him* in whom all fullness of life actually dwells. Everything needed for continual growth, for perpetual freshness, and for abundant fruitfulness are found in Him. All power, all purity, and all fullness—absolutely everything needed to make all grace abound toward us, in us, and through us—are stored up in Him who truly dwells within us.

All Christians have Christ and possess therefore all the resources of spiritual power and abundant fruitfulness, and yet not all Christians are abounding in fruit unto God. What is the reason for this? It is here: though we cannot make Christ more living, though we cannot add to His infinite fullness of life and purity and power, we may be hindering the manifestation of that life.

The truth is, we need two powers: a power to remove the hindrances and a power to produce the fruit; a power to separate from us the evil and a power to transform into us the good.

This twofold power is found in Christ. There is the power of His death and the power of His life. We do not bid goodbye to the first because we have been brought to live in the second. Nay, the condition of knowing the power of His resurrection lies in "being made comformable unto his death" (Phil. 3:10).

The true life, that which triumphs over sin and "does not cease from yielding fruit," is a life that springs up *out of death.*

Evan Hopkins, *The Law of Liberty in the Spiritual Life*

March 4

The death that He died, He died to sin.

Romans 6:10

It is impossible to exaggerate the importance of understanding the meaning of Christ's death. We must see that He not only died *for* sin but *unto* sin.

In the first of these senses, He died alone; we could not die with Him. He trod the winepress alone. As the sin offering, He alone became the propitiation for our sins.

But in the second, we died *with* Him. We must know what it is to be brought into sympathy with Him in His death unto sin. Oneness with Christ in that sense is the means of becoming practically separated not only from sinful desires but also from the old self-life. And this assimilation to the dying Christ is not an isolated act but a condition of mind ever to be maintained and to go on deepening. "Arm yourselves with the same mind: for he that hath suffered in the flesh hath ceased from sin" (1 Pet. 4:1).

We become practically partakers of His life in proportion as we enter into His death—as we are made conformable in heart and mind to His death.

Evan Hopkins, *The Law of Liberty in the Spiritual Life*

March 5

He must increase, but I must decrease.

John 3:30

I have long been impressed with the thirtieth verse of the third chapter of John. Some of the disciples of John the Baptist come to him, reporting that everybody has gone after Jesus; the Baptist has been eclipsed, his popularity has passed its peak. But the rugged old prophet graciously replies in part, "He must increase, but I must decrease."

Nothing is more needed among Christians than the lesson of the decreasing self. It is an egocentric age, a day of self-sufficiency. The world's creed is "Glorify yourself; express yourself." And just as a penny held close to the eye will hide the sun, so does the penny of self shut out God.

The business of the Christian is to express Christ. To do that, he must decrease, and Christ must increase. As at Cana, it is only when the wine of our own self-sufficiency gives out that we get the better wine which Christ provides. There must be the emptying of self if there is to be His infilling. Paul speaks of "having nothing, yet possessing all things." One must come to the first half of that phrase and realize his own nothingness before he truly can appropriate that other verse of Paul's, "All things are yours."

This is distasteful doctrine to a humanistic age that feels no need of the supernatural. The world asks, "Are you growing bigger?" Christ asks, "Are you growing less?" Paul was a self-sufficient man on the Damascus road that morning. But with his conversion a new process began: his en-Christment. The longer he lived, the less there was of Paul and the more there was of Christ, until he could say "Not I, but Christ liveth in me" and "To me to live is Christ."

He must increase; we must decrease.

Vance Havner, *Reflections on the Gospels*

MARCH 6

I long . . . to share in His sufferings.

PHILIPPIANS 3:10, WEY

Sometimes we suddenly recognize something in ourselves as self—self-love, self-choice, self-pity—which a year ago we should not have recognized at all. This shows that indeed our patient Lord is going on to perfect us. More light is flowing into our room, and so we see the dust more clearly. Even though a pang strikes us when we see the dust, let us thank God we do see it. We should not, if it were not for His light.

In other words, "there is always something more in your nature which He wills to mark with the Cross" (H. Maynard Smith, Frank, Bishop of Zanzibar). If we are following hard after Him, we shall be aware of this. Never a day will go by without some secret marking of the cross deep, deep within us. And to what end? "This spake he, signifying by what death he should glorify God" (John 21:19). When thou wast young (spiritually immature) thou wouldest bitterly have resented any interference with thy liberty—there was nothing trying to thee in that delightful freedom. But now, how different! Thou canst be trusted with what seems hardest to the natural mind, trusted not to fail.

All the time I have been thinking of our Lord's far-reaching words to Peter, the thought of Philippians 3:10 has been with me. Weymouth translates it, "I long to know Christ and the power which is in His resurrection, and to share in His sufferings and die even as He died"; and Way has "the power outflowing from His resurrection."

It is always first the power, then the crucified life. The God with whom we have to do is the God of limitless power. It is "the power of his resurrection" that assures us that even we shall be "made conformable unto his death."

AMY CARMICHAEL, *THOU GIVEST . . . THEY GATHER*

MARCH 7

The LORD has anointed Me . . . to proclaim liberty to the captives, and the opening of the prison to those who are bound.

ISAIAH 61:1

There is but one fountain for sin and for uncleanness: the cross of Christ. What then do we need in order that we may know the cleansing power of the cross of Christ? How may we be separated in heart and mind from the defiling influence of sin? Only by an apprehension of this blessed fact: that Christ died in order to separate us from sin's defilement.

It has often been shown that sin is to the soul what disease is to the body. The effect of disease on our physical organism is just a picture of what sin produces on our spiritual nature.

In the dysfunction of paralysis, we see the loss of the power of voluntary muscular motion. Sin has precisely the same effect on our souls. The effects of sin may be traced in the impairment of voluntary power, in the enfeebling of all moral energy, or in the hardening and deadening of the spiritual sense. And the result is that the whole tone of the spiritual life is lowered. Sin thus robs us of the power by which alone we are able to perform the functions that belong to our renewed being.

So with the soul. The new birth may have taken place, yet sin may have been allowed to come in and produce its paralyzing effects. It not only robs us of all spiritual energy, but it retards our progress; it hinders our spiritual growth.

Christ came not only to redeem the soul but to liberate every power and faculty we possess and which God originally created for His glory. Christ has come to open the prison doors—to burst the fetters that keep the soul in slavery to sin. The effect of His ministry was the emancipation of every moral and spiritual power, the loosening of every chain.

EVAN HOPKINS, *THE LAW OF LIBERTY IN THE SPIRITUAL LIFE*

March 8

Our old man was crucified with Him.

Romans 6:6

All truth would fall into right relationship to other truth if it were clearly understood that the cross is the focal point from which all truth radiates and that the normal position of every believer is, according to God's view and purpose, "crucified with Christ" (see Rom. 6:3, 6).

A careful reading of all the epistles of Paul will show that they are written on the basis of the cross set forth in Romans 6—the fact that God consigns the old fallen Adam to the cross and has nothing to say to him.

God deals with all believers on this ground: *in Christ you died*. But the church of Christ, as a whole, ignores this fact. It treats the fallen creation as capable of improvement, and the meaning of the cross—bringing to death the old Adam race as fallen beyond repair—is thus nullified.

How we need to see this plainly, for we find that in all those who do not thus apprehend the truth of Christ's death on the cross in its manward aspect, the old Adam life is busy appropriating truths which belong to the new creature in Christ Jesus; hence the confusion of views and strange mixture of truth and error held by various sections of the professing church. The precious blood of Christ was not meant to *shelter* the uncrucified flesh any more than it was intended as a cloak to sin.

Jessie Penn-Lewis, *The Cross: The Touchstone of Faith*

MARCH 9

I can of Myself do nothing.

JOHN 5:30

This is the position and privilege which the cross is purposed to bring us into—not only identification with Christ in His death as a judicial fact but a practical life where the "I" is kept in the place of death so that there results such a union with the risen Lord that, moment by moment, we rely upon Him as our new center, our source of action—as He depended upon His Father, saying, "I can do nothing of Myself."

The "old creation" life is very profuse. But as Christ becomes our center and the "I" is yielded to the cross, the whole life is brought into light to be placed under His control.

Let us lay down at the cross our natural abilities. Then we shall be freed from all pomposity and ostentation in our work, and we shall become simply dependent and helpless, actually relying upon the living Christ every minute.

Now the question for us is, shall God bring us individually to the bedrock fact of the "I" crucified for Christ to be the new center of our being? Shall He reach the very core so that "I" shall be recognized by us as displaced and crucified for the Holy Spirit to re-create and produce a new personality after the pattern of the Man Jesus Christ? Shall we ask Him to do it?

JESSIE PENN-LEWIS, *THE CENTRALITY OF THE CROSS*

MARCH 10

If we have been united together in the likeness of His death, certainly we also shall be in the likeness of His resurrection.

ROMANS 6:5

There is a deep spiritual meaning in those words of the apostle which we fail to grasp at first sight: "Always bearing about in the body the dying"—or the putting to death (*nekrosin*)—"of the Lord Jesus, that the life also of Jesus might be made manifest in our body" (2 Cor. 4:10). Death is here put before us as the condition of life. The continual manifestation of the life depends upon the constant conformity to the death.

Death means separation, and life means union. By being brought more and more into sympathy with Christ's death unto sin, we become more and more thoroughly separated from its service and defilement. It is not merely separation from sinning; it is a separation from the old self-life. The great hindrance to the manifestation of the Christ life is the presence and activity of the self-life. This needs to be terminated and set aside. Nothing but "the putting to death of the Lord Jesus Christ" can accomplish this. Conformity to His death means a separation in heart and mind from the old source of activity and the motives and aims of the old life.

This conformity is the condition for the manifestation of the divine life. As we have already observed, "the life of Jesus" does not need our energy or our efforts to make it more living. All that God requires is that we should fall in with those conditions which are essential for the removal of the hindrances. Let those conditions be complied with, and at once the life springs forth spontaneously and without strain or effort. Though we can neither originate nor strengthen it by direct efforts of our own, we may indirectly increase its manifestations by complying with the divinely appointed conditions.

EVAN HOPKINS, *THE LAW OF LIBERTY IN THE SPIRITUAL LIFE*

March 11

Whoever desires to come after Me, let him deny himself.

Mark 8:34

As we are led on by Him, we find the message of the cross opening out with an ever-widening meaning to meet an ever-deepening need. At first we apprehend our death with Christ simply in relation to the bondage of sin. We listen to the declaration of Paul in Romans 6:6 that "our old man is crucified with him," and we reckon ourselves dead unto sin. Thereby we prove with joy that the living Christ is "able to save completely them that draw near to God through him" (Heb. 7:25, margin).

But sooner or later, we find out that our lives are still in some measure *self*-centered. Self shows itself. Self-energy or self-complacency in service, self-pity when we are suffering, self-seeking in desiring the praise of men, self-introspection and self-judgment in hours of trial, self-sensitiveness in contact with others, self-defense when we are injured. Yes, and sometimes, above all, a self-consciousness that makes life almost a burden.

In the energy of self, desiring to be wholly the Lord's, we may sometimes consecrate ourselves to Him and with new vigor seek to work for Him, oblivious of the *self*-source of our activities until we are spent out. Or, finding little spiritual fruit from all our labor, our eyes are opened to see the uselessness of all our "creaturely activity" for Him.

The Lord Jesus touched the core of the trouble when He said, "If any man would come after me, let him deny himself." The Lord did not say his *sins*. He who knew what was in man struck to the very center of a man and said "deny *himself*."

Let a man see himself as crucified with Christ, and quickly *another* Himself—the Lord Christ—will take the central place in the heart and quietly bring all things under His sway!

Jessie Penn-Lewis, *The Cross of Calvary*

March 12

. . . if indeed we suffer with Him, that we may also be glorified.

ROMANS 8:17

Even when we have apprehended our death-position with Christ, we may have failed to see this conformity to His death as an experience *day by day.* This daily conformity brings into one's life not only victory over sin but the spirit of Calvary.

The absence of this continuing conformity brings about the anomaly of the cross being preached with no marks of the Calvary spirit. This is the danger of teaching identification without the consequent conformity to death which brings true power, for we may rely upon the fact that we have "died with Christ" and assume that it is entirely wrought in us at once, not realizing that "conformity to His death" must become deeper and deeper until the "fellowship of his sufferings" becomes a real experience in one's life.

"Always delivered to death for Jesus' sake." "Oh," you say, "you are not putting before us the attractive side." But why do you always cry for what is attractive from the human view in following Christ? Was Calvary in its reality *attractive*? Was Christ *attractive* on His way to the cross?

If our eyes were opened by the Spirit of God to the divine vision of the suffering Lord, we should see beauty in the lamb-spirit of Jesus. We should see the heavenly side of fellowship with Christ in His death path and count it joy to follow in His steps. We should then crave to "suffer with him" because thus, and only thus, we will be "glorified together" (Rom. 8:17).

JESSIE PENN-LEWIS, *DYING TO LIVE*

MARCH 13

In the place where He was crucified there was a garden.

JOHN 19:41

This is my Easter word for you. You will find your garden very near to the place where you will be crucified.

"Always bearing about in the body the dying of the Lord Jesus, that the life also of Jesus might be made manifest in our body" (2 Cor. 4:10). Whenever we have been most earnest and most sensitive about bearing about in our body that dying, we have known most of the power and sweetness and unearthly joy of the life of our Lord.

AMY CARMICHAEL, *CANDLES IN THE DARK*

As near Thy Cross a Garden lay,
So, as we follow in the way,
We find a garden. Pain and loss
Were not the last words of the Cross.

Beyond the sharpness and the strife,
The Easter lily reigns in life.
And singing birds are in the trees;
Were ever singing birds like these?

O Lord, the solemn mystery
Of Cross and Garden beckons me.
Thou who didst never turn Thee back,
Keep my feet steadfast in the track.

AMY CARMICHAEL, *MOUNTAIN BREEZES*

March 14

Narrow is the gate and difficult is the way which leads to life.

Matthew 7:14

At first the road to the cross seems broad, and we can all go together. But as we get nearer to that place of repentance, the path gets narrower. There is not room for us all abreast. We can no longer be lost in the crowd. Others fall behind. At last when we come to the One who is the Door Himself, there is not room even for two, you and that other one. If you are going to enter, you will have to stand there utterly alone. It must be you alone who repents, without waiting for any other.

But we do not want to be the one to repent. The devil tells us that the person by our side is so very wrong, and he makes us unwilling to repent unless that one repents first. But we can never get through the Door that way! You must be the one to repent and to do so first, as if you were the only sinner in the world. The other person may be wrong, but your reactions to his wrong—whether resentment, criticism, or unforgiveness—are wrong too, and in God's sight more culpably so. For "Thou shalt love thy neighbor as thyself" is second only to "Thou shalt love the Lord thy God with all thy heart" (Matt. 22:37–39), and those reactions in your heart are not love.

Jesus never fails as a Savior when we come to Him as sinners. But if in any degree we are not finding Him a real Savior who brings us fully out of darkness and defeat into light and liberty, it is because on one point or another we are not willing to be broken and see ourselves as sinners.

Roy Hession, *We Would See Jesus*

March 15

They could not enter in because of unbelief.

Hebrews 3:19

Many in the church of Christ think it must take a long time to get into full salvation. Yes, it will take a long time if you are to do it yourself—indeed, you never will.

No, no, friend, if you come and trust God, it can be done in a moment. By God's grace, give yourself up to Him. Don't say, "What's the use? It will do no good"; but put yourself as you are, in sin and weakness, into the bosom of your Father. God will deliver you, and you will find that it is only one step out of the darkness into the light. Say, "Father, what a wretch I have been in being with Thee and yet not believing Thy love to me!"

Yes, I come today with a call to repent, addressed not to the unsaved but to those who already know what it is to be pardoned. For have you not sinned in the hard thoughts you have had of God, and is there not a longing, a thirsting and hungering, after something better? Come then, repent, and just believe that God does blot out the sin of your unbelief.

Do you believe it? Oh, do not dishonor God by unbelief, but come today and confidently claim full salvation. Then trust in Him to keep you. This seems difficult to some, but there is no difficulty about it. God will shine His light upon you always, saying, "Son, thou art ever with me," and all you have to do is dwell in and walk in that light.

Andrew Murray, *Divine Healing*

March 16

What things were gain to me, these I have counted loss for Christ.

Philippians 3:7

In the course of history, God had sought to bring man to penitence by many and grievous disciplines, but all to no avail. Man had only stiffened his neck. And thus it was as if God said, "If man will not take the blame, there is only one thing left for Me to do: I must take the blame." And that is what God did in the person of His Son on Calvary's cross—He took on Himself man's blame.

As long as we love our righteousness and are not prepared to lose our reputation, our pride forbids us to repent. But when we see Jesus losing His reputation, His all, for us, then we are melted by the love of it and are willing to be broken and take a sinner's place. We are willing to be known as we really are.

In making his surrender to Jesus, Paul was not only motivated by the love of the cross but by the sight of better gains. The knowledge of Christ Jesus utterly excelled in value what he was giving up. "I count all things but loss . . . that I may know him, and the power of his resurrection."

Resurrection, like revival, simply means receiving life again. It presupposes there has been a dying, a going down, and tells us that where that is, so there is intended to be a coming up again, a living again. Paul, in effect, says that he wants to know the coming up again of the Lord Jesus after he has gone down to the cross. There was a coming up again for Jesus; so there is for you and me.

Roy Hession, *When I Saw Him*

MARCH 17

A Man wrestled with him.

GENESIS 32:24

This passage is often quoted as an instance of Jacob's earnestness in prayer. It is nothing of the sort. It is an instance of God's earnestness to take from us all that hinders our truest life—while we resist Him with all our might and main. It was not that Jacob wished to obtain aught from God, but it was that He—the angel Jehovah—had a controversy with this double-dealing and crafty child of His: desirous to break up his self-sufficiency forever and to give scope for the development of the Israel that lay cramped and coffined within.

There was much in him that needed to be laid aside, much self-sufficiency requiring to be broken down, much dross that had to be burnt out by a consuming fire; and so the love of God drew near to him on that solemn night to wrest these things from him at whatever cost.

Has not this "Man" that wrestled with Jacob found you out? Have you not felt a holy discontent with yourself? Have you not felt that certain things, long cherished and loved, should be given up, though it should cost you blood? Have you not felt that you should yield your whole being to God but there has been a rebellious uprising of self-will within you, as if it were impossible for you to make the surrender? Have you not felt as if some mighty power was wrestling with you, against you, and for your good?

Surely these convulsive throes, these heaven-born strivings, these mysterious workings are not of man or of the will of the flesh but of God. It is God that worketh in you and wrestleth with you. Glory be to Him for His tender patience, interest, and love!

F. B. MEYER, *ISRAEL*

MARCH 18

Put away the foreign gods that are among you. . . . Then let us arise and go up to Bethel; and I will make an altar there to God.

GENESIS 35:2-3

When, having left his idols behind, Jacob had got back to Bethel and had built again the altar of renewed consecration, we are told, significantly, that "God appeared unto him again, and blessed him." Are all the readers of these lines conscious that the blessing of the Almighty is resting upon them?

Has God revealed Himself to you again after the long, sad lapse of fellowship and communion? Is the backslider back again in the house of God and at the gate of heaven? If not, would it not be wise to do as Jacob did? Ask God to show you what your idols are. Tell Him that you want to be only, always all for Him. Put away not only your sins but your weights—i.e., anything that hinders you in the Christian race. If you cannot do this yourself, tell Him that you are willing for Him to take them from you.

If you cannot say that you are willing, tell Him that you are willing to be made willing. And when you have thus surrendered your will, give yourself again to Him; entreat Him to take full possession of your entire being. Lay yourself as an Isaac upon the altar of self-dedication, and remember that He takes all we give, and at the moment of our giving it.

It may be that He will appear to us at once, flooding our spirits with the old unspeakable joy; or He may keep us waiting for a little. But it matters comparatively little if only we can say with the assurance of an unwavering faith, "We are His; nothing shall henceforth separate us from the love of God."

F. B. MEYER, *ISRAEL*

MARCH 19

I will declare my iniquity; I will be in anguish over my sin. . . .
Blessed are those who mourn, for they shall be comforted.

PSALM 38:18; MATTHEW 5:4

The salvation of the Lord Jesus is a salvation from sin. The power, the grace, the blessing of Jesus is exhibited in the taking away of sin out of us and His implanting within us instead the holiness and the life of heaven.

It is not merely the sinner that is still seeking for forgiveness who must think of and confess his sins. No, it is especially the believer that has need to acknowledge rightly and with all earnestness the sins which he still commits and their antipathy to God.

Every sin is a need that calls for Jesus. By the confession of sin, you point out to Him the spot where you are wounded and where He must exhibit the healing power of His blood. Be not afraid to make mention of your sins by name before Him. Point out to Him that which you desire He should change in you. Sin which is not confessed is also not combated. When a saved soul goes to Jesus to speak with Him about sin and to make it known to Him, it breaks sin's power and makes Christ more precious. The very same light that enables you to feel the curse of sin more deeply also enables you to discern the perfect and final victory over it.

Beloved child of God, you perhaps do not yet know what a source of blessing is a deep conviction of sin. Do not be afraid of it; do not turn away from it. The blessed Spirit of God will give to you. Through the increasing grace of Jesus in you, through your deepening fellowship in the life of heaven, He will so reveal sin's incurable corruption that this very experience shall lead you to entire surrender to Jesus.

ANDREW MURRAY, *THE LORD'S TABLE*

March 20

When he was still a great way off, his father saw him and had compassion, and ran and fell on his neck and kissed him.

Luke 15:20

It is not easy to go at once to God when conscious of failure. In fact, the battle turns most upon this point, for once we go, we are saved in the very going! The devil, our conscience, our shame, and our regret all combine to keep us away. We have a sort of feeling that we ought to be miserable for a few hours first! It looks so presumptuous, a making light of sin, to dare to run to God at once; and yet, if we delay, we know one fall is but the precursor of many. The sin will be the same hideous thing—and worse—three hours hence.

The way of victory in the hour of defeat is to arise at once and go to the Father, saying, "Father, I have sinned," knowing that it is written, "I said after she had done all these things, Turn thou unto me . . . only acknowledge . . ." (Jer. 3:7, 13).

It is the immediate, frank confession to God that the devil seeks to keep us from. And as we do not know our Father well in the early days, too often he succeeds, and we stay away from God until in bitter sorrow we are driven back.

See that little child! It has fallen in the mud, and its clothes are soiled. Supposing it sat down in the mud and said, "It's of no use. I shall never walk and keep my garments white!"

No, little child of the Father, discouragement and repining only increase your sin. Get up and go back to your Father, pleading the precious blood.

Jessie Penn-Lewis, *Communion with God*

MARCH 21

I acknowledged my sin to you, and my iniquity I have not hidden.
I said, "I will confess my transgressions to the LORD."

PSALM 32:5

An honest heart will not try to cloak its sins and to make excuses for circumstances and about lack of training. It will not evade the truth of God and seek to establish its own righteousness. It will cry out, "God be merciful to me a sinner," while others may be saying, "I thank thee, that I am not as other men." It is honest with itself; it honestly desires to know the truth about itself, however humiliating that may be. It is honestly willing to put away sin and to accept salvation on God's terms.

Honest renouncing of sin *because it is sin* will make good ground for the word of life, for many grieve over the consequences of their sin far more than over the sin itself in its exceeding sinfulness.

An honest heart "heareth the word, and understandeth it" (Matt. 13:23), because the Spirit reveals the truth when there is an honest desire to obey it—for He will deign to teach a soul beset with honest difficulties, while He refuses to satisfy mere curiosity.

Honest dealing with sin, honest renunciation of all known sin, honest confession of sin, honest desire to know the truth and to do it, honest reception of the Word of God without reasoning—these conditions make good ground for the sowing of the seed. In such a heart the Word of God can work effectually.

JESSIE PENN-LEWIS, *FRUITFUL LIVING*

March 22

A full reward be given you by the Lord God of Israel,
under whose wings you have come for refuge.

Ruth 2:12

When she "happened to come to the part of the field belonging to Boaz," he took special note of her and extended to her unusual favors. He welcomed her into his fields; he gave her permission to drink from the vessels provided for the reapers; he assured her that he had charged his young men not to make improper advances to her or molest her. Then he invited her to eat with him and his reapers; he personally passed parched grain to her, and that in such quantity that she was not only satisfied herself but also had something left over. Finally, he instructed his reapers to let her glean right among the sheaves.

The magnanimity of Boaz to the poor gleaner, Ruth, is nothing to be compared to the vast grace of the Lord Jesus toward the one who is humble enough to confess himself a failed Christian and take the sinner's God to be his God. Once we start taking that ground, we find ourselves the object of His special attention in a way that is not the case when we are protesting our sufficiency.

As we bow before Him in our acknowledged failure and poverty, knowing that only Jesus can do the sinner any good, we find love, encouragement, and help coming to us from every direction in a way that is quite extraordinary and quite undeserved. Handfuls of precious promises are left on purpose all over the place, and as we stoop to gather them, we hear the words sounding again and again, "Do not reproach her; do not reproach her."

And we find that, though we are but poor gleaners, the field in which we are gleaning is indeed the field of grace; for Jesus is doing things for us that we neither expected nor deserved, and they are but the promise of more to come.

Roy Hession, *Our Nearest Kinsman*

March 23

There is no creature hidden from His sight, but all things are naked and open to the eyes of Him to whom we must give account.

Hebrews 4:13

Lord God, You search and know us. You are He who knows the hearts and tries the reins. Your eyes see through the heart of the ungodly and the righteous alike. You are the omniscient One, the Searcher of hearts.

With fear and yet from the depths of my heart, I say to You, "Holy God, I wish to tolerate no single sin, however secret or deeply rooted it may be. Lord, I crave Your help; I place myself in the light of Your flaming eyes, before which no sin can stand. Search me, O God, and know my heart."

Lord, make me know the sin to which I am blind—my characteristic sins also, about which I am so sensitive when any other person speaks of them.

Lord, use friend or foe; use what means You will, O my Father—only search me, and know my heart! Cleanse me from secret errors, and let no hurtful way abide with me, but lead me in the way that is everlasting (Ps. 139:23–24).

Yes, gracious Lord, give me such an overmastering conviction of the entire corruption of my nature that I shall be constrained to receive in its completeness the perfect redemption of Christ. Amen.

Andrew Murray, *The Lord's Table*

March 24

Thus says the Lord God, the Holy One of Israel:
"In returning and rest you shall be saved."

Isaiah 30:15

There are two conditions here if God's salvation is to come to us in a new way. First, there is returning—which is simply repentance, returning to the Lord. And then resting. For many of us, however, it is too often "in returning and *resolving*"—in repenting and making new promises. But that is to put us again on the ground of works in spite of having repented. But when we have seen the blood of Jesus, we do not talk like that; it is in returning and *resting*.

Now that we have returned, we can take it that we are right with God by the power of the blood of Jesus; we can rest with regard to our righteousness before God. We can also rest with regard to all the consequences of our sin and folly. Once the man in the middle of the mess he has created has repented, he can rest with regard to that mess, for God not only forgives but delights to take over the situation that has been created and make a new thing out of it. As someone has said, "Jesus not only forgives the messer but unmesses the mess." And so it is that the returning one can rest on that count too and see the Lord do wondrous things for him.

Roy Hession, *When I Saw Him*

MARCH 25

I will not contend forever, nor will I always be angry.

ISAIAH 57:16

The effects of sin and folly in our lives are irrecoverable apart from the grace of God. Having stained ourselves with guilt, what can we do to regain peace? Having messed up things, what can we do to get them straight again? The answer, if only we will face it, is that we can do nothing. We have limitless power to commit sin (what giants we are in that realm if we choose to be!), but we have no power at all to atone for it or undo its effects.

We sometimes think that if we can become better Christians and be nicer to our fellows that that will restore things. But, for myself, I find the moment I feel I have got to become a "little bit better" to qualify, I am defeated before I start; for I know from experience that it is becoming that "little bit better" that always defeats me.

But be encouraged; you are not going to remain empty. In coming back to God as an empty sinner, saying, "I'm all wrong; I'm the one to blame," you become a candidate for the gracious provision of One who has the right to redeem everything.

He is saying, "Everything has gone wrong for you, and that is because of your own sin. But what of that? 'Is My hand shortened so that it cannot now redeem? Or have I no power to deliver?'" (Isa. 50:2). I think I can hear those who receive this message answering in surprise, "We always knew You could redeem, but we never thought You would; for it has all been so much our own fault." And in reply Jehovah seems to say, "I am your Redeemer, made for such a situation as this."

ROY HESSION, *OUR NEAREST KINSMAN*

MARCH 26

If the Son makes you free, you shall be free indeed.

JOHN 8:36

How tremendously great is the remission and redemption of sins through Jesus Christ!

Many Christians do not sufficiently realize the work which Jesus Christ is doing for us at this very moment. Many of us believe that He died for our sins. We believe in His death and resurrection, but we forget that after His resurrection He ascended into heaven and sat down on the right hand of the Father and began to live for us as truly as He died for us.

The devil makes accusations against us day and night. But Jesus is our Advocate. In Him we are the righteousness of God (2 Cor. 5:21). If, after having been forgiven for a sin, we are still worrying about it, even for five minutes more, we are robbing both Him and ourselves of much joy. "Resist the devil, and he will flee from you" (James 4:7). No better weapon could be found to use against him than this text.

The consciousness of sin may degenerate into defeatism: "It's too bad, but that's the way I am." The devil rejoices when we are defeated but is afraid of the consciousness of victory. The devil makes us conscious of sin. The Spirit of God makes us conscious of sin and then conscious of victory.

CORRIE TEN BOOM, *AMAZING LOVE*

March 27

Blessed is the man to whom the Lord does not impute iniquity.

Psalm 32:2

What Jesus had to do to settle things with the law took Him outside the city, to the place of disgrace, to die on a cross between two thieves as if He was one Himself. The supreme thing He did there was to rob sin of its power to condemn us. He did it by bearing the curse attached to the broken law Himself, thus exhausting it.

In Romans 6:10 there is a sentence which tells us just this: "The death that He died, He died to sin once for all." It does not say there that He died *for* sin merely but *to* sin; that is, He died to sin's power to condemn Him any longer for the multitude of sins He took upon Him. The moment His blood was shed, the moment He said, "It is finished," Satan and the law could not hold Him any longer, because the price had been paid. But if the law has lost its power to condemn our substitute, it has likewise lost its power to condemn all those whose substitute He was!

I want to extol the mighty power of the blood of Jesus. Its efficacy extends not only to the sin itself but to the hangover of shame. The situation a man has created for himself may still continue and be only in process of recovery, but the man in the middle of it can be at perfect peace with God. By the power of the blood of Jesus, the element of guilt in the situation has been completely expunged. He can pray with confidence and joy about it as if it had not been his fault at all and expect God to work on his behalf. Though wars may still arise against him, he knows the blessedness of the man to whom the Lord does not impute iniquity (Rom. 4:6–8).

Roy Hession, *Our Nearest Kinsman*

MARCH 28

We have redemption through His blood, the forgiveness of sins.

EPHESIANS 1:7

Usually we equate redemption with the forgiveness of sins. Thank God, redemption does include that. But if you import into the New Testament word "redemption" these Old Testament associations on which it is based, you find it is a far bigger thing than that which deals only with the forgiveness of sins. Redemption is that activity of the grace of God that not only forgives a man's sins but also restores and overrules all the loss occasioned by his sin.

And what loss we have subjected ourselves to because of our folly, sin, and pride! We lose our experience of blessedness. We lose our happy relationships with others in the home, in the church, in the world outside; and we set people against us. We make mistakes and wrong choices because of our self-will and can find ourselves in grievous and complicated situations as a result.

But with God our failure is never final! Jesus Christ is the Redeemer of lost men and lost situations, whether the situation has been wrong for half a lifetime or only a day. When He moves in to redeem, He not only forgives the sin we confess but also overrules for good the whole situation in which we have landed ourselves! Yes, and when He starts doing that sort of thing, He does it in style. He often gives back to a man far more than he forfeited so that the repentant sinner cannot go on blaming himself but is lost in wonder, love, and praise for all that grace has done for a poor failure like himself. Oh, this great and marvelous God of redemption!

ROY HESSION, *OUR NEAREST KINSMAN*

MARCH 29

Though your sins are like scarlet, they shall be as white as snow.

ISAIAH 1:18

I had spoken the night before on the subject "The problem of sin has been solved on the cross of Jesus Christ."

And now Jack said, "I believe that there is remission of sins through Jesus Christ, but redemption? No, I can't see that. We have to carry the consequences of our sins as long as we live."

After dinner we continued our talk in the garden. There were only three of us now; John, with whom I had been working for the past two weeks, and Jack. It was a sad story.

"We were not very good boys in high school. I dated a lot of different girls, and one time things went wrong. I had to marry the girl; and four months later the baby came. Nobody knows that I am married, and no one must find it out. I want to become a minister; but if people hear about this, my whole career will be gone. I am living a lie, and don't know what to do about it. I'll have to bear the consequences of my sin as long as I live."

Then John began to speak. "Jesus does not patch things up. He renews. If you will ask Him to go back with you to that dark spot in your life, He will change its darkness into light. If you will now accept in faith that Jesus is the victor over the past, present, and future of everyone who surrenders his life completely to Him, He will change that dark spot in your life into a blessing."

All three of us then prayed, and Jack said, "I don't understand these things; but here I am, Lord. I know that You have said, 'He who comes to Me I will by no means cast out.'"

An hour later, as I was leaving, Jack said to me, "Corrie, I can laugh again. I haven't been able to laugh for a year. But now I am free."

And I knew that it was true.

CORRIE TEN BOOM, *AMAZING LOVE*

March 30

My beloved is mine, and I am his.

Song of Solomon 2:16

The only hope of a decreasing self is an increasing Christ. There is too much of the self-life in us all; chafing against God's will, refusing God's gifts, instigating the very services we render to God, simulating humility and meekness for the praise of men. But how can we be rid of this accursed self-consciousness and pride? Ah, we must turn our back on our shadow and our face toward Christ! We must look at all things from His standpoint. Surely if we love Christ with a constraining passion, we shall think His thoughts and feel His joys and no longer live unto ourselves but unto Him.

The Son of God is not content to love us. He cannot rest until He has all our love in return. "He looketh in at the windows" of the soul "and showeth Himself through the lattice." Our Beloved speaks and says unto us, "Rise up, my love, my fair one, and come away." And as our response, He waits to hear us say, "My beloved is mine, and I am his."

F. B. Myer, *John the Baptist*

March 31

If anyone desires to come after Me, let him deny himself, and take up his cross daily, and follow Me.

Luke 9:23

The word "must" is surely unpopular nowadays. Neither children nor adults like to be told what they must do. Yet there are certain compulsions in God's Word, and there is no way around them. They must be met if we are going to obey God!

The believer must die to self, reckon himself dead indeed unto sin, deny himself, count himself crucified with Christ, that Christ may fill his life and be all in all. The Christian is only the friend of the Bridegroom, and his delight is in hearing the Bridegroom's voice. This means more than the mere giving up of amusements, money, time: it means renouncing one's own will and self. Peter forsook his nets and boat on his first call; it was quite a while before he gave up *himself.*

Said George Müller, "There was a day when I died—utterly died to George Müller, his opinions, preferences, and will; died to the world, its approval or censure." Luther used to smite his breast and say, "Martin Luther does not live here: Jesus Christ lives here."

Between conversion and consecration stands Christ, and He is the key to both. We are *saved* by simply believing and receiving Him; we are *consecrated* as we yield to Him and are able to say "Not I, but Christ."

Vance Havner, *Reflections on the Gospels*

April

Abiding with Christ

The Testimony of Hudson Taylor

At a time when the interior of China was closed to foreigners and when ignorance, fanaticism, and race prejudice made it exceedingly hazardous to venture into the interior of China, Hudson Taylor established a chain of missions in almost all the great provinces of the interior. The church records no more amazing story of sacrifice and achievement than that of the humble doctor who laid the foundations of the kingdom of God in the interior of China!

But Hudson Taylor was not always victorious, even though he had already achieved great things as a missionary. In his letters to loved ones, he often poured out the pain of his soul over the fact of his spiritual poverty. If ever a man strove to imitate the Master, he was that man! But all to no avail.

In 1869 a great change took place. It was so radical, so complete, so overwhelming that all Mr. Taylor's fellow workers were soon aware of the fact. A tide of divine life swept through the mission as a result. "He was a joyous man now, a bright, happy Christian. He had been a toiling, burdened one before, with latterly not much rest of soul. It was resting now on Jesus and letting Him do the work which makes all the difference. Whenever he spoke in meetings after that, a new power seemed to flow from him; and in the practical things of life a new peace possessed him. He cast everything on God in a new way and gave more time to prayer. . . . From him flowed the living waters to others."

But what caused this great change?

To his sister he wrote, "I prayed, agonized, strove, fasted, made resolutions, read the Word of God more diligently, sought more time for meditation and prayer—but all was without effect. Then came the question, is there no rescue? Must it be thus to the end?

"All the time I felt assured there was in Christ all I needed, but the practical question was, how was I to get it out? I knew full well that there was in the Root abundant fatness. As the light gradually dawned on me, I saw that faith was the only prerequisite to lay hold on His fullness and make it my own. *But I had not this faith!* I strove for it, but it would not come; tried to exercise it but in vain. Seeing more and more the wondrous supply laid up in Jesus, the fullness of our precious Savior, my helplessness and guilt seemed to increase.

"When my agony of soul was at its height, a sentence in a letter from dear McCarthy was used to remove the scales from my eyes, and the Spirit of God revealed the truth of our oneness with Jesus as I had never known it before. He wrote, 'But how to get faith strengthened? Not by striving after faith, but by resting on the Faithful One.' As I read, I saw it all: 'If we believe not, He abideth faithful.' I looked to Jesus and saw (and when I saw, oh, how joy flowed!) that He had said, 'I will never leave you.' *Ah! there is rest*, I thought.

"But this was not all He showed me, nor one half. As I thought of the Vine and the Branches, what light the blessed Spirit poured direct into my soul: I saw not only that Jesus would never leave me but that I was a member of His body, of His flesh, and of His bones. The Vine, now I see, is not the root merely but all—root, stem, branches, twigs, leaves, flowers, fruit; and Jesus is not only that—He is soil and sunshine, air and showers, and ten thousand times more. Oh! the joy of seeing this truth. I do pray that the eyes of your understanding may be enlightened, that you may know and enjoy the riches freely given us in Christ."

F. J. Huegel, *Bone of His Bone*

April 1

If anyone is in Christ, he is a new creation.

2 Corinthians 5:17

The gospel proclaims a new creation: a new tree—union with a new root—being grafted on to a new stock. This is not to improve the old but to be translated into a new position.

Take another illustration. Here is a man, let us suppose, who has failed in business. He is not only hopelessly insolvent; his credit is gone, and his name is disgraced. All efforts of his own to retrieve his position are utterly fruitless; he is beyond all hope of recovery in that direction. But hope comes to him from another quarter. Let us suppose he is taken into partnership by one whose name stands high in the commercial world. He becomes a partner in a wealthy and honorable firm. All his debts are paid by that firm, and the past is canceled. But this is not all. He gets an entirely new standing. His old name is set aside, forgotten, buried forever. He has now a new name. In that name he transacts all his business. His old name is never again mentioned.

We have here a faint shadow of what the gospel bestows. To be a believer in Christ is to have passed out of our old position—to lose our old name—and to take our stand on an entirely new ground. We are baptized "into the name of the Lord"; we are "in Christ." This is not a privilege that comes to the believer by degrees; it is complete and absolute at once. And the moment the transition takes place, the believer stands not on the ground of probation but on the ground of redemption.

This truth is fundamental. The "in Christ" of standing is the foundation of all practical godliness, of all Christian service. We must start here, or we cannot take a single step in the way of holiness.

Evan Hopkins, *The Law of Liberty in the Spiritual Life*

April 2

Having been justified by faith, . . . we have access by faith into this grace in which we stand, and rejoice in hope of the glory of God.

Romans 5:1–2

Justification has done for the justified a twofold work, both aspects of which are all important for the man who asks, "*How can* I walk and please God?"

First, it has decisively broken the claim of sin upon him as guilt. He stands clear of that exhausting and enfeebling load. The pilgrim's burden has fallen from his back at the foot of the Lord's cross, into the Lord's grave. He *has* peace with God, not in emotion but in covenant, through our Lord Jesus Christ. He has a permanent and unreserved introduction into a Father's loving and welcoming presence in the merit of his Head.

But, as we have already noted, justification has also been to him, as it were, the signal of his union with Christ in new life. Not only therefore does it give him an eternal occasion for gratitude; it gives him a *new power* with which to live the grateful life—a power that is not in justification itself but in what it opens up. It is the gate through which he passes to the fountain; it is the wall which protects the fountain; the roof which shields him as he drinks. The fountain is his justifying Lord's exalted life, His risen life, poured into the man's being by the Spirit who makes Head and member one. And it is as justified that he has access to the fountain and drinks as deep as he will of its life, its power, its purity.

H. C. G. Moule, *The Epistle to the Romans*

APRIL 3

Christ also suffered once for sins, the just for the unjust.

1 PETER 3:18

It is a true instinct of man's nature that teaches him that guilt needs compensation; but the mistake into which he falls, if left to himself, is that he seeks to make that compensation by means which he himself has devised. While the voice of conscience tells us that some amends are needed for the guilt of our sin, it is only revelation that shows us how those amends can be made; it is only there that we learn *what* sacrifice is sufficient to atone for human guilt.

The believer sees that Christ, by dying for him, has completely delivered him from the penalty of sin. So it is his privilege to see that, because he is identified with Christ in that death, he is also delivered from sin as a ruling principle. Its power is broken. He is, in that sense, "free from sin" (Rom. 6:18, 22).

Freedom from sin's dominion is a blessing we may claim by faith, just as we accept pardon. We may claim it as that which Christ has purchased for us, obtained for our immediate acceptance. We may go forth as set free from sin and as alive unto God in Jesus Christ our Lord. This is freedom from sin as a ruling principle.

EVAN HOPKINS, *THE LAW OF LIBERTY IN THE SPIRITUAL LIFE*

April 4

Abide in Me, and I in you.

John 15:4

This verse [John 15:4] lays down for us a divine principle, which is that God has done the work in Christ and not in us as individuals. The all-inclusive death and the all-inclusive resurrection of God's Son were accomplished fully and finally apart from us in the first place. It is the history of Christ which is to become the experience of the Christian, and we have no spiritual experience apart from Him.

Every true spiritual experience means that we have discovered a certain fact in Christ and have entered into that. Anything that is not from Him in this way is going to evaporate very soon. "I have discovered that in Christ; then, praise the Lord, it is mine! I possess it, Lord, because it is in Thee." Oh, it is a great thing to know the facts of Christ as the foundation for our experience!

So our attention must be fixed on Christ. "Abide in Me, and I in you" is the divine order. Faith in the objective facts makes those facts true subjectively. As the apostle Paul puts it, "We all . . . beholding . . . the glory of the Lord, are being transformed into the same image" (2 Cor. 3:18). Our business is to look away to Him. As we do so, He undertakes to fulfill His Word in us.

How do we abide? "Of God are ye in Christ Jesus." It was the work of God to put you there, and He has done it. Now stay there! Do not be moved back onto your own ground. Never look at yourself as though you were not in Christ. Look at Christ, and see yourself in Him. *Abide in Him.* Rest in the fact that God has put you in His Son, and live in the expectation that He will complete His work in you.

Watchman Nee, *The Normal Christian Life*

April 5

There is therefore now no condemnation to those who are in Christ Jesus, who do not walk according to the flesh, but according to the Spirit.

Romans 8:1

To be "in Christ" is to have the consciousness of His favor. This is a matter not of standing but of experience—and yet not of feeling but of faith. We are commanded to abide in Christ. Those who have taken their stand in Christ—who are justified—are now required to remain, to dwell, or abide, in Him for *sanctification*.

It is possible, alas! not to abide in Him. And what happens when the believer ceases to abide? He then lives the self-life. There is such a thing as a religious self-life. Is it not the life that is too often manifested even by those who have a saving knowledge of Christ?

Many have a true aim, seeking to glorify Christ and to be made like Him, and yet they are continually being disappointed. Failure and defeat meet them at every turn. Not because they do not try, not because they do not struggle—they do all this—but because the life they are living is essentially the *self-life* and not the *Christ life*. They are brought into condemnation. This arises from the fact that the "law of sin" in their members is stronger than their renewed nature.

To be "in Christ" is to have the individual human spirit apprehended, or laid hold of, by the Holy Spirit of God. We are thus not only brought into harmony with God but linked with the power of God. The ability we lack when we struggle to overcome in the self-life is no longer lacking in the Christ life. This is to be free from the law of sin and death—this is to be spiritually minded.

Evan Hopkins, *The Law of Liberty in the Spiritual Life*

April 6

We have this treasure in earthen vessels.

2 Corinthians 4:7

An *earthen* vessel, although illuminated! A body of fragile clay, although indwelt by the Lord of glory!

As regards the service for Christ, "weakness, and fear, and much trembling" seem always to be the necessary condition of the vessel for the fullest "demonstration of the Spirit and power." A trembling vessel energized by the Holy Spirit is the picture before us in the life of Paul.

The manifestation of the life of Christ in earthen vessels is transparent and simple. So natural and open and free. It allows no room for insisting that others should accept all that is said as being "from the Lord" and promotes neither a spirit of bondage nor a fear of exercising the mental powers given to men by God Himself.

We need therefore to recognize the humanity and individuality of the earthen vessel alongside of the blessed indwelling of the risen Lord. Then we may faithfully declare "Thus says the Lord" about all that is written in His Word (not *our* view of what the Word means but the Word itself simply as it is written) while humbly saying about all light given personally to the soul, "I *think* also that I have the Spirit of God."

Jessie Penn-Lewis, *Power for Service*

April 7

He who believes in Me, as the Scripture has said,
out of his heart will flow rivers of living water.

John 7:38

What is the source of all practical holiness? It must have a source. Every river has a spring. In vital union with all fruit, there must be a root. What then is the source of our fruitfulness?

It is Christ Himself. There is only one source of all holy living; there is only one holy life. "I am the life"—not simply because "I am the pattern of a perfect life" or because "I am the bestower of the gift of life" nor yet because "I am the vital principle itself." Christ is the spring itself. "With thee is the fountain of life" (Ps. 36:9).

It is Christ living within us. "Not I," says the apostle, though I am redeemed. "Not I," though I am regenerate and have eternal life. "I live; yet not I, but Christ liveth in me" (Gal. 2:20).

It was this that Christ promised in the fourth chapter of Saint John's Gospel: "The water that I shall give him shall become in him a well of water springing up into everlasting life" (John 4:14). There is no progress in our appropriation of Christ as the life; there is, however, a progress in our heart knowledge of that fact. We see first the life in its source (John 1:4), then in its bestowal (John 3:16), then in its indwelling (John 4:14), and then in its practical outflow (John 7:38). It is in this last stage that we have the fruit, the outcome of an indwelling Christ.

Here then is the source of all practical holiness. It is important to lay the emphasis on that word "liveth." "Christ *liveth* in me."

Evan Hopkins, *The Law of Liberty in the Spiritual Life*

APRIL 8

Christ in you . . .

COLOSSIANS 1:27

Nothing less than this is His relation to His saints. He makes reconciliation for them. He presides over them. He is their unifying Center. But within all these operations, the innermost fact is this: He is in them by His Spirit, who unites the member and the Head so that "he who is joined to the Lord is one spirit" (1 Cor. 6:17). He is so present to all His own that nothing less than this word "in" satisfies the revealed thought.

In many a beautiful phrase, He is presented to us in His wonderful proximity: "come *unto* me"; "the LORD is *near*"; "I am *with* you all the days"; "the Lord stood *with* me, and strengthened me"; "to depart, and to be *with* Christ"; "we shall ever be *with* the Lord"; "*together with* him." But these bright circles surround this yet more radiant center: "Christ *in* you."

The indwelling of Christ in the Christian is presented to us as a normal—nay, as a necessary—fact of all living Christianity: "Know ye not that Jesus Christ is in you, unless you are somehow counterfeits?" (2 Cor. 13:5). If we are in simplicity at His feet, He, thus indwelling by the Spirit, is in our being. And the indwelling "in the heart"—what is it but this fact realized by the faith which sees and claims it? It is not an attainment; it is a recognition. "Come, and let us walk in the light of the Lord." Come, and let the Lord, humbly welcomed without misgiving, "dwell in us and walk in us" every hour of life.

H. C. G. MOULE, *COLOSSIAN AND PHILEMON STUDIES*

April 9

I am the vine, you are the branches.

John 15:5

It was in connection with the parable of the vine that our Lord first used the expression "Abide in me." That parable, so simple and yet so rich in its teaching, gives us the best and most complete illustration of the meaning of our Lord's command and the union to which He invites us.

The connection between a vine and its branches is a living one. No external, temporary union will suffice; no work of man can effect it. The branch, whether an original or an engrafted one, is such only by the Creator's own work, in virtue of which the life, the sap, the fatness, and the fruitfulness of the vine communicate themselves to the branch.

And just so it is with the believer too. His union with his Lord is no work of human wisdom or human will but an act of God, by which the closest and most complete life union is effected between the Son of God and the sinner. "God hath sent forth *the Spirit of his Son* into *your hearts.*" The same Spirit which dwelt and still dwells in the Son becomes the life of the believer; in the unity of that one Spirit and the fellowship of the same life which is in Christ, he is one with Him. As between the vine and branch, it is a life union that makes them one.

And Jesus, to whom we owe our life—how completely does He give Himself for us and to us! All His fullness and all His riches are for you, O believer; for the vine does not live for itself, keeps nothing for itself, but exists only for the branches. All that Jesus is in heaven He is for *us.*

Andrew Murray, *Abide in Christ*

APRIL 10

Christ, having been raised from the dead, dies no more . . .
but the life that He lives, He lives to God. Likewise you also, reckon yourselves
to be dead indeed to sin, but alive to God in Christ Jesus our Lord.

ROMANS 6:9–11

The sixth chapter of Romans presents not an *aspect* of truth but the *foundation truth* upon which every believer must stand to know anything about victory. It not only reveals the very heart of Calvary but the very heart of the resurrection. Calvary means the death identification of the believer with Christ so that he lives and moves in a spiritual sphere in resurrection life.

We need to see that there is a life side to the sixth chapter of Romans—the resurrection side. On the resurrection side of the cross, death has no more dominion. The negative side of death should not be dwelt upon to the exclusion of the positive *life side* of union with Christ. The death is to be reckoned an accomplished fact, every moment. But "Christ being raised dieth no more." He is *alive*, and the believer identified by faith with Him in death is united to Him in His life on the life side of the cross.

The believer must reckon that he *has* died—not that he is *going* to die. If he again and again asks God to "put to death" some one point, he will never realize the positive life power. Perhaps you are saying, "I have not died to this and that." Take your position now on Romans 6:6, and then reckon yourself "*alive unto God.*"

JESSIE PENN-LEWIS, *THE CROSS: THE TOUCHSTONE OF FAITH*

April 11

He . . . will subdue our iniquities.

Micah 7:19

As I have an Advocate, so I have an accuser. Let the devil accuse, but it is too late, for God Himself has cast all my sins into the very deeps of the sea, forgiven and forgotten (Mic. 7:19).

Satan accuses us to our own hearts as well as before God. How many Christians listen to him, pray and even sing themselves into feelings of guilt and self-accusation? Instant confession means instant forgiveness and cleansing, rendering the accuser impotent.

Does this sound too easy? Is not the fight one of strife and wrestling? Does not Scripture say, "Ye have not yet resisted unto blood, striving against sin" (Heb. 12:4)? Yes, it is a tremendous struggle in which we need the whole armor of God until the very last minute of our lives, but it is always available in the person of Jesus Christ.

Some Christians laugh about their sins instead of weeping. But we are told, "Be ye perfect" (Matt. 5:48). Holiness is not an idea or suggestion; it is a definite command. Bring your sins to the source of forgiveness and cleansing. Don't play with them.

Then look forward with Paul: "I leave the past behind and with hands outstretched to whatever lies ahead I go straight for the goal—my reward the honour of being called by God in Christ" (Phil. 3:14, Phillips).

Corrie ten Boom, *Plenty for Everyone*

April 12

. . . that the God of our Lord Jesus Christ, the Father of glory, may give to you the spirit of wisdom and revelation in the knowledge of Him.

EPHESIANS 1:17

The normal Christian life must begin with a very definite "knowing," which is not just knowing something about the truth or understanding some important doctrine. It is not an intellectual knowledge at all but an opening of the eyes of the heart to see what we have in Christ.

Such knowledge comes by divine revelation. It comes from the Lord Himself. For the written Word of God to become a living Word from God to you, He had to give you a "spirit of wisdom and revelation in the knowledge of him" (Eph. 1:17).

What you needed was to know Christ in that way, and it is always so. So there comes a time, in regard to any new apprehension of Christ, when you know it in your own heart, you "see" it in your spirit.

When once the light of God dawns upon your heart, you see yourself in Christ. It is not now because someone has told you and not merely because Romans 6 says so. It is something more even than that. You know it because God has revealed it to you by His Spirit. You may not feel it; you may not understand it; but you know it, for you have seen it. Once you have seen yourself in Christ, nothing can shake your assurance of that blessed fact.

While Christians may enter into the deeper life by different ways, one thing is certain: any true experience of value in the sight of God must have been reached by way of a new discovery of the meaning of the person and work of the Lord Jesus. That is a crucial test and a safe one.

WATCHMAN NEE, *THE NORMAL CHRISTIAN LIFE*

APRIL 13

Knowing this, that our old man was crucified . . . , reckon yourselves to be dead.

ROMANS 6:6, 11

God's Word makes it clear that "knowing" is to precede "reckoning." "Know this . . . reckon." The sequence is most important. Our reckoning must be based on knowledge of divinely revealed fact, for otherwise faith has no foundation on which to rest. When we know, then we reckon spontaneously.

Having said then that revelation leads spontaneously to reckoning, we must not lose sight of the fact that we are presented with a command: "Reckon ye . . ." There is a definite attitude to be taken. God asks us to do the accounting, to put down "I have died" and then to abide by it. Why? Because it is a fact. When the Lord Jesus was on the cross, I was there in Him. Therefore I reckon it to be true. I reckon and declare that I have died in Him.

Paul said, "Reckon ye also yourselves to be dead unto sin, but alive unto God." How is this possible? "In Christ Jesus." Never forget that it is always and only true in Christ. If you look at yourself, you will think death is not there, but it is a question of faith not in yourself but in Him. You look to the Lord and know what He has done. "Lord, I believe in Thee. I reckon upon the fact in Thee." Stand there all the day.

WATCHMAN NEE, *THE NORMAL CHRISTIAN LIFE*

April 14

. . . rooted and built up in Him.

Colossians 2:7

When we first received Christ by a simple act of faith, we were put *into* Him by the operation of the Spirit of God. Christ is in us, and our spirits are joined to Him as the risen One. But we are also to abide in Him as a sphere in which we are to walk day by day. As we began, so we are to continue—simply trusting and relying upon Him and abiding in Him. The life side of the cross means to be *alive* to God—"in Christ Jesus."

"Having in Him your root," continues the apostle [Col. 2:7, CH]. You cannot be rooted in one place today and in another place the next. Therefore see to your roots.

"Having in *Him* your root"—this clearly shows the need of our understanding the cross as the basic position from which we must never be moved. It is into His death that we are to be rooted. We cannot ever pass on into a life where we get past the cross or advance to any goal leaving the cross behind. To do so is like a tree refusing to root itself into the ground. We are to reckon ourselves "dead indeed unto sin" and living unto God, but it is "in Christ Jesus." In Him we must be rooted and in Him have our foundation, whereon we are continually to be built up; i.e., we must ever be striking our roots deeper into His death.

We are put into Him in His death and then into Him in His life, on the resurrection side of the cross. Therefore, "persevere steadfastly in your faith." When you first received Christ Jesus the Lord, you believed *into* Him; now stay in Him, be rooted in Him, have your foundation in Him. Have all your Spirit life built up in Him.

Jessie Penn-Lewis, *The Centrality of the Cross*

April 15

. . . the righteousness of God, through faith in Jesus Christ.

ROMANS 3:22

A young woman student came to me with a distressed face and a heavy heart. "I have been listening," she said, "to what has been said about victory and peace and power, and I am longing for it, but I can't get it. I am finishing my work here this summer; I am going out into the field of evangelism. But if I don't get what you are talking about, I shall feel that my entire course at Moody Institute will have been a failure, and I dare not go out into the work."

We talked together about the simple matter of surrender and faith, first giving yourself wholly to God, and then just believing that God is doing His part. Said she, "I know it is just a question of faith, but *I haven't got that faith.* That's the thing that's keeping me out. I can't seem to get the faith for victory."

"Are you saved?" I asked her.

"Oh, yes," she said.

"What makes you think you are saved?"

"Why," she said, "I know I am; John 3:16 settles that. God has told us that anyone who believes on Jesus as Savior is saved. I just take it on the Word of God."

"Well, then," I answered, "you have all the faith you need, and you are using it. For it's the faith that you are already using and have used for years for your salvation that is the only faith you need for victory."

"Do you mean that!" she exclaimed. "Is it just the same as salvation?" And her burden dropped then and there; and in the days that followed, she praised God that the faith she already had, and had had all the time, was the only faith she needed.

CHARLES TRUMBULL, *VICTORY IN CHRIST*

April 16

Those who receive abundance of grace and of the gift of righteousness will reign in life through the One, Jesus Christ.

Romans 5:17

Abundant life—a reigning in life—was the purpose of Calvary. The death Christ died He died unto sin for *us*, and He died "once for all" (Rom. 6:10, margin). So they [Paul's readers] were to *reckon* themselves dead unto sin with Him and utterly refuse to let it reign over them. Abiding in Him as their very life, they would *reign* in life in Jesus Christ their Lord.

"But I have reckoned thus, and it seems nothing but reckoning a lie!" cries some longing heart.

Ah, soul, maybe your eyes are in the wrong direction. You are looking within, occupied more with your reckoning than with the work of your Savior. The Holy Spirit will not bear witness to your "reckon" apart from the *object* of your reckoning.

Look away to Calvary. The Lord Jesus died on your behalf and, as your representative, carried you with Him to His cross. Relying upon the Holy Spirit and in faith in the Word of God, "let not sin therefore reign," for God has said that through Christ's death and your sharing of that death, "sin shall not have the mastery over you" (Rom. 6:14, CH).

Hidden in Christ upon His cross and joined to Him in His life, your part, O child of God, is the continual choice of your will—for "to whom ye yield," his "servants ye are" (Rom. 6:16). In the hour of sore temptation, in the center of your being, you must promptly retire, so to speak, to the cross; and hiding in Him who carried you there, refuse to be drawn out of your place in Him. Do not struggle with anything that comes to you, but hand over all to Him whose life you do share, and you shall find that He is able to deliver and to keep you day by day.

Jessie Penn-Lewis, *The Cross of Calvary*

APRIL 17

The anointing which you have received from Him abides in you, . . . and just as it has taught you, you will abide in Him.

1 JOHN 2:27

How often it is that the precious words "Abide in me" are heard with a sigh! It is as if we understand so little what they really mean. We long for someone who could make it perfectly clear that the abiding is in very deed within our reach. If we would but listen to the word we have from John this day, what hope and joy it would bring! It gives us the divine assurance that we have the anointing of the Holy Spirit to teach us all things, and this includes teaching us how to abide in Christ.

"Alas!" someone answers, "this word does not give me comfort; it only depresses me more. For it tells of another privilege I so little know how to enjoy. I do not understand how the teaching of the Spirit is given—where or how I can discern His voice."

Thoughts like these come from an error which is very common among believers. They imagine that the Spirit, in teaching them, must reveal the mysteries of the spiritual life first to their intellect and only afterward in their experience. But God's way is just the opposite of this. What holds true of all spiritual truth is specially true of the abiding in Christ: *we must live and experience truth in order to know it.*

"*If ye abide* in my word, *ye shall understand* the truth": in these and other words of God, we are taught that there is a habit of mind and life which precedes the understanding of the truth. True discipleship consists in *first* following and *then* knowing the Lord. The believing surrender to Christ, and the submission to His Word to expect what appears most improbable, is the only way to the full blessedness of knowing Him.

ANDREW MURRAY, *ABIDE IN CHRIST*

April 18

. . . You in Me, and I in you.

John 14:20

Christ dwelling in the heart by faith." Let us clasp and cherish the words and use them in the most practical needs of life. "Not I, but Christ liveth in me"; "Christ dwelleth in me."

I listened lately with deep attention to a Christian man's quiet narrative, given to me in private, of his experience of discovery in this matter. "The fear of man" had been a burden to him. It was brought home to him that the secret of deliverance was to recollect that his Lord was in him and that his Lord was not afraid. Sudden and wonderful was the revolution within. Some circumstances attended it which I cannot for a moment think to be, in God's purpose, normally meant for all believers. But the essence of the thing—is it not meant for all? For it is but an extension and application, in the light of the Holy Spirit, of the truth of the indwelling in the heart by faith.

Come in then, Lord, oh, come and dwell, and let Thy presence evermore expand within.

O Jesus Christ, grow Thou in me,
And all things else recede;
My heart be daily nearer Thee,
From sin be daily freed.

H. C. G. Moule, *Ephesian Studies*

April 19

Christ . . . is our life.

Colossians 3:4

Our aim, our longing, our hunger and thirst are for a holiness which shall indeed be real—real before God in its root and real before man in its fruit. We seek a holiness which shall win the world to own that Christ can make a poor human life blessed and fruitful, loving, cheering, useful, humble, tender, while yet strangely strong, with a power not its own, to rebuke the evil which it meets. We want to be holy in a way which shall never glorify ourselves but always our Master. We want to have a "heart" that does "not condemn us" (1 John 3:21)—not the delusion of a supposed sinlessness but the happy, honest certainty that our central and steadfast desire and choice is to please Him, to do His dear will.

Then let us *go up* to fetch our secret down. Believer, your talisman for that life, the only life worth living, is in the heaven of heavens. It is seated on the right hand of God. It is "Christ which is your Life." It is *He*: as He died for you, as He lives for you, as He lives in you, as you live in Him; as He is coming for you; as you are going to be glorified with Him. Seek Him with the seeking which is also a perpetual finding, and use Him as He is so found, and you shall have your desire.

H. C. G. Moule, *Colossian and Philemon Studies*

April 20

As you therefore have received Christ Jesus the Lord, so walk in Him.

Colossians 2:6

It is not only by faith that we first come to Christ and are united to Him, but it is by faith that we are to be rooted and established in our union with Christ. No less essential than it is for the commencement is faith for the progress of the spiritual life. Abiding in Jesus can only be by faith.

There are earnest Christians who do not understand this; or, if they admit it in theory, they fail to realize its application in practice. While they firmly grasp the truth "The sinner shall be justified by faith," they have hardly found a place in their scheme for the larger truth "The just shall *live* by faith." They have never understood what a perfect Savior Jesus is and how He will each day do for the sinner just as much as He did the first day when he or she came to Him.

The life of grace is always and only a life of faith; and in the relationship to Jesus, the one daily and unceasing duty of the disciple is to believe, because believing is the one channel through which divine grace and strength flow out into the heart of man.

The old nature of the believer remains evil and sinful to the last; it is only as he daily comes, all empty and helpless, to his Savior to receive of His life and strength that he can bring forth the fruits of righteousness to the glory of God. Therefore, "*as* ye have received Christ Jesus the Lord, *so* walk ye *in him*." As you came to Jesus, so abide in Him—by faith.

Andrew Murray, *Abide in Christ*

April 21

. . . the mystery which has been hidden . . . Christ in you, the hope of glory.

Colossians 1:26–27

This is the end, or purpose, of the cross: we are crucified with Christ to make room for Him to dwell in our hearts by faith, and this indwelling of the Lord Christ is called a "mystery"—a word signifying "secret," something hid from our understanding until revealed to us.

This mystery was not made known under the dispensation of Law. Then every man stood by his own works before God, except a few, like Abraham, who in the Spirit foresaw the day of Christ and were glad; they saw the promises afar off and embraced them. But during the dispensation of the church, it is God's purpose that the mystery should be proclaimed to all nations.

Paul precedes his testimony "Christ *liveth* in me" by the words "*I have been crucified with Christ*," showing clearly that the revelation of the mystery of Christ living in us depends upon a true and real planting into His death. Once the believer perceives this focal point of Calvary in relation to his practical experience, all the truths of God fall into their place in beautiful harmony.

The very energy of God comes into his life, and as he proves with joy the might of the risen Christ thus working through him, his whole outlook changes. "I have been taught the secret . . . I can do all things in Him" (Phil. 4:12–13, CH) becomes the glad triumphant cry, "to me *life is Christ*" (Phil. 1:21, CH) the one increasing joy.

Oh, blessed life! How restful, how glad, how free when once the secret is known and the soul learns to live by faith in the Son of God.

Jessie Penn-Lewis, *The Cross of Calvary*

April 22

The righteousness of God is revealed from faith to faith.

Romans 1:17

This gospel, this good news is, in its essence, *Jesus Christ.* It is supremely *He*, not *it*; person, not theory. Or rather, it is authentic and eternal theory in vital and eternal connection everywhere with a person.

Christ is all. Faith is man's acceptance of Him as such. "Justification by faith" is not acceptance because faith is a valuable thing, a merit, a recommendation, or a virtue; it is acceptance because of Jesus Christ, whom man, dropping all other hopes, receives. It has absolutely nothing to do with earning the gift of God; it has all to do with taking it.

So the gospel "*unveils God's righteousness*"; it draws the curtains from His glorious secret. And as each fold is lifted, the glad onlooker looks on "*from faith to faith.*" He finds that this reliance is to be his part—first, last, midst, and without end. He takes Jesus Christ by faith; he holds Him by faith; he uses Him by faith; he lives and dies in Him by faith. That is to say, always by Him—by Him received, held, used.

H. C. G. Moule, *The Epistle to the Romans*

APRIL 23

Reckon yourselves to be dead indeed to sin,
but alive to God in Christ Jesus our Lord.

ROMANS 6:11

What is union with Christ? It results from an exercise of identification by faith. We go for elucidation away back to Leviticus 1:4: "He shall put his hand on the head of the burnt offering, and it will be accepted on his behalf to make atonement for him."

Those oft-repeated offerings of the Old Testament pointed on to, and drew their significance from, the once-for-all sacrifice of Christ in the New Testament. We shall meet those Old Testament believers on exactly the same ground. We believers will be there—at the cross of Calvary. "By means of [His] death, for the redemption of the transgressions under the first covenant," as Hebrews 9:15 has it.

It was all a God-given, God-ordained, prophetic picture of what was afterward to be; and old Isaac Watts has captured its significance for us in his great hymn:

My faith would lay her hand
On that dear head of Thine,
While like a penitent I stand
And there confess my sin.

Thus by this heavenly identification by faith, we are joined to Him—reckoning ourselves as dead to sin and, moreover, as being alive in resurrection to "newness of life" (Rom. 6:4, 11). Christian, as a matter of complete certainty, you were raised with Christ. The only question, for you and me, is whether we are living up to our high privilege, whether walking after "the power of His resurrection."

GUY KING, *COLOSSIANS: TRUE LIFE IN CHRIST*

April 24

. . . that Christ may dwell in your hearts through faith.

Ephesians 3:17

Is there need that we should remind one another that this truth is for our century as much as for the first? With simplicity and humility I do remind my reader, and God knows I would be daily reminded myself, that *every one of us* is divinely intended to live a Christian life of which the inmost secret is this: Christ dwelling in the heart by faith—the Spirit strengthening us thereto in the inner man.

I shrink from an elaborate attempted analysis of the blessed mystery in itself. I would only say a little about what must assuredly be some of its results where it has begun to be. It must produce a deep and absolutely genuine humility. It must produce an inner calm which shall greatly tell upon the air and manner of outward life, aye, on look and on tone of discourse. It must produce an abiding Christ-consciousness at the back, so to speak, of the manifold experiences of life; with this presence in the heart, by faith, we shall not find it a chimerical hope day by day and hour by hour to "do all to the glory of God."

Our life in its activities and interests may, and very possibly will, go on as before; we shall walk and talk and work and rest and sigh and smile as men really living in a real society. People will find us doing, not dreaming: attentive, active, full of the sense of duty and responsibility—only *kept* amidst it all by a power not our own, in a tone and temper which mean that "the Lord is there."

H. C. G. Moule, *Ephesian Studies*

April 25

Abraham believed God, and it was accounted to him for righteousness.

Romans 4:3

The righteousness of Abraham resulted not from his works but from his faith. Oh, miracle of grace! If we trust ever so simply in Jesus Christ our Lord, we shall be reckoned as righteous in the eye of the eternal God. We cannot realize all that is included in those marvelous words. This only is evident: faith unites us so absolutely to the Son of God that we are *one* with Him forevermore. All the glory of His character—not only what He was when He became obedient unto death but what He is in the majesty of His risen nature—is reckoned unto us.

Some teach imputed righteousness as if it were something apart from Christ, flung over the rags of the sinner. But it is truer and better to consider it as a matter of blessed identification with Him through faith; so that as He was one with us in being made sin, we are one with Him in being made the righteousness of God. In the counsels of eternity, that which is true of the glorious Lord is accounted also true of us who, by a living faith, have become members of His body—of His flesh and of His bones. Jesus Christ is made unto us righteousness, and we are accepted in the Beloved.

There is nothing in faith, considered in itself, which can account for this marvelous fact of imputation. Faith is only the link of union; but inasmuch as it unites us to the Son of God, it brings us into the enjoyment of all that He is as the Alpha and Omega, the Beginning and the End, the First and the Last.

F. B. Meyer, *Abraham*

April 26

If anyone desires to come after Me, let him deny himself, and take up his cross.

Matthew 16:24

I fear there are many Christians who are content to look upon the cross with Christ on it merely dying for their sins and who have little heart for any fellowship with the crucified One. They hardly know that He invites them to it. Or they are content to consider the ordinary afflictions of life—which the children of the world often have as much as they—as their share of Christ's cross. They have no conception of what it is to be *crucified* with Christ!

They do not know that bearing the cross means likeness to Christ in the principles which animated Him in His path of obedience. The entire surrender of all self-will, the complete denial to the flesh of its every desire and pleasure, the perfect separation from the world in all its ways of thinking and acting, the losing and hating of one's life, the giving up of self and its interests for the sake of others—this is the disposition which marks him who has taken up Christ's cross, who seeks to say, "I am crucified with Christ; I abide in Christ the crucified One."

We know how Peter knew and confessed Christ as the Son of the living God, and yet the cross was to him still an offense, something which he could not countenance (Matt. 16:16–17, 21–23). The faith that believes in the blood that pardons, and even in the life that renews, can only reach its perfect growth as it abides beneath the cross and, in living fellowship with Him, seeks for perfect conformity with Jesus the crucified.

Andrew Murray, *Abide in Christ*

April 27

He who does not take his cross and follow after Me is not worthy of Me.

Matthew 10:38

If, the moment I am conscious of the shadow of self crossing my threshold, I do not shut the door, and in the power of Him who works in us to will and to do, keep that door shut, then I know nothing of Calvary love.

If there be any reserve in my giving to Him who so loved that He gave His Dearest for me; if there be a secret "but" in my prayer, "Anything but that, Lord," then I know nothing of Calvary love.

If I ask to be delivered from trial rather than for deliverance out of it, to the praise of His glory; if I forget that the way of the Cross leads to the Cross and not to a bank of flowers; if I regulate my life on these lines, or even unconsciously my thinking, so that I am surprised when the way is rough and think it strange, though the word is "Think it not strange," "Count it all joy," then I know nothing of Calvary love.

Amy Carmichael, *If*

April 28

God forbid that I should boast except in the cross of our Lord Jesus Christ.

Galatians 6:14

When the Lord Jesus said to His disciples, "I am with you always," it was as the crucified One, who had shown them His hands and His feet, that He gave this promise. And to each one who seeks to claim His promise, it is of the first importance that he should realize that it is the crucified Jesus who offers to be with him every day.

Could one reason why we find it so difficult to expect and enjoy the abiding presence be because we do not glory in the cross by which we are crucified to the world? We have been crucified with Christ; our "old man was crucified with Him" (Rom. 6:6); "those who are Christ's have crucified the flesh with its passions and desires" (Gal. 5:24). Yet how little we have learned that the world has been crucified to us and that we are free from its power. How little we have learned, as those who are crucified with Christ, to deny ourselves, to have the mind that was in Christ when He emptied Himself and took the form of a servant, then humbled Himself and became obedient even to the death of the cross (Phil. 2:7–8).

Let us learn the lesson that it is the *crucified* Christ who comes to walk with us every day and in whose power we too are to live the life that can declare, "I have been crucified with Christ; Christ crucified lives in me."

Andrew Murray, *Secrets of Intercession and Prayer*

April 29

Let this mind be in you which was also in Christ Jesus, who . . .
made Himself of no reputation.

Philippians 2:5–7

No tree can grow except on the root from which it sprang. Even as we need to look to the first Adam and his fall to know the power of the sin within us, we need to know well the second Adam and His power to give within us a life of humility as real and abiding and overmastering as has been that of pride.

The life of God which in the incarnation entered human nature is the *root* in which we are to stand and grow; it is the same almighty power that worked there, and thence onward to the resurrection, which works daily in us. Our one need is to study and know and trust the life that has been revealed in Christ as the life that is now ours and waits for our consent to gain possession and mastery of our whole being.

It is of inconceivable importance that we should have right thoughts of what Christ is—of what really constitutes Him the Christ—and specially of what may be counted His chief characteristic, the root and essence of all His character as our Redeemer. There can be but one answer: it is His *humility*.

If this be the root of the tree, its nature must be seen in every branch and leaf and fruit. If humility be the first, the all-including grace of the life of Jesus—if humility be the secret of His *atonement*—then the health and strength of our spiritual life will entirely depend upon our putting this grace first also and making humility the chief thing we admire in Him, the chief thing we ask of Him, the one thing for which we sacrifice all else.

Andrew Murray, *Humility*

April 30

He who says he abides in Him ought himself also to walk just as He walked.

1 John 2:6

To abide in Christ is to maintain in principle the same relationship toward Him that He maintained toward the Father. This means, firstly, *a life of submission* in which we gladly consent to the limitations of "that good, and acceptable, and perfect, will of God." We accept a bondage which we find to be perfect freedom. This was truly His life who said, "I delight to do thy will, O my God" (Ps. 40:8). It must be ours also if we would abide.

Then it must be also *a life of renunciation* of ourselves, our abilities, our resources. We have to come to the place of weakness and emptiness, that His strength may be made perfect in us. This is the place of abiding. He is the vine; we are the branches. The vine has everything; the branch has nothing. "As the branch cannot bear fruit of itself . . . so neither can ye" (John 15:4). The attitude of self-renunciation characterized the life of the Savior. "The Son can do nothing of himself" (John 5:19, 30); "My teaching is not mine" (John 7:16); "neither have I come of myself" (John 8:42). We are called to follow Him.

Finally, abiding involves *a life of faith* which looks to Christ for all and finds its all-sufficiency in Him. Alongside the statement of Christ "Apart from me ye can do nothing" (John 15:5), we must put Paul's triumphant declaration "I can do all things through Christ which strengtheneth me" (Phil. 4:13).

Paul set forth the true life of renunciation and faith when He said, "I live; and yet *no longer I*, but Christ liveth in me. . . . I live by the faith of the Son of God [Darby], who loved me, and gave himself up for me" (Gal. 2:20). This is truly the abiding life.

Arthur Wallis, *In the Day of Thy Power*

May

Trusting and Obeying Christ

The Testimony of F. B. Meyer

The visit of Messrs. Stanley Smith and Studd to Melbourne Hall will always mark an epoch in my own life. Before then my Christian life had been spasmodic and fitful: now flaming up with enthusiasm, and then pacing wearily over leagues of grey ashes and cold cinders. I saw that these young men had something which I had not but which was within them a constant source of rest and strength and joy.

And never shall I forget a scene at seven o'clock in the grey mist of a November morning as daylight was flickering into the bedroom, paling the guttering candles, which from a very early hour had been lighting up the page of Scripture and revealing the figures of the devoted Bible students. The talk we had then was one of the formative influences of my life.

"You have been up early," I said to Charlie Studd.

"Yes," said he. "I got up at four o'clock this morning. Christ wakes me to have a good time with Him."

"Well," I inquired, "how can I be like you?"

C. T. Studd replied, "Have you ever given yourself to Christ, for Christ to fill you?"

"Yes," I said, "I have done so in a general way, but I don't know that I have done it particularly."

He answered, "You must do it particularly also."

I knelt down that night and thought I could give myself to Christ as easily as possible. I gave Him the iron ring of my will with all the keys of my life on it, except one little key that I kept back. And the Master said, "Are they all here?"

I said, "They are all there but one, the key to a tiny closet in my heart, of which I must keep control."

He said, "If you don't trust Me in all, you don't trust Me at all." I tried to make terms; I believe that my whole life was just hovering in the balance. He seemed to be receding from me, and I called Him back and said, "I am not willing, but I am willing to be made willing."

It seemed as though He came near and took that key out of my hand and went straight for the closet. Within a week from that time, He had cleared it right out. But He filled it with something so much better! Why, what a fool I was! He just took away the thing which was eating out my life and instead gave me Himself. Since then I have reckoned on Him to keep; but full consecration is a necessary condition of any deep experience of His keeping power.

F. B. Meyer in Norman Grubb,
C. T. Studd: Cricketer and Pioneer

MAY 1

He said to Simon [Peter],
"Launch out into the deep and let down your nets for a catch."

LUKE 5:4

Peter would be prepared to obey the slightest precept that came from the Master's lips; but how could One who had spent His days in the carpenter's workshop of a mountain village be competent to take command of a boat and direct the casting of a net! Was he to renounce himself in this also? The morning was no time for fishing; the glare of light revealed the meshes of the nets, and the fish were to be found not in the deep but the shallower part of the lake.

There is no escaping the test. At a certain moment in our experience, often long after we have become disciples, the Master comes onboard the ship of our life and assumes supreme control. For a moment or an hour there may be question and hesitation. We have been accustomed to making our own plans, being masters in our own craft; shall we—may we, dare we—hand over the entire command to Christ?

To what point may He not steer us! On what venture may He not engage us! At what inhospitable part of the shore may He not land us! Happy are we if, after such a moment of hesitation, we reply, "Nevertheless, at thy command I will put out even to the deep and let down the nets for a draught."

Christ must be Master. His will must rule, though it seems to contradict the dearest traditions of the soul. There cannot be two captains in the boat if it is to make a successful voyage and return at last to the shore laden with fish. Today and now, let that question be decided! He has a place and a use for you, but you must surrender yourself to His disposal. Make Christ Captain, while you take to the oars!

F. B. MEYER, *PETER*

May 2

. . . to be strengthened with might through His Spirit . . . that you may be filled with all the fullness of God.

Ephesians 3:16–19

Why do we need a supreme *empowering* just in order to receive our Life, our Light? Does the hungry wanderer need power in order to eat the food without which he will soon sink? Does the bewildered mariner need power to welcome onto his deck the pilot who alone can steer him to the haven of his desire?

No; but there is another aspect of the matter here. For the heart, though it immeasurably needs the blessed Indweller, has that in it which *dreads* His absolute indwelling. *Can it trust Him* with complete internal authority? Will He not use it for purposes terrible to the human heart, asserting His position by some infliction, some exaction awful and unpitying? So the hand, stretched out to "open the door" (Rev. 3:20), the *inner* door—for the King is presumed to be already received into the porch and hall, the more public chambers of the being—falls again and shrinks from that turning of the key which is to set the last recess quite open to the *Master*.

Here is the need for the Spirit's empowering work. Come, Holy Spirit, and *show* to the hesitating heart "the glory of God in the face of Jesus Christ"—that lovely glory, shown in that fair countenance; then it shall hesitate no more. Beholding His love in His look, it shall not dread His power in His grasp. It shall be strong to welcome Him wholly in, for it shall see, in the light of the Spirit, that "*in His presence* is the fullness of joy" and that "to serve Him is to reign."

H. C. G. Moule, *Ephesian Studies*

May 3

You were not redeemed with corruptible things, like silver or gold, from your aimless conduct received by tradition from your fathers, but with the precious blood of Christ.

1 Peter 1:18–19

The right that the Lord Jesus has obtained for you is so infinitely high, so broad, so unlimited, that if you will only think about it, you will respond to it. Just as I desire that every member of my body—the eye, the ear, the hand, the foot—should always be at my service, so the Lord desires that you, as a member of His body, along with every power and faculty, should always, without a moment's break, serve Him. You are so far from being able to do this that you may not even realize the possibility of it. Cease trying to do it on your own, and begin each day by committing yourself to the almighty keeping and control of your Lord.

Christ is not an owner who is *outside* of you, or who is only in heaven above; He is your *Head* and *lives in you* with His holy nature and by His Holy Spirit. And the one thing to which He calls you is to trust Him, to wait for Him, to rely confidently upon Him to complete in the outward things of our lives His hidden and unnoticed work of protection and perfection.

Our great need is to recognize ourselves as His possession and, by a reverent confession of this, to have the heart filled by the consciousness of it. Let the wonderful ownership of Jesus, His blood-bought right, so possess you that it will every moment be the keynote of your life and the power of an enduring attachment to Him.

Andrew Murray, *The Power of the Blood of the Cross*

May 4

We who live are always delivered to death for Jesus' sake, that the life of Jesus also may be manifested in our mortal flesh.

2 Corinthians 4:11

What our Lord asks us to do is to offer ourselves to Him and for Him. What will He do for us? He will receive us into the fellowship of His cross as the most glorious thing He possesses—by which He entered into the glory of the Father.

Are you willing to make the cross your abode, the place where you will pass every hour of your life in fellowship with the crucified Jesus? Or does it seem to you to be too hard to surrender yourself, your will, your life so utterly up to death as to bear about daily the dying of the Lord Jesus? I pray you do not think this is too hard for you. It is the only way to a close fellowship with the blessed Jesus and, through Him, a free entrance to the eternal Father and His love.

It need not be too difficult for you! In fellowship with Jesus, it will become joy and salvation. I urge you, become willing. Let us ascend to the altar to die so that we may live. Or is it your fear that you are not fit to complete such a sacrifice? Listen then to the glorious comfort which the Word of God gives you today: "The altar sanctifies the gift." Even the Old Testament altar had power to sanctify every gift which was laid upon it. "How much more shall the blood of Christ, who through the eternal Spirit offered Himself without spot to God," sanctify the cross as an altar on which the sacrifice of your body may be sanctified!

The cross is the place of the blessed presence of God, and dying with Christ leads to a life with Him in the love of the Father.

Andrew Murray, *The Power of the Blood of the Cross*

May 5

Blessed are those . . . who seek Him with the whole heart!

PSALM 119:2

Many are stopped from seeking the higher Christian life by a reluctance to give up the world completely and be fully conformed to the will of Christ. Maybe they find the yoke of Christ too heavy, even when they bear it in a half-and-half sort of way. By the arithmetic of unbelief, they figure that if half-hearted service is a burden, then full service would be twice as heavy and would break them down completely!

They don't see that the Master gives grace and strength to those who are fully given to Him. They overlook the lessons of the past, that the Lord is the strength of those who lean completely on Him, enabling them to pass through floods on dry land and through fire untouched. But those who stop halfway are left with enemies all around them—unconquered, un-expelled, ready to rise up and attack.

Imagine a farmer's fields overrun with weeds, but instead of waging a war of extermination and destroying the weeds down to the roots, he only did a half-and-half job by cutting down a few of them. The rest would go to seed and produce even more weeds the next year. And suppose he justified his actions by saying, "It takes me so much time and work to keep these weeds under control from year to year that it is not worth the trouble!"

Such a farmer would be the laughingstock of the whole countryside, and yet his reasoning would be the same as that of a half-hearted disciple who shrinks from full consecration because he thinks it would be so much harder than the half-and-half life he lives now.

WILLIAM BOARDMAN, *THE HIGHER CHRISTIAN LIFE*

May 6

*An angel of the Lord stood by him . . . saying, "Arise quickly!" . . .
So he went out and followed him.*

Acts 12:7–9

There are some who would gladly follow the Lord completely and who understand what it means to be entirely given up to Him but do not see how they can maintain it. They don't see the hand of God outstretched to lift them up and sustain them; they don't dare to trust His promise, so they are afraid to start.

In some ways they are like Peter in the prison at Jerusalem. They are in bondage to sin just as he was in bondage to Herod; they know they are chained to the world just as Peter was chained to soldiers on either side. Their prison is dark, and its iron gate shut.

In this situation the gospel comes to them, as the angel of the Lord came to Peter while he slept between his keepers, and shakes them, saying, "Get up and follow me."

But here is the difference: Peter got up, put on his clothes, and followed, almost as in a dream. But these people just sit there, still in their chains, and say, "But what about these chains—how will they be broken off? And the soldiers on each side of me—who will protect me from them? And how do I get past the iron gate and the sentries?"

The difficulties along the way frighten and weaken them. If only they would get up at the call of the gospel and give themselves completely to follow the Lord Jesus, He would go with them. And then, just like Peter in the prison, the way would open up in the light of His presence, every enemy would sleep on, every barrier would swing wide open, and they would step easily and delightedly into a way of happiness and a path of peace.

William Boardman, *The Higher Christian Life*

MAY 7

God has not given us a spirit of fear.

2 TIMOTHY 1:7

If ever a man had reason and excuse for being afraid, it was young Timothy. Naturally timid as he was in himself, having upon his young shoulders the responsibilities and cares of his Ephesian church, face to face with all the perils and perplexities of a time of persecution—no wonder if he quaked before the situation in which he found himself.

However, Paul writes to brace him up; he assures him that he need not fear with such a God above him and before him and behind him and beneath him and beside him and within him. "Whenever I am afraid, I will trust in You," says David in Psalm 56:3, but Paul would prefer the prophet's word for him: "I will trust and *not be* afraid" (Isa. 12:2).

We will not dare to criticize Timothy for any tendency to fear, for are we not also much inclined that way? How often we refrain from some right word or action because we are so dreadfully afraid of what other people might think or say or do! Do we not hesitate again and again from starting upon some good course or undertaking because of that stupid fear of failing?! Well, this "spirit of fear" has no right to be there.

Of course a *right* fear was theirs. The fear of God is a thing about which the Bible has much to say: indeed, Psalm 111:10 and Proverbs 9:10 combine to impress upon us that "the fear of the LORD is the beginning of wisdom." Yet this fear has very little place among the moderns. The old religion was shot through with this godly fear. The presence of this fear and the absence of all other fear make up together that quality of fearlessness which is such a marked feature of religion.

GUY KING, *II TIMOTHY: TO MY SON*

May 8

"Lord, save us! We are perishing!" But He said to them, "Why are you fearful, O you of little faith?"

MATTHEW 8:25-26

Many believers need to learn that faith *delivers* from fear. Theoretically we believe in the Christ within, but when the crisis comes, we grow panicky and cry, "Master, we perish!" But faith and fear are contradictory. In proportion as we have one, we do not have the other. No Christian need fear anything, "for God hath not given us the spirit of fear; but of power, and of love, and of a sound mind" (2 Tim. 1:7). For every fear, "faith is the victory."

We are not thinking of fear merely as a feeling but as an attitude that paralyzes the will and restrains and cramps the life until one becomes a cowering slave. Neither is faith merely a feeling but the attitude which steps forth in dependence upon God even though feelings and circumstances may point the other way. The conquest of fear is not wrought in a day. The Christian who sets out to live by faith will find many nervous qualms and inhibitions trying to choke his courage; but as he exercises faith, the faith grows stronger and the fear weaker until it no longer becomes a serious problem. Here, as everywhere else, the practice of His presence plays its part.

Of course, it is all done through the indwelling Spirit, but still there must be practice and persistence. God will empower and sustain, but the decision of the will is our part, and all the prayers and devotional readings on earth will not make up for our definite stepping out upon the promises.

VANCE HAVNER, *REFLECTIONS ON THE GOSPELS*

May 9

O you of little faith, why did you doubt?

Matthew 14:31

Elijah had been animated by a most splendid faith because he had never lost sight of God. "He endured, as seeing him who is invisible." Faith always thrives when God occupies the whole field of vision. But when Jezebel's threats reached him, we are told most significantly, "he arose, and went for his life." In afteryears Peter walked on the water until he looked from his Master to the seething waves. "*When he saw the wind boisterous*, he was afraid; and beginning to sink, he cried, saying, Lord, save me." So here, while Elijah set the Lord always before his face, he did not fear, though a host encamped against him. But when he looked at his peril, he thought more of his life than of God's cause, and was afraid of man that should die and of the son of man that should be made as grass, and forgot the Lord, his Maker, which made heaven and earth.

Let us refuse to look at circumstances, though they roll before us as a Red Sea and howl around us like a storm. Circumstances, natural impossibilities, difficulties are nothing in the estimation of the soul that is occupied with God. They are as the small dust that settles on a scale and is not considered in the measurement of weight. O men of God, get you up into the high mountain, from which you may obtain a good view of the glorious Land of Promise, and refuse to have your gaze diverted by men or things below!

F. B. Meyer, *Elijah*

May 10

Meditate in it day and night. . . . Be strong and of good courage; do not be afraid, nor be dismayed, for the Lord your God is with you.

Joshua 1:8–9

In this passage we also see from the Lord's words the linking together of His presence and the resulting courage and fearlessness necessary for victory. To be freed from all fear and dismay of the forces of the enemy, our great remedy is to have God's Word strengthening us day and night so that we lose sight of man and all fear of man. This Word is strength to you. You would be strong Christians if you were so filled with the Word of God that everything you heard around you would instantly cause to spring into your mind the passage which would meet or explain the need—so that whatever question was asked you or whatever doubt came to you, in one moment there would come the right answer to your mind from the Scriptures.

Are you being kept by God at this point? You know so much about victory, you know so much about identification with Christ and His cross; but are you strong and very courageous? Are you dismayed, are you afraid, are you fearful? Will you allow all fear to be swept from you and go forward meditating on this Book day and night? It means when you awake in the morning, the revelation that is fresh will be in your mind. When you go to sleep, it means that you will not have troublesome thoughts in your mind to prevent you from sleeping. One great, strong, mighty resource for unbroken victory is to be filled with divine strength by this Word dwelling in you richly.

Jessie Penn-Lewis, *The Conquest of Canaan*

May 11

Behold, I am with you and will keep you wherever you go; . . .
I will not leave you.

Genesis 28:15

Recall, for a moment, if there was not a sacred epoch in your history when God took up the trailing tendrils of your love and twined them around Himself, and you realized His presence and clung to Him as never before. It is at such a moment that the Almighty offers His company for the untrodden path. Happy is he who accepts the proffered help and transfers the feeling of dependence from the earthly to the heavenly Friend.

When one is willing to be taken up by Him, there need be no further anxiety or care; for directly a human spirit yields itself to its Almighty Lover, that moment He takes it, and assumes all responsibility, and makes Himself answerable for all its needs. There is but one condition: "Seek ye first the kingdom of God, and his righteousness; and all these things shall be added unto you."

Would that all the children of God might know what it is to hand over, moment by moment as they occur, all worries, anxieties, and cares to the compassionate Lord, sure that He takes them straight from their hands! We need never feel then as if all depended on our tired brain or failing strength, because the Lord Himself would supply all our need according to His riches in glory.

There is indeed no real independence for the believer. To be independent of Christ is to be cast forth as a branch to wither. The secret of rest and fruit and power is an abiding union with Him—which time cannot impair and death cannot dissolve.

F. B. Meyer, *Israel*

May 12

Seek first the kingdom of God and His righteousness,
and all these things shall be added to you.

Matthew 6:33

Many Christians seem to think of worry as a "white sin," as though God had made an exception in that case and we were allowed to fret and grieve, with no provision being made for our relief. People think they simply must worry, but God's Word is explicit that we are to be anxious about nothing (Phil. 4:6). Why did Jesus say "Let not your heart be troubled" if we cannot help it?

So our Lord tells us, "Take no thought for your life, what ye shall eat, or what ye shall drink" (Matt. 6:25). Of course we know that "thought" here means *anxious* thought and not the forethought and planning that are necessary for any business. It is not work but worry that kills—the feverish tension and uneasiness that soon wear down mind and body. The man who lives in the will of God need never worry about food, clothes, and the vexations of daily experience. It does no good, it is positively forbidden in the Word, and God has promised to supply all the believer's needs (Phil. 4:19).

The Lord Jesus speaks in this passage of the birds and the lilies as illustrations of God's care. Here cynics have objected that the sparrow falls just the same. But the idea is that no matter what happens, we are in God's care. Come what will, our lives are hid with Christ, and no matter what happens to our health or our money, we ourselves—our spirits—are safe in Him.

No Christian should worry. His sole business is to know the will of God and do it. Truly the peace of God will garrison the hearts and minds of those who are careful for nothing but thankful for everything.

Vance Havner, *Reflections on the Gospels*

MAY 13

Who walks in darkness and has no light?
Let him trust in the name of the LORD and rely upon his God.

ISAIAH 50:10

Every advancing soul must come sooner or later to the place where it can trust God, the bare God, if I may be allowed the expression, simply and only because of what He is in Himself and not because of His promises or His gifts.

The only way in which this place can be reached, I believe, is by the soul being compelled to face in its own experience the loss of all things both inward and outward. I do not mean necessarily that all one's friends must die or all one's money be lost; but I do mean that the soul must find itself, from either inward or outward causes, desolate and bereft and empty of all consolation. It must come to the end of everything that is not God and must have nothing else left to rest on, within or without.

The soul's pathway is always through death to life. The caterpillar cannot in the nature of things become the butterfly in any other way than by dying to the one life in order to live in the other. And neither can we. Therefore, it may well be that some region of death and desolation must needs be passed through if we would reach the calm mountain heights beyond. And when we know this, we can walk triumphantly through the darkest experience, sure that all is well, since God is God.

HANNAH WHITALL SMITH, *THE CHRISTIAN'S SECRET OF A HAPPY LIFE*, IN JESSIE PENN-LEWIS, *THE STORY OF JOB*

May 14

I will open rivers in desolate heights. . . .
I will plant in the wilderness the cedar and the acacia tree.

Isaiah 41:18–19

Life is not easy for any of us if we regard the external conditions only. But as soon as we learn the divine secret, rivers flow over bare heights in magnificent cascades, fountains arise in the rock-strewn sterile valleys, the wilderness becomes a pool and the dry land springs, the plain is covered with noble trees and the desert with the beautiful undergrowth of a forest glade. What makes the difference?

Faith is conscious that God is there and that His presence is the complement of every need. To her eye, common desert bushes burn with His Shekinah.

Faith recognizes the reality of an eternal choice—that God has entered into a covenant which cannot be dissolved and that His love and fidelity are bound to finish the work He has commenced.

Faith knows that there is a loving purpose running through every moment of trial and that the great Refiner has a meaning in every degree of heat to which the furnace is raised—and she anticipates the moment when she will see what God has foreseen all the time and toward which He has been working.

Faith realizes that others are learning from her experiences lessons which nothing else would teach them and that glory is accruing to God in the highest, because men and angels see and know and consider and understand together that the hand of the Lord has done this and the Holy One of Israel has created it.

F. B. Meyer, *Christ in Isaiah*

May 15

I will show you my faith by my works.

James 2:18

Alas! over how many of the promises of God to us can it not be said, "The word preached did not profit them, because they were not united by faith to it" (Heb. 4:2, margin)? Faith puts to the proof the statements of God by acting upon them, and in the acting finds their substance and reality. Faith tests the unseen things and translates them into real experience.

Faith is the key to all the treasuries of God. The gospel is practically God's statement of what *is* in the spiritual world. Faith is simply believing God's Word, however contrary it may appear to the things of sense and sight. Faith in God's statement to us is proved by action. We act according to what is told us by God, which we believe and must of necessity obey. Living faith involves action; without action it may be said to be dead, for a mental assent to the truths of God will never give them substance in our lives. If we do believe God's words, we shall act according to those words.

We must not forget, however, that the faith that is the "proving of things not seen" demands direct communication with God. Souls have often been shipwrecked here. They have rested their faith upon the word as spoken by *others* rather than upon *God Himself* in His Word.

The faith that can act as Moses did must have the word of the living God as its basis—the declaration of the living God given in His written Word but by the Holy Spirit applied as His direct word to the soul.

Jessie Penn-Lewis, *Face to Face*

May 16

Jesus said to them, "Do you believe that I am able to do this?" They said to Him, "Yes, Lord." Then He touched their eyes, saying, "According to your faith let it be to you." And their eyes were opened.

Matthew 9:28–30

Here is the key to a life of blessing: "according to your faith." But, mind you, faith in the Lord Jesus, for He had just asked, "Believe ye that I am able to do this?" The value of faith depends upon the object of faith; and when Christ is the object, faith never fails. All things are possible to the person who believes if he believes in Him with whom all things are possible.

Back of all the misery of the world today lies unbelief in Christ. We will not come unto Him that we might have life. Sinners miss life here and hereafter because they believe not, and Christians live meager and defeated lives because they believe so little. In the midst of it all stands Jesus, the answer to every problem; but we do not believe like the blind men that He is able to do wonders in our lives, or, if we believe it theoretically, we do not believe it practically, so our eyes are not opened. Some seek special experiences, signs, and wonders but will not live daily by faith, looking unto Jesus.

Here is the measure of blessing: *according to your faith.* If there is much faith, there is much blessing. If there is little faith, there is little blessing. There is no other way. Simple faith in Jesus is the key to every problem, the answer to every issue, from the smallest to the greatest. He Himself said so; how long will it take us to learn it?

Vance Havner, *Reflections on the Gospels*

May 17

If you love Me, keep My commandments.

John 14:15

Is not this [a refusal to obey] the true cause of failure in so many Christian lives? We catch sight of God's ideal; we are enamored with it; we vow to be only His; we use the most emphatic words; we dedicate ourselves upon the altar. For a while we seem to tread another world, bathed in heavenly light. Then there comes a command clear and unmistakable. We must leave some beloved Cherith and go to some unwelcome Zarephath; we must speak some word, take some step, cut off some habit—and we shrink from it. The cost is too great. But as soon as we refuse obedience, the light dies off the landscape of our lives and dark clouds fling their shadows far and near.

We do not win salvation by our obedience—that is altogether the gift of God, to be received by faith in the finished work of Jesus Christ our Lord. But being saved, we must obey. Our Savior adjures us, by the love we bear to Himself, to keep His commandments. And He does so because He wants us to taste His rarest gifts and because He knows that in the keeping of His commandments, there is great reward.

Search the Bible from cover to cover, and see if strict, implicit, and instant obedience has not been the secret of the noblest lives that ever lit up the dull monotony of the world. The proudest title of our King was "Servant of Jehovah." And none of us can seek to realize a nobler aim than that which was the inspiration of His heart: "I come to do thy will, O my God."

F. B. Meyer, *Elijah*

May 18

He who has my commandments and keeps them,
it is he who loves Me. And he who loves Me will be loved by My Father,
and I will love him and manifest Myself to him.

John 14:21

It is hardly possible to overestimate the value of simple, unquestioning obedience in the growth of character. The rejection of Saul, the first king of Israel, and the selection of David hinged on the fact that the one did not obey the voice of the Lord in performing His commandments and that the other was a man after God's heart and fulfilled all His will.

The stress of our Lord's farewell discourse is on the reiterated word "obey." Obedience is the test of love; the condition of divine revelation; the precursor of the most sacred intimacy into which God can enter with the human spirit.

In proportion as we obey, we become possessed of noble elements of character which exist in our hearts as vapor until they are condensed in some act of obedience and become henceforth a permanent property. Disbelief and disobedience are interchangeable terms (Heb. 4:11, margin); from this we may infer that as our obedience is, so will our faith become. Live up to what you know to be your duty; fill in the outlines of God's commands; never stay to count consequences or to question results. If God says "Go unto Pharaoh, and tell him" and you obey, you will not only be set to greater tasks, but you will acquire a character which no amount of meditation or prayer could afford.

F. B. Meyer, *Moses*

May 19

Everyone who loves is born of God and knows God.
He who does not love does not know God, for God is love.

1 John 4:7–8

No man is a Christian who does not love the Lord Jesus. "If any man love not the Lord Jesus Christ, let him be Anathema" (1 Cor. 16:22). This is the touchstone of trial for each one of us—not what we profess or say but whether we love, and how much.

How may we love Christ more? Spend much time alone in contemplating what He has done for you and what He is as the "chiefest among ten thousand" and the "altogether lovely." Stir the inner fire by means of memory, and let hope pile on it the fuel of promise until it begins to blaze. Cultivate the habit of speaking aloud to Him in an empty chamber or a lonely walk until He be interlaced in the tiniest episodes of existence. Open your heart to the entrance of the Holy Spirit shedding abroad the love of God in the heart, and gather the rays of that love into a burning focus so that you may love God back with love which has come from His heart into yours. And very specially, accustom yourself to do, for the sake of His dear love, many things which cost you self-sacrifice and effort. As we show love to others, we understand His love to ourselves.

The key to the knowledge of the love of Jesus is not in singing rapturous hymns or in seeking to arouse intense emotion but in quietly doing daily deeds of self-denial for His sake. He measures the least act of love not by the magnitude of the deed itself but by the strength of the love which prompts it. It is astonishing how quickly we graduate in the school of love when we begin to put in practice all we know.

F. B. Meyer, *Tried by Fire: Exposition of 1 Peter*

May 20

Jehovah . . . thy burnt-offering doth reduce to ashes.

Psalm 20:1–3, YLT

A thing turned to ashes is utterly gone; we cannot recover it. I see in this a very deep thought of God. It is perhaps the deepest of all His thoughts for us while we are here in the flesh. It leads to the great "not my will, but thine, be done" of Gethsemane and Calvary.

Some of us are a long way from even beginning to understand this. None of us are anywhere near a full understanding, but I do want to lay these words on your hearts, even on the hearts of you who are still young. If you want to be one of those of whom the Lord can ask anything in the days to come, begin now by laying your little offerings upon His altar. Lay down your little choices, your will about very little things. He will not call these love-offerings little. He will accept them, and cause His face to shine upon you, and give you peace.

Something of this is in that wonderful word in Psalm 43:4: "*the altar of God, . . . God my exceeding joy*" (ASV). It is not a sad thing to be allowed to lay a sacrifice on the altar and see it accepted and turned to ashes. It is a joyful thing; it is the most joyful thing in all the world.

Amy Carmichael, *Thou Givest . . . They Gather*

May 21

Be obedient, . . . as bondservants of Christ, doing the will of God from the heart.

Ephesians 6:5-6

God's demand upon every one of His servants is surrender with no conditions, no terms—nothing but the yielding of our will and of our life to Him to do His will in the strength of His might. In the old feudal days, when the vassal did his homage to his lord, he did this: he put his hands together and put them within the hands of his lord in token of absolute submission to his will and readiness for activity in his work. *That is the only true position for a Christian's hands*, the hands and heart and will, the spirit and life. Not one hand but both, completely within the hands of the Sovereign; the infinitely more than feudal Lord; the despot; the glorious, absolute, unconstitutional despot of His servants; the infinitely trustworthy, infinitely sovereign Lord Jesus Christ.

Are you prepared to live for His service at home or abroad, in the commonest round of the most ordinary life or in the high places of the field? Are you prepared to live as those who have put their hands into His and have recognized distinctly that the center of life is shifted from self to Jesus Christ; who have distinctly laid down at His feet all those desires which attract notice for self's sake? You belong to Him if you are His. All your gains are to go into your Master's purse, and He is to decide where and how and how long you are to serve.

My glorious Victor, prince Divine,
Clasp these surrendered hands in Thine.
At length my will is all Thine own,
Glad vassal of a Savior's throne!

H. C. G. Moule in Andrew Murray,
The Key to the Missionary Problem

May 22

Present your bodies a living sacrifice, holy, acceptable to God.

Romans 12:1

It is a great thing when I discover I am no longer my own but His. Real Christian life begins with knowing this.

Presenting myself to God implies a recognition that I am altogether His. This giving of myself is a definite thing. There must be a day in my life when I pass out of my own hands into His, and from that day forward I belong to Him and no longer to myself. I consecrate myself to the will of God to be and to do whatever He requires.

We have only one life to live down here, and we are free to do as we please with it; but if we seek our own pleasure, our life will never glorify God. A devoted Christian once said in my hearing, "I want nothing for myself; I want everything for God." Do you want anything apart from God, or does all your desire center in His will? Can you truly say that for you the will of God is "good and acceptable and perfect" (Rom. 12:2)?

For it is our wills that are in question here. That strong self-assertive will of mine must go to the cross, and I must give myself wholly to the Lord. We cannot expect a tailor to make us a coat if we do not give him any cloth or a builder to build us a house if we let him have no building material; and in just the same way, we cannot expect the Lord to live out His life in us if we do not give Him our lives in which to live. Without reservations, without controversy, we must give ourselves to Him to do as He pleases with us.

Watchman Nee, *The Normal Christian Life*

May 23

. . . that God may be all in all.

1 Corinthians 15:28

True and saving faith is twofold: it gives all and takes all. If I fail to *give* all to Christ, then no matter how bold and noisy I may be in claiming the promises, my faith is dead and powerless. My boldness, like Peter's before the crucifixion, will be put to shame when tested, and like Peter, I will end up weeping bitterly. On the other hand, if I fail to *take* Christ for all, all my giving will be in vain, ending only in terrible disappointment.

The Word of God presents us with two great assets: one of commands and one of promises. Faith trusts implicitly in both. Faith obeys the one and accepts the other. In the commandments God reveals Himself as a requiring God, in the promises as a giving God. Faith relies on Him in His commandments and promises, yielding explicit obedience to the one and putting forth a confident hand to take the other. Any "faith" which accepts one and rejects or neglects the other is not really faith at all.

God demands that our heart and life be wholly given and consecrated to Him, and true faith responds, "Yes, Lord, take it all. All I have and am are Yours." God gives us His Son to be our Savior, and true faith takes Him at once and is satisfied, saying,

Thou, O Christ, art all I want;
More than all in Thee I find.

He who gives all and takes all *has* all. He who gives but does not take or takes but does not give has nothing but disappointment and sorrow.

William Boardman, *The Higher Christian Life*

May 24

Paul, a bondservant of Jesus Christ, called to be an apostle, separated to the gospel of God . . .

Romans 1:1

The apostle Paul never wearied of describing himself as *the slave of Jesus Christ*. He had been a rebel chieftain. With fire and sword he had ravaged the flock of God. He had measured his strength with Jesus of Nazareth but had met more than his match. The stronger One had come upon him, taken away his armor, and bound him with fetters from which he could not get free.

Break free?—he would not if he could, nor could he if he would. From that hour in which he had been smitten to the ground on the road to Damascus, he had been content to be led from city to city, from continent to continent in the triumphal progress of his Lord, a trophy of His mighty power to bring the most stubborn under His yoke. "Thanks be unto God," he cries, "who always leadeth us in triumph."

Is this your conception of your life? Captured! Apprehended by Jesus Christ! Set apart for Himself! Do you realize that you are bound by the most sacred fetters to your Conqueror and are following His chariot through the earth? Life would assume a new aspect if you realized this and that all you are in your person and own in your property have become Emmanuel's.

F. B. Meyer, *Paul*

May 25

Do not love the world or the things in the world.

1 John 2:15

The Rechabites dwelt in tents. They drove their vast flocks from place to place and were content with the simple life of the wandering shepherd. It was thus that the great patriarchs had lived before them (Heb. 11:9, 13). And ever since their days, the tent life has been the chosen emblem of the life that is so strongly attracted to the other world as to be lightly attached to this.

It is difficult to say what worldliness consists in. What would be worldly to some people is an ordinary part of life's circumstances to others. But all of us are sensible of ties that hold us to the earth. We may discover what they are by considering what we cling to; what we find it hard to let go, even into the hands of Christ; what we are always striving to augment; what we pride ourselves in. It may be name, fame, notoriety, pride of fashion, rank, money.

But whatever it is, if it hinders us from living on the highest level—if it is a weight that impedes our speed heavenward—it should be laid deliberately on God's altar that He may do with it as He will and that we may be able, without frustration or hindrance, to be wholly for God.

F. B. Meyer, *Jeremiah*

May 26

I delight to do Your will, O my God.

Psalm 40:8

It is a great rebellion against God to think that your will may ever rightly differ from His. You are therefore to consider yourself as a being that has no other business in the world but to be that which God requires you to be; to have no desires, to seek no self-ends, but to fill that place and act that part which the divine pleasure has ordained.

To think that you are your own or at your own disposal is as absurd as to think that you created yourself. In *Him* you live and move and have your being.

When a man has that confident inner assurance that God's will for his life is the design of an infinite wisdom and love, it will be as necessary, while in the possession of this faith, to be thankful and pleased with everything that God chooses as it would be to wish his own happiness. For what more could be asked than that every circumstance of life be the choice of an infinite wisdom and love?

Hence the vital necessity, both for our salvation and for our eternal well-being, of placing ourselves completely under the power and control of the Holy Spirit, allowing Him to live through us that very purpose for which God at first created us and for which we were redeemed when, like lost sheep, we had gone astray.

William Law, *The Power of the Spirit*

May 27

They departed to go to the land of Canaan. So they came to the land of Canaan.

Genesis 12:5

For many days after leaving Haran, the eye would sweep a vast monotonous waste, broken by the scantiest vegetation; the camels treading the soft sand beneath their spreading, spongy feet and the flocks finding but scanty nutriment on the coarse, sparse grass.

At one point only would the travelers arrest their course. In the oasis where Damascus stands today, it stood then—furnishing a welcome resting place to weary travelers over the waste.

But Abraham would not stay here. The luxuriance and beauty of the place were very attractive, but he could not feel that it was God's choice for him. And therefore, before long he was again on the southern track to reach Canaan as soon as he could.

Our one aim in life must ever be to follow the will of God and to walk in those ways in which He has preordained for us to walk. Many a Damascus oasis tempts us to tarry. Many a Peter, well-meaning but mistaken, lays his hand on us, saying, "This shall never happen to thee; spare thyself." Many a conspirator within the heart counsels a general mutiny against the lonely, desolate will. And it is well when the pilgrim of eternity refuses to stay short, in any particular, of perfect consecration and obedience to the extreme demands of God.

When you go forth to go into the land of Canaan, do not rest until into the land of Canaan you come. Anything short of complete obedience nullifies all that has been done. The Lord Jesus must have all or none, and His demands must be fulfilled up to the hilt. But they are not grievous.

F. B. Meyer, *Abraham*

May 28

Know that the Lord *has set apart for Himself him who is godly.*

Psalm 4:3

The outward separation of the body from the world of the ungodly is incomplete unless accompanied and supplemented by the inner separation of the spirit. It is not enough to leave Ur, Haran, and Egypt. We must be rid of Lot also. Though we lived in a monastery, shut away from the homes and haunts of men, with no sound to break upon the ear but the summoning bell of worship and the solemn chant, yet so long as there was an alien principle in our breast, a Lot in our heart life, there could not be that separation to God which is the condition of the growth of faith and of all those higher forms of the true life which make earth most like heaven.

O souls that sigh for saintliness as harts pant for water brooks, have you counted the cost? Can you bear the fiery ordeal? The manufacture of saints is no child's play.

As Abraham was separated from one after another of nature's resources, so must it be with all aspirants for the inner chambers of the palace of God. We must be prepared to die to the world with its censure or praise; to the flesh with its ambitions and schemes; to the delights of a friendship which is insidiously lowering the temperature of the spirit; to the self-life in all its myriad subtle and overt manifestations; and even, if it be God's will, to the joys and consolations of religion.

All this is impossible to us of ourselves. But if we will surrender ourselves to God, willing that He should work in and for us that which we cannot do for ourselves, we shall find that He will gradually and effectively, and as tenderly as possible, begin to disentwine the clinging tendrils of the poisoning weed and bring us into heart union with Himself.

F. B. Meyer, *Abraham*

May 29

Sanctify in your hearts Christ as Lord.

1 Peter 3:15, RV

The Lord must, for our salvation at all, be so in living union with us that we are in Him and *He in us.* But His presence in us has its degrees and advances, its less and more, its outer and inner.

To drop a metaphor, a life may be truly Christian and yet far from fully Christian; the man may have come really to Christ and have really cast anchor on Him and have really confessed Him and be really seeking to serve Him yet be keeping back, perhaps quite unconsciously, whole regions of the life from Him. He may be living rather as His *ally* than as His *vassal.* He may be rather treating Him as an august visitor in His servant's house than behaving as the loving *bondservant* in a house where Christ is always the Master at home.

And Saint Paul cannot rest about the Ephesians till they have, all of them, accepted the Lord simply on *His* own terms in this matter. They will never satisfy their apostle, for they cannot possibly satisfy the Lord if they do not welcome the blessed, the beloved, the adorable Indweller *to the heart*—not only to the convictions or even to the conduct but to the heart. He must be inducted into the central chamber, for it is His proper place. And He must be always there.

There let Him sit, supreme and at the center. In many a Christian's experience, it is as if the Christian life began anew, and in an almost heaven, when the will chooses deliberately and without reserve to seat Him *there.*

H. C. G. Moule, *Ephesian Studies*

May 30

You are worthy to take the scroll, and to open its seals;
for You were slain, and have redeemed us to God by Your blood.

Revelation 5:9

These words remind us of the claim which Christ makes on us. A person may have a right to something without exercising that right; he lays no claim to it. But it is not thus with Jesus Christ. He comes to us with the urgent request that we should surrender ourselves to Him.

You know how, in every ordinary purchase, the buyer has the right to ask that what he has purchased shall be given to him. Jesus Christ asks that in all things His will and not ours should be supreme. That message comes to us again today. He beseeches us to make an end of slavery to other lords and to give ourselves up to Him as His purchased possession.

Each of us must deal with this claim, this request by the Lamb of God. How you deal with it will decide what your life will be in time and in eternity. A voice comes to us from heaven, saying, "He is worthy; He has been slain; He has redeemed us to God by His blood." Oh, that our hearts might no longer hesitate but by faith in that divine blood might respond to His call and reply, "You are worthy, O Lord! Here I am; take what You have purchased. I yield myself to You as Your possession."

Andrew Murray, *The Power of the Blood of the Cross*

May 31

Do not hesitate to go, and enter to possess the land.

Judges 18:9

The soul is first possessed by Christ, and then it begins to possess Christ. We are apprehended by our divine Captor, and then we come to apprehend Him. We open our hearts to receive Him into their depths and then learn to appropriate Him by a living faith. In other words, consecration must precede appropriation.

But when once the act of consecration is complete, we may begin to possess Him. This blessed habit may be initiated in a single act, but it is built up by a series of such acts, which are maintained through the grace of the Holy Spirit, till it becomes as natural for us to look up to Jesus and to claim whatever we need as to breathe.

Ah soul, why pine in poverty and starvation? Is it not because you have withheld yourself from Jesus? Arise and yield yourself to Him! Let Him possess you, and then you may claim a reciprocal possession of your Lord. Thus shall you begin to enter upon your eternal inheritance and commence to expend yourself on pursuits that shall engage you when sun and moon are no more!

F. B. Meyer, *Joshua*

June

Holiness and Victory in Christ

The Testimony of H. C. G. Moule

Handley Carr Glyn Moule, principal since 1881 of the new Theological College of Ridley Hall at Cambridge and for nearly nineteen years Bishop of Durham, was "a recognized theologian of unquestioned Evangelical principles." He had taken an important part in D. L. Moody's epochal mission to the university in November 1882, and the unprecedented effect of Moody and Sankey lay fresh in memory when Evan Hopkins and others conducted a holiness convention at Cambridge.

Moule had understood from hearsay that this teaching "lacked balance" and "had a dangerous drift." But he was impressed by the "grave and reverent" manner of "the godly visitors," nor could he deny evidence of blessing among undergraduates. His puzzlement grew: "Cambridge was moved in an extraordinary measure and manner by the deepest inquiries and aspirations. The watchwords of surrender and holiness were everywhere."

At Easter 1884 appeared Evan Hopkins's book *The Law of Liberty in the Spiritual Life*. During the summer Handley Carr Glyn Moule wrote for the *Record* four long anonymous articles on "the contemporary stir of thought, discussion, and aspiration upon the great theme of holiness." He reviewed exhaustively Evan Hopkins's "singularly careful treatise" with "sincere respect but with sometimes stringent criticism."

A certain wistfulness crept into these articles. Moule's diary of those summer months records a pathetic catalogue of depression relieved by fitful "hope and peace and gladness." He had "begun to feel, after [his] years of converted life and ministerial work, guilty of discreditable failure in patience and charity and humbleness, and [he knew] not what."

In September 1884 Moule and his wife and their two little girls went to stay in Scotland with relatives, the Learmonths at Park Hall. Livingstone Learmonth, after attending the Keswick of 1882, had founded for neighbors and friends an annual convention on his estate. To Moule's annoyance the convention came around in the course of their visit, and there was no escape "without breach of courtesy."

A disgruntled Moule sat at the back of the barn, genuinely afraid that he would be party to heresy, "but there was a great deal of mixed motive, of jealousy and prejudice in it too." Moule very nearly refused to attend next evening. Courtesy alone drove him to enter the barn again. "God be thanked that I did."

Evan Hopkins stepped to the rostrum, unaware that his anonymous *Record* critic sat below—broken, hungry of soul, faced with "the sins of [his] converted life and its tremendous secret and open failures." Hopkins's simple, luminous address "was one long, ordered piling up of the promises of God" to a soul in Handley Moule's sorry case, encouraging him "to expect large and deep deliverances from himself, on the simple condition of surrender into the most trustworthy and tender hands, the hands of a perfect Redeemer, Conqueror, Keeper, and indwelling Friend."

Moule was honest. "And so I listened, and so I yielded, and believed."

In response to Hopkins's closing call, Moule stood, "a helpful act of *definition*." To his wonder, his wife stood too. As he walked back to the house, took his lamp, and mounted to bed, he "was wonderingly conscious of being in the grasp of an absolute Master, and of having grasped, in Him, a supreme secret of peace and life and victory."

Dr. John Charles Pollock, *The Keswick Story*

JUNE 1

Be holy, for I am holy.

1 PETER 1:16

There is only one way of becoming holy, as God is, and it is the obvious one of opening the entire being to the all-pervading presence of the Holy One. None of us can acquire holiness apart from God. It dwells in God alone. Holiness is only possible as the soul's possession of God, nay, better still, as God's possession of the soul. It never can be inherent or possessed apart from the divine fullness, any more than a river can flow on if it is cut off from its fountainhead. We are holy up to the measure in which we are God possessed.

Would you be holier? There is but one way: you must have more of God in you. Holiness is the beauty of the Lord of hosts. You cannot separate the one from the other. To have it, you must have Him. Nor will it be hard to obtain either, for He longs to enter into your being. Your longing is the faint response of your heart to His call.

Man never desired so much of God as God desired of man. God's holiness has revealed itself in a human form in the person of Jesus Christ our Lord, and so it is as able as it is eager to enter human lives through that blessed Spirit who is preeminently the channel by which we are filled up unto all the fullness of God. Ask your heavenly Father for this Spirit. He is more eager to give Him than a father to give food to his hungry child. And having asked, dare to believe that you have received, and "go in this thy might" (Judg. 6:14).

F. B. MEYER, *TRIED BY FIRE: EXPOSITION OF 1 PETER*

JUNE 2

Present yourselves to God.

ROMANS 6:13

The whole object of Christ's work is to bring us near to God. And the first thing the apostle gives us to do, since we have died with Christ and been raised with Him, is to come with this new life and bring it to God. The object for which Christ died was to get us very near to God and into fellowship with Him.

"Present yourselves to God." How often must I do it? It must be every moment. It must become a habit of my life. I have to do it every day until the consciousness takes possession of me that I have a divine life from God. I bring it to God because God does not give me life in myself so that I can have it as my private possession. His life works in me only so far as I yield to Him and abide in communion with Him. Present yourselves to God every day, until your whole soul is filled with the living faith of your true position.

The everlasting God has begun a life in me and is carrying it on every moment of the day, so every moment I can count on *God* to maintain it. Don't you see that it is *we* who have been guilty of breaking off the connection with God, resulting in broken communion?

If I can learn to walk all the day in God's presence, presenting myself to Him momentarily as alive from the dead, God will make the resurrection life of Christ work in me day and night—secretly, quietly, gently, and effectively. You who are justified, you who know you have life in Christ, present yourselves to God. Everything must come from Him.

ANDREW MURRAY, *THE SPIRITUAL LIFE*

June 3

He who dwells in the secret place of the Most High shall abide under the shadow of the Almighty.

Psalm 91:1

It is not easy to abide in Christ all at once. It is the growth of years, the result of perpetual watching and self-discipline, the outcome of the blessed Spirit's tender influence on the inner life. The clinging of the soul to Christ comes as the result of prolonged habit and self-discipline beneath the culture of the Spirit of God.

Never leave your room in the morning without lifting up your heart to Him and saying, "Teach me, O blessed Spirit, to abide in Christ for today. Keep me in abiding fellowship with Him. Even when I am not directly thinking of Him, may I still be abiding." Expect that He will do this. And when drifting from these moorings, lift up your heart and say, "O my Lord, who art the life and the light of men, give me more of Thy Spirit, that I may better abide in Thee."

Abiding in Christ means a life of communion with Him. To tell Him all; to talk over all anxieties and occurrences with Him; to speak with Him aloud as to a familiar and interested friend; to ask His counsel or advice; to stop to praise, to adore, and utter words of love; to draw heavily upon His resources, as the branch on the sap and life of the vine; to be content to be only a channel, so long as His power and grace are ever flowing through; to be only the bed of a stream hidden from view beneath the hurrying waters, speeding without pausing toward the sea. This is abiding in Christ.

This is what David must have meant when he said, "One thing have I desired of the Lord, that will I seek after; that I may dwell in the house of the Lord all the days of my life, to behold the beauty of the Lord, and to enquire in his temple" (Ps. 27:4).

F. B. Meyer, *Joseph*

June 4

Those who live according to the Spirit [set their minds on] the things of the Spirit. For . . . to be spiritually minded is life and peace.

Romans 8:5–6

The secret of walking after the Spirit is, briefly, to "mind" the Spirit and put spiritual things first.

Madame Guyon has a helpful illustration of what it means to abide in Christ. She says that when you enter a room, you may sense how pleasant and warm it is, but as you stay in it, you have no consciousness save of ease. But go into the cold outside, and you will soon know that you are not "abiding" in the room.

Walking in the Spirit, therefore, does not always mean any consciousness in the senses but a keen intuitive knowledge of God and His will. It is not a life of great spirit phenomena but of quiet rest in God in the common things of daily life. The believer thus ceases to be governed by circumstances and to measure external acts by their external values. Your great and blessed rest lies in simply and quietly doing the will of God, for in the life of union with God, the person cheerfully, gladly does the common everyday things with the same fervency of spirit as he would do what is called "the Lord's work."

Jessie Penn-Lewis, *The Centrality of the Cross*

June 5

To Him who is able to do exceedingly abundantly above all that we ask or think, according to the power that works in us . . .

Ephesians 3:20

What is the secret strength of the Christian life? From where does it derive its power? Let me give you the answer in a sentence: *the Christian's secret is his rest in Christ.* His power derives from his God-given position. We *sit* forever with Christ that we may *walk* continuously before men. Forsake for a moment our place of rest in Him, and immediately we are tripped and our testimony in the world is marred. But abide in Christ, and our position there ensures the power to walk worthy of Him here.

If you desire an illustration of this kind of progress, think first of all not of a runner in a race but of a man in a car or, better still, of a cripple in a power-driven invalid carriage. What does he do? He *goes*—but he also *sits.* And he keeps going because he remains sitting. His progress follows from the position in which he has been placed. This, of course, is a far from perfect picture of the Christian life, but it may serve to remind us that our conduct and behavior depend fundamentally upon our inward rest in Christ.

This explains Paul's language here. He has first learned to sit. He has come to a place of rest in God. As a result, his walking is not based on his efforts but on God's mighty inward working. There lies the secret of his strength. Paul has seen himself seated in Christ; therefore his walk before men takes its character from Christ dwelling in him.

Watchman Nee, *Sit, Walk, Stand*

June 6

We have been sanctified through the offering of the body of Jesus Christ once for all.

HEBREWS 10:10

The victorious life, the life of freedom from the power of sin, is not a gradual gift. There is no such thing as a gradual gift. And victory is a gift. It is not a growth.

Please do not misunderstand me as saying that in the victorious life there is no growth. That would be absolutely false, wholly untrue to the Word of God. But we only begin to grow normally, grow as God wants us to grow, after we have entered into victory. Then we have the chance to grow for the first time as we ought to grow.

Then we can "grow in grace" in a thousand and one ways—grow as long as we live, learning more of the Lord all the time and of His Word, and be growing as He wants us to grow—but not growing in freedom from the power of sin. For we can have that victory today as completely as we can ever have it in this world. If Jesus is not able to do it for us today, then He will never be able to do it for us. But praise God, He is! And He is "the same yesterday, and today, and forever."

CHARLES TRUMBULL, *VICTORY IN CHRIST*

June 7

Unless a grain of wheat falls into the ground and dies, it remains alone; but if it dies, it produces much grain.

John 12:24

There is no gradual deliverance from sin, no gradual process of death to sin or deliverance from the world or the flesh. The Spirit of God does not say, "A little bit today and a little bit tomorrow," but to all sin and all workings of the flesh, as soon as you become aware of either, "Drop it!" Romans therefore bids you reckon yourself dead to sin.

But John 12:24 speaks of a gradual and progressive law of death in respect to fruitfulness. It speaks not of parting with that which is wrong but with that which is lawful, that which we have by nature: life. It is this life which the Lord calls those who follow Him to lay down for His sake; i.e., the life we have by nature has to go into death to enable the life of God in us to bring forth fruit.

The life of God in us, set free to act through us as the life of nature is buried in death, quickens everything it touches. One of the old writers describes this life as a "tincture." Take, for instance, one drop of ink or a drop of milk, and it will tincture a glass of water.

Oh thus to live that everything we say or do has the tincture of the life of God in it. It makes the ordinary, everyday life full of God. The one who knows it is so occupied with being "faithful in that which is least" that he does not think whether he is used or not. Such a one does not clamor for power or for more power, for he has only to see to the dying—the abiding in the death of Christ—while unknown to him the life of God in him is tincturing all the doing and bringing forth fruit eternal.

Jessie Penn-Lewis, *The Centrality of the Cross*

JUNE 8

This is the will of God, your sanctification.

1 THESSALONIANS 4:3

Believers are called unto holiness. "This is the will of God, even your sanctification." "God chose you from the beginning in sanctification of the Spirit." Without holiness grace fails in its purpose, and without it no man can see the Lord. The experience is set forth in various terms and under many forms, but in all its manifold representations, the same root ideas persist and prevail. Holiness is an attitude of dedication and an experience of grace in which the heart is cleansed from sin and made perfect in love.

A mistake made by many earnest Christians about holiness is that it comes by a gradual growth in grace and a steady progress of spiritual discipline. They are always growing toward it, but they never get into it—always struggling and striving to attain but never entering into possession. The positive expectation is always seen to be afar off, and they die without having possessed. The hopeful future never becomes the positive now. The time never comes that calls for a definite step and a positive act of faith.

But holiness does not come by growth, neither is it identified with growth. Growth is a process of life; holiness is the *gift* of abundant life. Growth is the result of health; holiness *is* health. Holiness implies a crisis, a new experience, a transformed life. It is not an achievement or an attainment but a gift of grace in the Holy Ghost. It comes not by works but by faith.

SAMUEL CHADWICK, *THE WAY TO PENTECOST*

June 9

It is God who works in you both to will and to do.

Philippians 2:13

The Bible teaches that by trusting in Christ, we receive an inward influence that stimulates and directs our activity; that by faith we receive His purifying influence into the very center of our being; that through and by His truth revealed directly to the soul, He quickens our whole inward being into the attitude of a loving obedience; and this is the way, the only practical way, to overcome sin.

But someone may say, "Does not the apostle exhort as follows: 'Work out your own salvation with fear and trembling. For it is God which worketh in you both to will and to do of his good pleasure'? And is not this an exhortation to do what in this article you condemn?" By no means.

This passage of Scripture happily recognizes both the divine and human agency in the work of sanctification. God works in us to will and to do, and we, accepting by faith His inworking, will and do according to His good pleasure.

It must be understood that the whole of spiritual life that is in any man is received directly from the Spirit of Christ by faith, as the branch receives its life from the vine! Forget this religion of resolutions! It is a snare of death. Forget this effort to make the life holy while the heart does not have in it the love of God! We need to learn to look directly at Christ through the gospel and so embrace Him by an act of loving trust as to involve a universal agreement with His state of mind. This and this alone is sanctification.

Charles Finney, *Power from On High*

JUNE 10

In lowliness of mind let each esteem others better than himself.

PHILIPPIANS 2:3

"For three years I had put all my time, money, and everything into the mission," he [Rees Howells] noted, "and had been over every night. And now, when there were great prospects, God was asking me to step down and help behind my friend, as he had previously helped behind me. The mission was growing and would become still more popular, and the people naturally would attribute all the success to my friend.

"It was a great inward conflict to allow my friend to get the outward success. This was the next grade of self the Holy Ghost was going to deal with; and it was a hard process, allowing self to be replaced by His divine nature. For three days I could not willingly accept it, but I knew I would be pulled through. It was God's way of working one up to having as much joy in a hidden life as in an open and successful one. If my aim in life was to do God's will, then I could truly say either way would be equal joy."

The story of Madame Guyon, in which the process of sanctification was to be seen very plainly, proved a help to him at this time. Even in the dungeon in France, she would say, "I ask no more, in good or ill, but union with Thy holy will."

God brought Rees through and made another deep change in his nature. Like Jonathan, he was able to love the man who took his place. He talked it over with his friend and told him how God was leading him and that from henceforth the mission would be his while he stood behind him in prayer. "Build it as a great mission. The Lord will win souls through you, and I will be praying for you. I want the mission to become a greater success through you than it was through me."

NORMAN GRUBB, *REES HOWELLS: INTERCESSOR*

June 11

These things indeed have an appearance of wisdom in self-imposed religion . . . but are of no value against the indulgence of the flesh.

Colossians 2:23

How shall I meet and conquer the indulgence of the flesh? No mere abstract question is in view. The most awful of realities was before Saint Paul and the Colossians: the presence of sin, the power of temptation, the mystery of our moral bondage in the fall.

Saint Paul was still as sure as ever that we are called, in Christ, to a life which must be always watchful and always self-controlled—the exact opposite of a self-seeking independence. But he had learned, in the light of the Lord, that the heart of such a life is found in the holy liberty wherewith Christ has made us free by making us one with Him.

The man who is kept awake by grace to his own awful weakness and to the foes that beset him will indeed not only pray but watch. But he will do so as one whose secret and resource of moral power in the watching life is altogether Jesus Christ our Lord. He will oppose *Him* to the enemy, who seems sometimes all but omnipotent. He will draw upon his *Head* for the strength and victory which shall make the weak "limb" able to "do great acts." He will retire into *Christ* and abide there for deliverance and peace that he may continually serve Him in holy purity in the stress of real life. He will remember that in *Christ* he died; in *Christ* he lives. And his life now, yea, in this formidable "flesh," will be lived in peace and power on the ascetic principle of heaven: "by the faith of the *Son of God*, who loved me, and gave himself for me."

H. C. G. Moule, *Colossian and Philemon Studies*

June 12

This is the victory that has overcome the world—our faith.

1 John 5:4

The children of Israel did not get their inheritance by crossing the Red Sea; the Jordan also had to be crossed, in the same way, *by faith*. Only then could they learn the lesson that *by faith* they were to conquer their foes in the land—the same way they had gained deliverance from their enemies in Egypt. It proved to be a hard lesson to learn.

The Red Sea didn't stop them. They stood on the far side, looking back at the water which had opened to let them pass but had closed on their enemies, and they sang a song of triumph.

Then they came to the borders of Canaan. When the spies Moses had sent out described the giants and walled cities, they saw it all through the magnifying glass of fear and lost their strength. Difficulties rose up in their minds and swelled to impossibilities, and they decided to go back to Egypt.

It is the same with us. We break from the bondage of the world, run to the Savior for pardon, and find it. We are happy in it—we sing a song of triumph after passing through the sea, and we go forward. But at some point we see the Canaanites—the giant sins in the walled cities of our hearts. And when we think of conquering them, we see it as *our* job, not the Lord's, and we shrink from it as hopeless. We content ourselves as well as we can with a life of wandering in the wilderness simply because we fail to move forward in faith to victory, trusting in God alone to give it.

In this way many people are stopped almost before they have started. They see the land before them but have not yet taken the first decisive step toward its possession. May God help us to conquer in spite of Satan's hindrances.

William Boardman, *The Higher Christian Life*

June 13

Work out your own salvation with fear and trembling.

Philippians 2:12

We are to be holy. We are *to act* in the light and wonder of so vast an act of love [as Christ's cross], in the wealth and resource of "so great salvation." We are to set spiritually to work. We are to learn that all-important lesson in religion, the holy and humble energy and independence which come to the man who "knows whom he has believed" and is aware that he possesses "all spiritual blessing" in Him (Eph. 1:3). We are to rise up and, if need be, walk alone, bereft of human help, in the certainty that Christ has died for us and reigns for us and in us.

Our Paul may be far away in some distant Rome, and we may sorely miss him. But we have at hand Jesus Christ, who "took bondservant's form" and obeyed even unto death for us, and who is on the eternal throne for us, and who lives within us by His Spirit. Looking upon Him in the glory of His person and His work, we are not only to wonder, not only even to worship; we are to work—to "work out" our spiritual blessings into a life which shall be full of Him and in which we shall indeed be "saved" ourselves and help others around us to their salvation.

In the "fear and trembling" of those who feel the blissful awfulness of an eternal Presence, we are to set ourselves, with the inexhaustible diligence of hope, to the business of the spiritual life. We are to bring all the treasures of a manifested and possessed Redeemer to bear upon the passing hour and to let Him be seen in us, "Christ our Life," always formative and empowering.

H. C. G. Moule, *Philippian Studies*

JUNE 14

Whoever hears these sayings of Mine, and does them,
I will liken him to a wise man who built his house on the rock.

MATTHEW 7:24

In 1 Corinthians 3:10–15 we have set before us the solemn responsibility of the believer to be careful about his building. Christ is the only sure foundation, for He is the chief cornerstone (Eph. 2:20), the tried stone, the sure foundation (Isa. 28:16). But the building must not only be *on* the Lord but must be built *by* Him, for except the Lord build the house, they labor in vain that build it (Ps. 127:1).

God works, however, through consecrated apprentices, and here Paul tells us that a man may build upon the true foundation with gold, silver, and precious stones or with wood, hay, or stubble. The fire of judgment will test the life, and although the believer himself shall be saved, if he has built of wood, hay, or stubble, his lifework shall be destroyed.

Think of how we waste spare time, filling it with unenduring materials when we could make it a permanent blessing. We build unworthily, cheaply, because we will not pay the price for the best materials. God offers us gold already tried in fire (Rev. 3:18), but there are no bargain rates and reduced prices. It takes hours of prayer and Bible study and obedience and self-denial. If our lifework is to be fireproof, it will not be so built by sentence prayers and one-minute Bible readings before breakfast.

One day we shall thank God we built with enduring material. It is so easy to let up here and there and work in a little wood or stubble, but blessed is the man who will not substitute even the good for the best.

VANCE HAVNER, *REFLECTIONS ON THE GOSPELS*

June 15

There remains very much land yet to be possessed.

Joshua 13:1

In the occupation of Canaan, the method adopted seems to have been, first, a careful survey of the land not yet possessed; then its apportionment among the several tribes according to their size; and lastly, the actual appropriation and acquisition of each portion by the efforts of the tribe to which it was assigned.

It would be interesting, did space permit, to examine the area designated by the divine Spirit. It included all the region of Philistia, inhabited by some of the stoutest foes that Israel ever encountered and who were a perpetual source of weakness and danger till the times of the kings. There were also the rich pasturelands of the south and, in addition, the luxuriant plain of Phoenicia and the fertile upland valleys, cooled by the snowcapped summits and watered from the rivulets of Lebanon—all portions of the land on which Israel had always a very slender hold. Compare this outline sketch of the divine intentions with the territories then actually held and afterward possessed by Israel, and the difference between God's ideal and their real inheritance becomes very striking.

The mountains of vision and the valleys of blessing; green pasturelands and the waters of rest; the cities we may occupy and the foes we may expel—all are mapped out for us. And we shall do wisely to carefully ponder it, that we may be humbled as we see the slow progress we have made and may be stirred up to apprehend all that for which we were apprehended in Christ Jesus.

F. B. Meyer, *Joshua*

JUNE 16

My cup runs over.

PSALM 23:5

We all can recognize those words as a beautiful description of the abiding presence of Jesus in the heart—His peace, joy, and presence filling us to overflowing, with no shadow between. But here comes the point of it in this message of revival: we are to recognize that "cups running over" is the *normal* daily experience of the believer walking with Jesus.

But that just isn't so in the lives of practically all of us. Those cups running over get pretty muddled up; other things besides the joy of the Lord flow out of us. We are often much more conscious of emptiness or dryness or hardness or disturbance or fear or worry than we are of the fullness of His presence and overflowing joy and peace. And now comes the point. What stops that moment-by-moment flow? The answer is only one thing: sin.

But we by no means usually accept or recognize that. We have many other more convenient names for those disturbances of heart. We say it is nerves that cause us to speak impatiently—not sin. We say it is tiredness that causes us to speak the sharp word at home—not sin. We say it is the pressure of work that causes us to lose our peace, get worried, act or speak hastily—not sin.

What are "cups running over"? Of course the Spirit witnessing to Jesus in the heart. He is our peace, joy, life, all, and it is the Spirit's work never to cease witnessing to Him within us. What then can stop the Spirit's witness? Can nerves or tiredness or pressure of circumstances or difficult people? Paul's cry was, "Who or what can separate me from the love of God? Can tribulation or persecution or things present or things to come?" "No!" he says.

NORMAN GRUBB, *CONTINUOUS REVIVAL*

JUNE 17

God . . . gives us the victory through our Lord Jesus Christ.

1 CORINTHIANS 15:57

The victorious life is the normal one for a Christian. Sin finds power through unbelief, which uses the excuse, "I'm only human." It is the same attitude of mind as that adopted by the pickpocket who said, "I'm a good Christian. Once upon a time I would have stolen fifty watches every month. Since I have been converted, I steal only four or five."

Every temptation offers an occasion for victory. It is a signal to fly the flag of our Victor, an opportunity to make the tempter know anew that he is defeated. The prince of this world is judged.

No condemnation can hang over the head of those who are in Christ Jesus, for the new spiritual principle of life in Christ lifts me out of the old vicious circle of sin and death (Rom. 8:1).

Although we know about this vicious circle of sin and try again and again to live up to the Christian life (indeed we may be successful for a time), yet we fall because of our sinful nature, and the power of the enemy keeps us on the deadly treadmill of sin. Jesus came to lift us out of it and to put us into the blessed circle of the Holy Spirit.

If we then sin, we confess it immediately; and "we find God utterly reliable and straightforward—he forgives our sins" (1 John 1:9, Phillips), and the blood which His Son shed for us keeps us clean from all sin. Should we fail again, our Advocate lives, and His blood is available to cleanse us from our sins.

CORRIE TEN BOOM, *PLENTY FOR EVERYONE*

June 18

Son, you are always with me, and all that I have is yours.

Luke 15:31

We may talk a great deal about the father's love to the prodigal, but when we think of the way he treated the elder brother, it brings to our hearts a truer sense of the wonderful love of the father.

The elder son, being ever with his father, had, if he liked, the privilege of two things: unceasing fellowship and unlimited partnership. But he was worse than the prodigal, for although always at home, yet he had never enjoyed or understood the privileges that were his. All this fullness of fellowship had been waiting for and offered to him, but he had not received it. While the prodigal was away from home in the far country, his elder brother was far from the enjoyment of home while he was at home.

Full salvation includes unceasing fellowship: "ever with me." An earthly father loves his child and delights to make his child happy. "God is love," and He delights to pour out His own nature on His people. It is the very nature of the sun to shine, and it can't help shining on and on. "God is love," and, speaking with all reverence, He can't help loving. We see His goodness toward the ungodly and His compassion on the erring, but His fatherly love is manifested toward all His children.

My message is that the Lord your God desires to have you living continually in the light of His countenance. Your business, your temper, your circumstances of which you complain as hindering, are they stronger than God? If you come and ask God to shine in and upon you, you will see and prove that you may walk all the day and every day in the light of His love. That is full salvation.

Andrew Murray, *Divine Healing*

June 19

Be still.

Psalm 46:10

Going to and fro" and "walking up and down"—so the adversary describes his occupation. The picture given is that he has been roaming around in the "heat of haste." He has been hurrying through the inhabited earth "as a roaring lion seeking whom he may devour" or as an "unclean spirit seeking rest" and finding none.

This fallen archangel imparts his feverish spirit to those who are yet under his control, for "the wicked are like the troubled sea, when it cannot rest. . . . There is no peace, saith my God, to the wicked" (Isa. 57:20–21).

We should pay special heed to this self-given description of the adversary's character and note the contrast between his feverish heat of haste and the calm walk of the Son of God in His life on earth.

The devil rushes to and fro with restless energy through the realms he has betrayed, causing tumult and unrest wherever he goes. The Son of God walked in calm peace through the world He came to save, and rest and blessing and life were given by Him on every hand.

No feverish heat of haste ever comes from God; and just as far as the soul becomes a "partaker of the divine nature" will it partake of the calm, restful power so strikingly manifested in the Man Christ Jesus.

Jessie Penn-Lewis, *The Story of Job*

JUNE 20

If we love one another, God abides in us, and His love has been perfected in us.

1 JOHN 4:12

At the close of a meeting in Berlin some time ago, a man came into the inquiry room. He appeared depressed and downhearted and had great difficulty in saying what it was that troubled him so deeply. I became impatient with him, asking rather abruptly, "Come along, what's your problem? I don't have much time. Let's talk together; perhaps I can help you." His answer made me tremble.

"I was one of the guards at Ravensbrück," he replied, "during the time you were a prisoner there. A few months ago, I was saved and brought all my sins to Jesus. He has forgiven me, and I have prayed that I might be allowed to ask forgiveness from one of my victims. I know everything about the transportation of the Dutch women—you numbered about a thousand—from Vught in Holland in 1944. Can you forgive me for my cruelties?"

At that moment it was as though a wave of God's love streamed through my heart, and I said to him, "Brother, I forgive you with my whole heart!" I took his hand—the hand that had been so cruel.

Could I have done that with my love? No! But with the love of Jesus in my heart, I was able to do so. Without Him I would have hated this man, but connected to Jesus I could joyfully love him with God's plentiful love.

CORRIE TEN BOOM, *PLENTY FOR EVERYONE*

June 21

Let all those who seek You rejoice and be glad in You.

Psalm 70:4

This morning Psalm 70:4 spoke to me. That's not just a holy aspiration; it's a command. And He who commands enables. Let all those who seek the Lord *rejoice*, today, every day. Joy is to be the keynote of our lives. He calls us then to make an act of faith every time we would naturally be pulled down into the pit of joylessness, for there is an end set to the sin and sorrow and confusion of the world as well as to our own private trials. We only see today. He whom we worship sees tomorrow.

You will find the truest joy comes in utter self-forgetfulness—what our Lord called the *denial* of self. This is what He is working in you to create and maintain. But He never forgets the cost.

Now may God give you the joy of Psalm 4:7: "Thou hast put gladness in my heart, more than they have when their corn and their wine are increased." May that joy flow over and wash away self in all its subtle forms and give you that dearest of all graces, *selflessness*.

Amy Carmichael, *Candles in the Dark*

JUNE 22

He who has begun a good work in you will complete it.

PHILIPPIANS 1:6

O my soul, if You would enjoy the comfort of this promise, be much occupied with this fact: *"He has begun."* The Christian speaks too often of his conversion and his faith and his self-surrender. Contemplating all this from the side of man, he keeps himself too little occupied with the thought *"He* has begun."

My soul, understand what this means: He has sought me and found me and made me His own, and what He has thus done to me points back to that which He did for me—He gave His own Son, and by His blood He bought me for Himself as His possession. And that again points back to eternity. He chose me and loved me before the foundation of the world. My soul, ponder what this means: "He has begun."

Then you shall be able to joyfully exclaim, "He will complete it; 'the LORD will perfect that which concerns me'" (Ps. 138:8). My life shall then become a life of humility, thanksgiving, confidence, joy, and love. You see that there is nothing in yourself, and you learn to expect all from God and thank Him for all. You learn to rely upon Him in everything. The end will be to you as certain as the beginning, because the end as well as the beginning has its root and stability in God. The selfsame faith, looking back, acknowledges the beginning as God's, and it also looks forward. "What He has done, He will perfect."

ANDREW MURRAY, *THE LORD'S TABLE*

June 23

Whatsoever toucheth the altar shall be holy.

Exodus 29:37, KJV

The smallness or unworthiness of the offering of him who brought it did not render it unacceptable to God. The altar, sanctified by blood, had the power to make it holy.

And thus when I fear lest my self-sacrifice be not indeed perfect, or lest in my dying to self I may not be entirely honest and true, my thoughts must be turned away from myself and fixed on the wonderful power which the blood of Jesus has bestowed on His cross: the power to sanctify all that touches it. The cross—the crucified Jesus—is the power of God when I, by increasing insight into what the cross means, really choose it and hold it fast. Then there proceeds from the cross, by the Spirit of Jesus, a power of life to take me up and hold me fast that I may live as one who has been crucified.

I may walk each moment in the consciousness of my crucifixion, my entire renunciation of self, because the Spirit of the crucified One makes His cross the death of the self-life and the power of the new life of God that rises out of death. From the cross as a sanctified altar, a sanctifying power is exercised over me. From the moment that I trustfully surrender myself to the cross, I become a sanctified person—one of God's saints.

In proportion as I believe in the sanctifying power of the cross and seek to live in fellowship with it, I become partaker of a progressive and increasing holiness.

Andrew Murray, *The Power of the Blood of the Cross*

June 24

. . . looking unto Jesus, the author and finisher of our faith.

Hebrews 12:2

I had just spoken to a group of young people on the riches we have in Jesus Christ. I invited them to remain for a period of discussion after the meeting. One said, "I am so unfaithful; I want to believe, but my faith wavers. Now that you have told us all these things, I feel certain again, but what about tomorrow? I don't know whether it will be so then."

I told him that I was a watchmaker by trade and that in our shop we received sometimes new watches that did not keep good time. These I did not repair myself but sent back to the manufacturer. When he had repaired them, they ran accurately. And that is also what I do with my faith. Jesus is the "author and finisher of our faith." If there is something wrong with my faith, I send it back to the heavenly manufacturer. When He has repaired it, it functions perfectly.

It is fortunate that Hebrews 12:2 does not read, "Let us look unto our own faith." If I should do that, I would perhaps say, "My faith is great." That would be pride, and the victory would be the devil's. Spiritual pride is very destructive. Or perhaps I would say, "Oh, my faith doesn't amount to anything; it doesn't do anything for me." That is defeatism; and it too is a victory of the devil.

Hudson Taylor once said, "We do not need a great faith but faith in a great God." Let us therefore look more and more to Jesus and not upon our own faith. Let us look not upon the storms around us but keep our eyes fixed upon Him. Then we shall be able to walk upon the waves of the turbulent sea of life. Faith is such a firm foundation that the safest place for a Christian to walk is the water that Peter trod as he went to meet Jesus.

Corrie ten Boom, *Amazing Love*

June 25

The things which are impossible with men are possible with God.

Luke 18:27

Your Christian life is every day to be a proof that God works impossibilities; your life is to be a series of impossibilities made possible and actual by God's almighty power. Have you learned to deal so closely with an almighty God that you know omnipotence is working in you?

The cause of the weakness of your Christian life is that you want to work it out partly and to let God "help" you. And that cannot be. You must come to be utterly helpless, to let God work; and God will work gloriously!

I could go through Scripture and prove to you how Moses, when he led Israel out of Egypt, how Joshua, when he brought them into the land of Canaan, how all God's servants in the Old Testament counted upon the omnipotence of God doing impossibilities. And this God lives *today*, and this God is the God of every child of His!

Yet some of us want God to give us a little help while we do our best instead of coming to understand what God wants and to say, "I can do nothing; God must and will do all." Have you said, "In worship, in work, in sanctification, in obedience to God, I can do nothing of myself, and so my place is to worship the omnipotent God and to believe that He will work in me every moment"? May God teach us this!

Andrew Murray, *Absolute Surrender*

June 26

The Lord is your keeper.

Psalm 121:5

Would you realize God's keeping grace? Give yourself entirely up to Him, renouncing all trust in yourself and all connection with evil. Choose definitely and forever the lot of the cross of Jesus. And then trust Jesus to keep you. Whenever temptation approaches, look up and say, "Jesus, I trust Your keeping power." Ask the Holy Spirit to keep you so constantly in this attitude that it may become the habit of your soul to look to Jesus when temptation assails. Trust Him to keep you trusting.

Nourish your faith by devout meditation on the promises of God. Do not look at your weakness or your foes but at the mighty bulwarks of God's salvation which He has appointed. Hear His gracious words, and hide them in your heart: "I the Lord do keep it; I will water it every moment: lest any hurt it, I will keep it night and day." Surely it were the height of blasphemy to affirm that the Almighty is not able or willing to keep the soul that trusts Him.

Thus will you await the consummation of your salvation, which shall be yours at the coming of the Lord. Already it is finished and prepared, but it waits to be revealed. And when amid the breaking light and exuberant gladness of perfect deliverance you review the pathway by which you have come, you will better realize your indebtedness to His wondrous grace in keeping that which you committed to Him against that day.

F. B. Meyer, *Tried by Fire: Exposition of 1 Peter*

June 27

If by the Spirit you put to death the deeds of the body, you will live.

Romans 8:13

Note the words well. Paul says nothing here of things often thought to be of the essence of spiritual remedies: nothing of "will worship, and humility, and unsparing treatment of the body" (Col. 2:23); nothing even of fasting and prayer. Sacred and precious is self-discipline—the watchful care that act and habit are true to the temperance which is a vital ingredient in the Spirit's fruit (Gal. 5:22–23). It is the Lord's own voice (Matt. 26:41) which bids us always "watch and pray"; "praying in the Holy Spirit" (Jude 1:20).

Yes, but these true exercises of the believing soul are after all only as the covering fence around that central secret—our use by faith of the presence and power of the Holy Spirit given to us. The Christian who neglects to watch and pray will most surely find that he knows not how to use this his great strength, for he will be losing realization of his oneness with his Lord. But then the man who actually and in the depth of his being is "doing to death the practices of the body" is doing so immediately not by discipline or by direct effort but by the believing use of the Spirit. Filled with Him he treads upon the power of the enemy. And that fullness is according to surrendering faith.

H. C. G. Moule, *The Epistle to the Romans*

June 28

Call upon Me in the day of trouble; I will deliver you, and you shall glorify Me.

PSALM 50:15

Christian man, by grace—that is to say, by the Holy Spirit of God—you have believed and live. You are a limb of Christ, who is your life. But you are a sinner still, always, actually, and potentially. For whatever the presence of the Spirit in you has done, it has not so altered you that if He should go, you would not *instantly* revert to unholiness. Do you, if I may put it so, use your regenerate self in an unregenerate way, meeting temptation and the tendency to sin by yourself alone, with only high resolves and moral scorn of wrong and discipline on body or mind?

God forbid we should call these things evil. They are good. But they are aspects, not the essence, of the secret. It is the Lord Himself dwelling in you who is your victory, and that victory is to be realized by a conscious and decisive appeal to Him. "Through God you shall do valiantly; for he it is that shall tread down your enemies" (Ps. 60:12).

And is this not proved true in your experience? When, in your regenerate state, you use the true regenerate way, is there not a better record to be given? When, realizing that the true principle is indeed a person, you resolve and struggle less and appeal and confide more—is not sin's reign broken, and is not your foot, even yours, because you are in conscious union with the Conqueror, placed effectually on "all power of the enemy"?

H. C. G. MOULE, *THE EPISTLE TO THE ROMANS*

June 29

. . . through sanctification by the Spirit.

2 Thessalonians 2:13

The scriptural method of sanctification is through the personal work of the Spirit of God. The law of the Spirit of life makes us free from the law of sin and death. It is God's work wrought in the heart by the Holy Spirit, who makes Christ our sanctification.

There are diversities of operation in all the works of the Spirit, and the method of entering into possession is as manifold as the temperaments and conditions of human life. No two experiences are ever really alike. Generally there is an awakening of heart and mind in which there come vision and persuasion. There is a conviction of need and a revelation of grace, a hunger and a search, a process and a crisis, an act of faith and an assurance of cleansing.

Holiness is in the spirit and of the divine Spirit. It is not in forms and ordinances, not in "will worship and voluntary humility." It is not in prohibitions and self-denial. It is a spirit, a life, a principle, a dynamic. The Spirit of God indwells the spirit of man. He clothes Himself with man, and man is clothed in the presence and power of the Spirit.

The body is the temple of the Spirit. Christ lives in men through the Spirit. He is no longer a model but a living Presence. Christian faith does not copy Him; it lives Him. The Spirit of God does not work upon us; He *lives* in us.

This is the contrast between the *works* of the flesh and the *fruit* of the Spirit. Works are by the sweat of man's brow; fruit is God's gift to man. Fruit does not come by toil but by appropriation, assimilation, and abiding. The Spirit of holiness makes the heart clean, the mind true, the faculties fit, and the life fruitful—by making His holiness ours.

Samuel Chadwick, *The Way to Pentecost*

June 30

Thanks be to God who always leads us in triumph in Christ, and through us diffuses the fragrance of His knowledge in every place.

2 Corinthians 2:14

What an ideal this is for us all, so to live that though we are unable to speak much or occupy a commanding position, yet from our lives a holy savor may be spread abroad which will not be ours but Christ's! Let us live so near Him that we may absorb His fragrance and then go forth to exhale it again in pureness, in knowledge, in longsuffering, in kindness, in the Holy Spirit, in love unfeigned, in the word of truth, and in the power of God. Just as a piece of clay or sponge may become so impregnated with some aromatic spice that it will scent the drawer, cupboard, or box in which it lies, so we may become impregnated with the sweetness of Jesus and spread it by an irresistible influence in every place where we are called to live or work.

What a test for daily living! Is my life fragrant of Jesus? Do I remind the Father of the blessed Lord? Does He detect Jesus in my walk and speech? And that there are in me the sweet savor of that daily burnt offering, that delight in God's will, that holy joy in suffering for His glory, that absorption in His purposes which made the life of the Son of Man so well pleasing to God?

F. B. Meyer, *Paul*

July

Being Filled with the Spirit of Christ

The Testimony of "Mr. Paul"

An American friend, now with the Lord, whose name we will call Paul, cherished the hope from his early youth that one day he would be called "Dr. Paul." When he was quite a little chap, he began to imagine himself first studying for his MA degree and then for his PhD. Then at length the glad day would arrive when all would greet him as Dr. Paul.

The Lord saved him and called him to preach, and before long he became pastor of a large congregation. By that time he had his degree and was studying for his doctorate, but despite splendid progress in his studies and a good measure of success as a pastor, he was a very dissatisfied man. He was a Christian minister, but his life was not Christlike; he had the Spirit of God within him, but he did not enjoy the Spirit's presence or experience His power.

He thought to himself, *I am a preacher of the gospel and the pastor of a church. I tell my people they should love the Word of God, but I do not really love it myself. I exhort them to pray, but I myself have little inclination to pray. I tell them to live a holy life, but my own life is not holy. I warn them not to love the world, and though outwardly I shun it, yet in my heart I myself still love it dearly.*

In his distress he cried to the Lord to cause him to know the power of the indwelling Spirit. But though he prayed and prayed for months, no answer came. Then he fasted and asked the Lord to show him any hindrance there might be in his life. That answer was not long in coming, and it was this: "I long that you should know the power of My Spirit, but your heart is set on something that I do not wish you to have. You have yielded to Me all but one thing that you are holding to yourself—your PhD."

Well, to Mr. Paul, this was his very life. He had dreamed of it from childhood and labored for it all through his youth. Now the thing he prized above all else was almost within his grasp. In two short months it would be his.

So he reasoned with the Lord: "Is there any harm for me to be a doctor of philosophy? Will it not bring much more glory to Thy name to have a Dr. Paul preaching the gospel than a plain Mr. Paul?" But God does not change His mind.

Then he resorted to bargaining with the Lord. He promised to go here or there, to do this or that—but still the Lord did not change. And all the while Mr. Paul was becoming more and more hungry to know the fullness of the Spirit. This state of affairs continued to within two days of his final examination.

It was Saturday, and Mr. Paul settled down to prepare his sermon for the following day. But study as he would, he could get no message. The ambition of a lifetime was just within reach of realization, but God made it clear that he must choose between the power he could sway through a doctor's degree and the power of God's Spirit swaying his life. That evening he yielded. "Lord," he said, "I am willing to be plain Mr. Paul all my days, but I want to know the power of the Holy Ghost in my life."

He rose from his knees and wrote a letter to his examiners, asking to be excused from the examination and giving his reason. Then he retired, very happy, but not conscious of any unusual experience. Next morning he told his congregation that for the first time in six years he had no sermon to preach and explained how it came about. The Lord blessed that testimony more abundantly than any of his well-prepared sermons. From that time God owned him in an altogether new way, for from that day he knew separation from the world no longer merely as an outward thing but as a deep inward reality. And as a result, the blessedness of the Spirit's presence and power became his daily experience.

WATCHMAN NEE, *THE NORMAL CHRISTIAN LIFE*

July 1

I will pray the Father, and He will give you another Helper.

John 14:16

Jesus said to them so tenderly, "I will pray the Father, and he shall give you another Comforter." Take these words into your heart, and ask that He may be made known to you. It is good to have mental knowledge, but such knowledge does not satisfy the heart. The greatest thing that is needed in the world today is the personal knowledge of a Comforter who will make known the unseen Savior.

Do you know the Comforter? Or are you just like the world when you are in trouble? Do you know the Holy Spirit? Or do you simply know a historical Christ and that the Holy Spirit was given on the Day of Pentecost? Do you know Him, the person?

You get to know Him by experience, not by theory or by a mental knowledge. Anything you know in that way can soon be stripped away from you, but something that you have proved and you know from experience, no human being in this world can take from you.

That, I say, is what God wants to do for us. He wants the Holy Spirit to be a real person in us to make Christ real to us in life so that we cannot help living in the living One. It is not what you believe or think, but it is what you are—what is wrought into you as part of you and what is greater than all you merely see. "Ye know him; for he shall be in you."

Dear listeners, are your hearts now saying, *Oh God, make me know Him*? I do not want to meet your intellects or your feelings or your views. I desire to disentangle you from all these and just say to you, "Do you know the Holy Spirit?"

Jessie Penn-Lewis, *The Work of the Holy Spirit*

July 2

The Spirit of truth . . . dwells with you and will be in you.

John 14:17

There are two levels of the Christian life. The one is that in which we experience something of the operations of the Holy Spirit similar to what many did under the old covenant but do not yet know Him as the Pentecostal Spirit, as the personal indwelling Guest who has come to abide permanently in the heart. On the other hand, there is a more abundant life in which the indwelling just referred to is known and the full joy and power of redemption are facts of personal experience. It will be only when Christians come to understand fully the distinction between these two conditions and discern that the second of these is in very deed the will of God concerning them that we shall dare to hope that the Christian community will once more be restored to its Pentecostal power.

So long as Christians imagine that the only thing lacking in their life is more earnestness or more persistence or more strength and that if they only obtain these benefits, they themselves will become all they ought to be, the preaching of a full salvation will be of little avail. It is only when the discovery is made that they are not standing in a right attitude toward the Holy Spirit—that they have only His preparatory operations but do not yet know and honor Him in His indwelling—that the way to something higher will ever be open or even be desired.

We may reckon upon it that where the reception of the Holy Spirit and the possibility of being filled with Him are proclaimed and appropriated, the blessed life of the Christian community will be restored to all its pristine power.

Andrew Murray, *The Full Blessing of Pentecost*

July 3

Having begun in the Spirit, are you now being made perfect by the flesh?

GALATIANS 3:3

It is to be feared that there are many Christians who hardly know that when they believed, they received the Holy Ghost. A great many Christians can say, "I received pardon, and I received peace." But if you were to ask them, "Have you received the Holy Ghost?" they would hesitate, and many, if they were to say yes, would say it with hesitation; and they would tell you that they hardly knew what it was since that time to walk in the power of the Holy Spirit. Let us take hold of this great truth: the beginning of the true Christian life is to receive the Holy Ghost.

God gives Christians the Holy Spirit with this intention: that every day all their life should be lived in the power of the Spirit. A man cannot live a godly life for one hour except by the power of the Holy Ghost. He may live a consistent, irreproachable life, a life of virtue and diligent service; but to live a life acceptable to God, in the enjoyment of God's salvation and God's love, to live and walk in the power of the new life—he cannot do this unless he be guided by the Holy Spirit every day and every hour.

But now listen to the danger: my human nature and will and effort can be very active in religion, and after being converted and receiving the Holy Ghost, I may in my own strength try to serve God. I may be very diligent and doing a great deal, and yet all the time it is more the work of human flesh than of God's Spirit. What a solemn thought that man can, without noticing it, be shunted off from the line of the Holy Ghost onto the line of the flesh. The great request for us to ask of God in self-examination is that we may be shown whether our religious life is lived more in the power of the flesh than in the power of the Holy Spirit.

ANDREW MURRAY, *ABSOLUTE SURRENDER*

July 4

He commanded them . . . to wait for the Promise of the Father.

Acts 1:4

There is a great difference between the *peace* and the *power* of the Holy Spirit in the soul. The disciples were *Christians* before the Day of Pentecost and as such had a measure of the Holy Spirit. They must have had the peace of sins forgiven and of a justified state, yet they did not have the power necessary to accomplish the work assigned them. They had the peace which Christ had given them but not the power which He had *promised.*

This may be true of all Christians, and right here is, I think, the great mistake of the church and of the ministry. They rest in conversion and do not seek until they obtain this heavenly empowering. This is why so many professors have no power with either God or man. They prevail with neither. They cling to a hope in Christ and even enter the ministry overlooking the admonition to wait until they are endued with power from on high.

But let anyone bring all the tithes and offerings into God's treasury, let him lay all upon the altar and put God to the proof therewith, and he shall find that God "will open the windows of heaven, and pour him out a blessing, that there shall not be room enough to receive it."

Charles Finney, *Power from On High*

July 5

I will open rivers in desolate heights, and fountains in the midst of valleys;
I will make the wilderness a pool of water, and the dry land springs of water.

ISAIAH 41:18

In our country, where we often suffer from drought, we find two sorts of reservoirs for catching and storing water. On some farms you have a spring or well but with a stream too weak to irrigate with. There a reservoir is made for collecting the water, and the filling of the reservoir is the result of the gentle, quiet inflow from the fountain day and night.

In other cases the farm has no spring, and the reservoir is built in the bed of a stream or in a hollow where, when rain falls, water can be collected. In such a place, the filling of the reservoir with a heavy fall of rain is often the sudden work of a very few hours and is accompanied with a rush and violence not free from danger.

There is a similar difference in the way in which the fullness, or baptism, of the Spirit comes and also the response to it. On the Day of Pentecost, or at times when new beginnings are made, suddenly, mightily, manifestly men are filled with the Holy Ghost. In the enthusiasm and the joy of the newly found salvation or revival, the power of the Spirit is undeniably present.

There are other Christians who have never been partakers of any such marked experience and in whom, nevertheless, the fullness of the Spirit is no less distinctly seen in their deep and intense devotion to Jesus, in a walk in the light of His countenance and the consciousness of His holy presence, in the blamelessness of a life of simple trust and obedience, and in the humility of a self-sacrificing love to all.

Happy are they who can recognize God in both and hold themselves always ready to be blessed in whichever way He comes!

ANDREW MURRAY IN LEONA CHOY,
ANDREW MURRAY: THE AUTHORIZED BIOGRAPHY

July 6

Be filled with the Spirit.

Ephesians 5:18

God has no suggestions, only commandments—with the sweetest command in Ephesians 5:18: "Be filled with the Spirit." God the Father glorifies Jesus in heaven, but the Holy Spirit glorifies Jesus on earth. He has no other dwelling place than in our hearts. When we are filled with the Holy Spirit, we then are used to glorify Jesus.

However, the Holy Spirit cannot and will not live in a dirty house. When there are unconfessed sins in our hearts, He cannot dwell there. What can we do with such sins as pride, self-pity, jealousy, sexual impurity, criticism, inferiority feelings, dishonesty, unpaid debts, etc.? God's faithfulness and truth are the guarantees of our forgiveness when the blood of Jesus Christ cleanses us from all the sins we confess. First John 1:7–9 is the first aid for the sinning Christian, but His blood will never cleanse an excuse.

After we have brought our last sin to the Lord, we must surrender. Then we can claim the fullness of the Holy Spirit. Claiming is an act of faith based on the express promise in God's Word. As we believe, so we receive.

It was Jesus Himself who said that the greatest proof of His own love to the world would be demonstrated through His promised power of the Holy Spirit.

Corrie ten Boom, *Plenty for Everyone*

July 7

. . . the Holy Spirit whom God has given to those who obey Him.

Acts 5:32

The New Testament tells us that there are four possible attitudes that we may take up toward the Holy Spirit: the first is to grieve Him (Eph. 4:30–31); the second is to resist Him (Acts 7:51); the third is that of quenching Him (1 Thess. 5:19–20). The fourth attitude that we can take to the Spirit's working is to be filled with Him.

When thinking of this matter of being filled with the Holy Spirit, it is important always to do so in the context of these three other attitudes to the Spirit. If we do not do so, we shall always be regarding the fullness of the Holy Spirit as a special blessing, extra to our inheritance in Christ, and that attitude will lead us only to striving and frustration.

If we are not filled with the Spirit at any given moment, it is only because of one thing: sin. Through sin we have grieved Him and are resisting Him where He has convicted us. Maybe we have been in a dry, unsatisfied condition for years, but it is all due to an accumulation of this same one thing—sin. But we have only to humble ourselves in repentance under the Holy Spirit's conviction, and He will witness in our hearts to Jesus and His blood and enable us to believe that His blood cleanses what we have confessed. Then where the blood cleanses, the Holy Spirit fills, and that without further waiting on our part.

Roy Hession, *Be Filled Now*

July 8

. . . not in the flesh but in the Spirit.

Romans 8:9

When God created man "a living soul," that soul, as the seat of his personality and consciousness, "was linked, on the one side, through the body, with the outer world; on the other side, through the spirit, with the unseen and divine. The soul had to decide whether it would yield itself to the spirit, by it to be linked with God and His will, or to the body and the solicitations of the visible. In the fall, the soul refused the rule of the spirit and became the slave of the body with its appetites" (Andrew Murray, *The Spirit of Christ*).

When the Holy Spirit comes to dwell in man, He seeks to reverse the condition of the fall by raising man's spirit again to the place of dominance. He wants to have right of way through our entire being, from center to circumference. We are so anxious to get the outward life changed—"you must do this, and you must not do that"—but God's way is to renew us from within outward.

However much knowledge you have of the things of God, nothing will ever make up for that personal, intimate, moment-by-moment recollectedness of perpetual fellowship with the living Christ. This is the key to a life in the Spirit. It is Christ becoming your wisdom, your strength, your holiness—Christ and you joined in one spirit!

We need to be brought to an end of our own wisdom, our own strength, our own power to work for God. It is only as the "own" life is laid down that God can fulfill His purpose of bringing every faculty with which He has endowed the soul under the control of His Spirit and into full use as the channel through which the indwelling Spirit works.

Jessie Penn-Lewis, *Communion with God*

July 9

If we live in the Spirit, let us also walk in the Spirit.

Galatians 5:25

I am sure there are many who cry to God for the Holy Spirit to come upon them as a Spirit of power for their work, and when they feel that measure of power and get blessing, they thank God for it. But God wants something more and something higher. God wants us to seek for the Holy Spirit as a Spirit of power in our own heart and life to conquer self and cast out sin and work the blessed and beautiful image of Jesus into us.

There is a difference between the power of the Spirit as a gift and the power of the Spirit for the grace of a holy life. A man may often have a measure of the power of the Spirit, but if there be not a large measure of the Spirit as the Spirit of grace and of holiness, the defect will be manifest in his work. He may be made the means of conversion, but he never will help people on to a higher standard of spiritual life.

But a man who is separated unto the Holy Ghost is prepared to say, "Father, let the Holy Ghost have full dominion over me, in my home, in my temper, in every word of my tongue, in every thought of my heart, in every feeling toward my fellow men. Let the Holy Spirit have entire possession."

I ask you to listen to the voice of heaven. May the Word enter into the very depths of our being to search us, and if God reveals to us that the self-life, self-will, self-exaltation are there, let us humble ourselves before Him.

Are you separated unto the Holy Ghost? Has that been your longing desire? Has that been your surrender? Has that been what you have expected through faith in the power of our risen and almighty Lord Jesus? If not, here is the call of faith, and here is the key of blessing: *separated unto the Holy Ghost.*

Andrew Murray, *Absolute Surrender*

July 10

. . . that we might receive the promise of the Spirit through faith.

Galatians 3:14

As by faith we receive the saving grace of Jesus, so by faith we may receive the filling, and the repeated fillings, of the Holy Spirit. But such faith always exists in union with an entire surrender of the will and devout fellowship with God through Scripture. Why should not each reader study once more Galatians 3 and at verse 14 claim his inheritance? Are we not joint heirs with Christ? There may be no emotional response, but the reckoning of faith cannot be ashamed.

Would that every minister and teacher were so filled that the Holy Spirit might fall as soon as he began to speak. It was said of Finney that on one occasion, when he was passing through a factory, a girl made a contemptuous remark about him which he overheard. He turned to look at her, and instantly she cried out under a deep conviction of sin which so spread among the work people that the whole place became a Bochim of tears and prayers (Judg. 2:1–5). "*Forasmuch as God gave unto them the like gift which he did unto us . . .*" (Acts 11:17). Have we received that same gift?

There are five tests which supply an infallible answer: the Lord Jesus will be an abiding presence in our lives; the prayer life will become increasingly real; the self-life will be kept on the cross; there will be unmistakable but quiet power in service; and the Spirit of grace and love will be conspicuously present in our behavior and conversation.

Have we received? If not, why not? "Let him that is athirst take of the river of life freely." It flows from the throne of God and of the Lamb.

F. B. Meyer, *Peter*

July 11

Did you receive the Spirit by the works of the law, or by the hearing of faith?

Galatians 3:2

Many Christians, seeking this blessed fullness of the Spirit, make the same mistake as is so constantly made by seekers after forgiveness and acceptance with God. They look within for evidences of the reception and indwelling of the Spirit and refuse to believe in His presence unless they detect certain symptoms and signs which they consider befitting. This is entirely wrong. The reckoning is not of feeling but of faith.

If we have complied with God's directions, we must believe, whether we feel any difference or not, that God has done His part and has kept His promise given us through Jesus Christ our Lord, and that He has not been slower to give the Holy Spirit than earthly fathers to give bread to their hungry children (Luke 11:13). When we leave the chamber where we have solemnly dedicated ourselves to God and sought to be filled with the Spirit, we must not examine our feelings to discover whether there is such a difference in us as we might expect, but we must cry, in the assurance of faith, "I praise Thee, blessed One, that Thou hast not failed to perform Thy chosen work; Thou hast entered my longing heart; Thou hast taken up Thine abode in me. Henceforth Thou shalt have Thy way with me to will and do Thine own good pleasure."

We should not seek to know the presence of the Holy Ghost by any signs pointing to Himself. He reveals not Himself but Christ. He glorifies Him (John 16:14). And the surest symptoms that He is within are sensitiveness as to sin, tenderness of conscience, and the growing preciousness of Jesus—the fragrance of His name, sympathy with His purposes. Do you have these in growing measure? Then you know somewhat of His gracious filling.

F. B. Meyer, *Elijah*

July 12

I will meditate on Your statutes . . . , for Your word has given me life.

Psalm 119:48–50

We must meditate on the words of God, because it is through the Word of God that the Spirit of God comes in fullness to be the mighty occupant of our inner man. This, after all, is the secret of strength—to be possessed of the strong Son of God, strengthened by His indwelling might, and filled by His Spirit.

We can do all things when Christ is in us in unthwarted power. The only limit lies in our faith and capacity or, in other words, in our absolute submission to His indwelling.

Our risen Lord is charged with power. It is stored in Him for us as in a cistern. As the force of the brain is communicated to the members by the energy of the vital current flashing along the nerves, so does the power of Jesus come to us, His members, by the Holy Spirit. And if we would have that blessed Spirit, we must seek Him not only in the fervid meeting or in the great convocation but through the Word—wherein His force is stored.

Meditate on it day and night till it yields to you strength and good courage, drawn from the nature of the glorified Redeemer. Your God has commanded your strength: claim it from Jesus through faith, by His Spirit and in His Word.

F. B. Meyer, *Joshua*

JULY 13

I am with you always.

MATTHEW 28:20

If we are to follow Christ—to have His mind in us and live out His life—we must seek to regard the fullness of the Spirit as a daily supply, as a daily provision. Only in this way can we live a life of obedience, joy, self-sacrifice, and power for service. There may be occasions when the fullness of the Spirit is especially evident, but being led by the Spirit—every day and all day—is the only way we can abide in Christ Jesus, conquer the flesh and the world, and live life with God and our fellow men in humble, holy, fruitful service.

Only when we are filled with the Spirit can we fully understand and experience the words of Jesus "I am with you always." If this seems unattainable, remember that what is impossible with men is possible with God (Luke 18:27). And if we cannot attain to it at once, let us at least make it, in an act of holy decision, our definite aim, our unceasing prayer, our childlike expectation.

"I am with you always" was meant for daily life, with the all-sufficient aid of that blessed Spirit of whom Jesus said, "He who believes in Me . . . , out of his heart will flow rivers of living water" (John 7:38). Our faith in Christ is the measure of our fullness of the Spirit. The measure of the power of the Spirit in us will be the measure of our experience of the presence of Christ.

ANDREW MURRAY, *SECRETS OF INTERCESSION AND PRAYER*

July 14

Walk in the Spirit.

Galatians 5:16

In our evangelical and rightful zeal to bring sinners to the crisis of the new birth and to lead the saints on to further crises of separation, consecration, sanctification, the baptism of the Holy Spirit, or whatever might be the special emphasis of our various Christian communities, we have often made too much of the spiritual *crises* and too little of the *walk*.

But the Scriptures leave us in no doubt of their emphasis. In almost every epistle the Holy Spirit leads us on *through* the crises—the way into Christ—to the *walk* with Him. Thus in Romans we are taught the way of justification and sanctification from chapters 1 through 7; then in 8 it says, "There is therefore now no condemnation to them which are in Christ Jesus, who walk not after the flesh, but after the Spirit."

Now to walk is a step-by-step activity. Given the main destination, all that matters is the next step. Christian living is concerned therefore just with the implications of the *present* moment, not with past or future. That means simple concentration on things as they are with me just this moment, then the next, then the next—and so on.

We *walk* moment by moment, step by step with Him, the past under the blood, the future in His keeping. We are in Jesus and He in us. Now then, if our walk at this moment is darkened with clouds because of the rising up of some motion of sin in us, then God just points to that. "There," He says. "Look at that—*just* that. Just get that quickly under the blood, and then walk again with Me."

Norman Grubb, *Continuous Revival*

July 15

. . . that you may be filled with all the fullness of God.

Ephesians 3:19

Through our surrender to God and the acceptance of the cross—typified by Jordan—the Holy Spirit gains possession of the citadel of the heart; and then He seeks to lead the believer into the real fellowship of the cross, working in steady progression from within to without, from center to circumference—dealing with new departments of the life, unveiling new needs, and revealing the cross in aspect after aspect as the answer to those needs. He applies the death of Christ as the severing power from the old life and ministers the life of the risen Christ for the building up of the new creation.

The believer may be said to be *filled* with the Spirit when he first receives the Spirit, but he is filled only to the extent of his capacity at the time. The capacity may be small, and it will *remain* small unless he apprehends that the Spirit leads to the cross so that the capacity may be deepened and a greater fullness of the Holy Spirit be truly known.

From faith to faith, the Holy Spirit leads the trusting one as he cooperates with Him by a glad and ready yes to all His dealings.

Jessie Penn-Lewis, *The Cross of Calvary*

JULY 16

How much more will your heavenly Father give the Holy Spirit to those who ask Him!

LUKE 11:13

Let us not fall into the extreme of saying that since God has given and we have received the Spirit, we are no longer to pray for more of Him. It is often questioned, "But how can you ask for that which you already have?" Our lungs are full of breath and yet call for a fresh supply every moment. Our fingers pulse with the fullness of blood yet continually call to the heart for a fresh supply. So our whole life of prayer should be the harmony of faith that praises for the Spirit that has been received and yet always waits for His fuller inflow out of Him in whom all fullness dwells.

It would indeed be sad if a believer, on once having received the Spirit, were to feel that the "how much more" of Jesus' promise was something he had now outgrown and that this chief of blessings he need no longer ask for. No! As the anointing with fresh oil is a daily need, just so the thought of Jesus baptizing with the Spirit is not a remembrance of what is a *past* thing, done once for all, but a promise of what may and should be a daily, continuous experience.

The faith that we have the Spirit within us, even when it has almost come like a new revelation and filled us with joy and strength, will lose its freshness and its power except as the inflow is maintained in living fellowship with the Father and the Son.

ANDREW MURRAY IN LEONA CHOY,
ANDREW MURRAY: THE AUTHORIZED BIOGRAPHY

July 17

. . . a fountain of gardens, a well of living waters, and streams from Lebanon.

Song of Solomon 4:15

The fountain and the well with the flowing streams were for irrigating the garden, thus providing the means of growth for the lawn, the flowers, and the trees. A well is a storage or a depository for living water, while a fountain bubbles forth to flow with streams. A well speaks of depth, and a fountain tells of energetic and continuous outflow.

This garden of the King had both a well and a fountain, which provided life-giving energy and outflow to all the plants. In the garden of Eden, we read of a river which divided into four heads and which thus watered all the garden. In the New Jerusalem we also see a river of life—"a pure river of water of life, clear as crystal, proceeding out of the throne of God and of the Lamb" (Rev. 22:1). The New Jerusalem is a garden city. The river of life with its continual refreshing describes the work and function of the Holy Spirit in the lives of the saints.

If the Lord Jesus had not ascended into heaven, there could have been no release of the life of the Spirit. Thus He said, "It is expedient for you that I go away: for if I go not away, the Comforter will not come unto you; but if I depart, I will send him unto you" (John 16:7). All the spiritual refreshment and irrigation which flow into the lives of believers today are the outflow of the Spirit of life from the Lord's presence as He represents us before the Father in heaven.

Watchman Nee, *Song of Songs*

JULY 18

Stand still, and see the salvation of the LORD, which He will accomplish for you today.

EXODUS 14:13

Not only am I in Christ, but Christ is in me. And just as physically a man cannot live and work in water but only in air, so spiritually Christ dwells and manifests Himself not in terms of "flesh" but of "spirit." Therefore, if I live "after the flesh," I find that what is mine in Christ is, so to say, held in suspense in me. Though in fact I am in Christ, yet if I live in the flesh—that is, in my own strength and under my own direction—then in experience I find, to my dismay, that it is what is in Adam that manifests itself in me. If I would know in experience all that is in Christ, then I must learn to live in the Spirit.

Living in the Spirit means that I trust the Holy Spirit to do in me what I cannot do myself. This life is completely different from the life I would naturally live of myself. Each time I am faced with a new demand from the Lord, I look to Him to do in me what He requires of me. It is not a case of trying but of trusting, not of struggling but of resting in Him. If I have a hasty temper, impure thoughts, a quick tongue, or a critical spirit, I shall not set out with a determined effort to change myself, but instead, reckoning myself dead in Christ to these things, I shall look to the Spirit of God to produce in me the needed purity of humility or meekness, confident that He will do so. This is what it means to "stand still, and see the salvation of Jehovah, which he will work for you."

WATCHMAN NEE, *THE NORMAL CHRISTIAN LIFE*

JULY 19

... strengthened with might through His Spirit in the inner man.

EPHESIANS 3:16

The Father in heaven loves to fill His children with His Holy Spirit. God longs to give each one individually, separately, the power of the Holy Spirit for daily life.

God wants us as His children to arise and place our sins before Him and to call upon Him for mercy. Oh, are you so foolish?—having begun in the Spirit, are you perfecting in the flesh that which was begun in the Spirit?

I have often been asked by young Christians, "Why is it that I fail so? I did so solemnly vow with my whole heart and did desire to serve God; why have I failed?" To such I always give the one answer: "You are trying to do in your own strength what Christ alone can do in you."

Are you living under the power of the Holy Ghost? Are you living as an anointed, Spirit-filled man? Are you consecrated, given up to the Spirit to work in you and to live in you? If your answer be no, then I ask a second question: are you *willing* to give up yourself to the power of the Holy Spirit?

You can do it at once. A great deal may still be dark and dim and beyond what we understand, and you may feel nothing; but go into God's presence. God alone can effect the change. God alone, who gave us the Holy Spirit, can restore the Holy Spirit in power into our life. God alone can "strengthen us with might by His Spirit in the inner man."

ANDREW MURRAY, *ABSOLUTE SURRENDER*

JULY 20

I will not leave you orphans; I will come to you. . . .
At that day you will know that I am in My Father, and you in Me, and I in you.

JOHN 14:18–20

In the course of our Lord's interaction with His disciples on earth, He spared no pains to teach and train them, to renew and sanctify them. In most respects, however, they remained just what they were. The reason was that up to this point He was ever still nothing more than an external Christ who stood outside of them; it was from there that He sought to work upon them by His word and His personal influence.

With the advent of Pentecost, this condition was entirely changed. In the Holy Spirit He came down as the inward indwelling Christ to become in the very innermost recesses of their being the "life" of their life. This is what He Himself had promised.

This was the source of all the other blessings that came with Pentecost. Jesus Christ, the Crucified, the Glorified, the Lord from heaven, came in spiritual power, by the Spirit, to impart to them that ever-abiding presence of their Lord that had been promised to them. And that was indeed in a way that was at once most intimate, all-powerful, and wholly divine—by the indwelling which makes Him, in truth, their life. He whom they had known in the flesh, living with them on earth, they now received by the Spirit in His heavenly glory within them. Instead of an outward Jesus near them, they now obtained the inward Jesus with them.

ANDREW MURRAY, *THE FULL BLESSING OF PENTECOST*

JULY 21

The Spirit who dwells in us yearns jealously.

JAMES 4:5

Nowhere does the Old Testament say [that the Spirit yearns jealously for us] in so many words, but it does say it in effect. It is not an empty, meaningless statement; it is the expression of a real and great truth.

The revisers have used a capital "S" for Spirit, though it is a small "s" in many translations. Some expositors think that it is referring simply to the human spirit that dwells in our bodies, but personally I follow the majority of the commentators in holding that the Holy Spirit is meant. I do so principally because such a description is, so far as I remember, never used of man's spirit, while it is the exact delineation of God's Spirit in a score of places—in Romans 8:11, for instance.

What a glorious truth it is and what infinite possibilities it opens out that, if we are Christians at all—however weak, however unsatisfactory, however young in the faith—the Holy Spirit of God actually does indwell us! Paul was astonished that the Corinthian Christians were ignorant of that fact (1 Cor. 6:19) and suggests that this ignorance was an explanation of the sad failure and low level of their lives. Well, have *we* grasped the truth?

But in what sense does He "yearn jealously"? You remember how in Exodus 20:5, 34:14, and other passages, He discloses Himself as "a jealous God"—but how so? Why, this is the jealousy of *love*!—love that covets the whole of our love and that cannot brook our coquetting with the world, His rival. J. B. Mayor's translation of this phrase brings out this same interpretation; he puts it "jealously yearns for the entire devotion of the heart." How grand to be so loved and how unworthy to squander any part of our love elsewhere than on Him. Away then with worldliness!

GUY KING, *JAMES: A BELIEF THAT BEHAVES*

July 22

. . . to know the love of Christ which passes knowledge.

Ephesians 3:19

Next to pride, lack of love—or, as we may put it in one word, lovelessness—was the sin for which the Lord had so often to rebuke His disciples. The new commandment that He gave them, the token whereby all men should know that they were His disciples, was love to one another.

How gloriously was it manifested on the Day of Pentecost when the Spirit of the Lord shed abroad His love in the hearts of His own. The multitude of those who believed was as one heart, one soul. All things they possessed were held in common; the kingdom of heaven with its life of love had come down to them. The spirit, the disposition, the wonderful love of Jesus filled them, because He Himself had come into them.

How closely the mighty working of the Spirit and the indwelling of the Lord Jesus are bound up with a life in love appears within the prayer of Paul on behalf of the Ephesians. In this prayer he asks that they might be strengthened with power "by the Spirit" in order that "Christ might dwell in their hearts." Then he immediately makes this addition: "that you, being rooted and grounded in love, may be able to comprehend . . . the love of Christ which passes knowledge" (Eph. 3:16–19). The filling with the Spirit and the indwelling of Christ bring by themselves a life that has its root, its joy, its power, its evidence in love, because the indwelling Christ Himself is Love.

Oh, how would the love of God fill the church and convince the world that she has received a heavenly element into her life if the filling with the Spirit and the indwelling of Christ in the heart were recognized as the blessing which the Father has promised us!

Andrew Murray, *The Full Blessing of Pentecost*

July 23

Love has been perfected among us in this: that we may have boldness in the day of judgment; because as He is, so are we in this world.

1 John 4:17

Perfect love is by the Spirit of love. There are two senses in which love may be in need of perfecting. It may be defective in quality or it may be deficient in quantity. If the love shed abroad in the heart is the very love of God Himself, it cannot be defective in quality, but it may be deficient in range and scope of operation.

The Spirit fills what is given. He does not wait for fullness of knowledge in us. Wherever there is a sincere purpose to serve Christ, He accepts the motive, however great the ignorance. There is a law of the Spirit of life, and it patiently waits through all the stages of the blade, the ear, and the full corn in the ear. He yearns for fullness of love, and as He led to repentance, so He leads to surrender and fullness of blessing.

Love is made perfect when the Spirit of love alone reigns in all the heart and life. We love because the Spirit of love dwells in us, and that love is made perfect when the indwelling Trinity of love permeates, dominates, and possesses us entirely to the praise of His glory and the excellence of His power.

Samuel Chadwick, *The Way to Pentecost*

July 24

The law of the Spirit of life in Christ Jesus has made me free from the law of sin and death.

Romans 8:2

The Holy Spirit is emphatically both Giver and Lord of the life that is in Christ. The believer is born of the Spirit, believes in the Spirit, prays in the Spirit, and walks in the Spirit. From first to last, he is sphered in the presence of the Spirit, and the Spirit dwells in him, just as in his natural life he lives in the air and the air dwells in him.

Delivered from the flesh, he lives in the Spirit. And what is the life in the Spirit? It is a life lived in the realm of the spiritual. It is a life in which there is no condemnation. Guilt is purged, sin is cleansed away, carnality is destroyed. There is not only an imputed righteousness by grace but a realized righteousness through faith. The things that bring condemnation have been put away, and life stands approved and accepted in the will of God.

Instead of condemnation there is the assurance of sonship and heirship in Christ Jesus. One's life of prayer finds a new intelligence, intensity, and power. The Spirit prays in the praying heart, and prayer in the Spirit prevails. Conquest takes the place of defeat, and the Spirit-filled life prevails in conflict as it prevails in prayer.

Consequently there comes to the heart a deep sense of security in the love of God and a Christlike compassion for the souls of the lost. The Spirit of Christ brings the mind of Christ and baptizes us into the fellowship of His redeeming love. This is the abundant life Christ came to bring—the life filled with His Spirit.

Samuel Chadwick, *The Way to Pentecost*

July 25

The love of God has been poured out in our hearts.

Romans 5:5

Many of us try hard at times to love. We try to force ourselves to love, and I do not say that is wrong; it is better than nothing. But the end of it is always very sad. "I fail continually," such a one must confess. The reason is simply this: because I have never learned to believe and accept the truth that the Holy Spirit can pour out God's love into my heart.

That blessed text—how often it has been limited! It has often been understood in this sense: it means the love of God *to me*. Oh, what a limitation! That is only the beginning. The love of God always means the love of God in its entirety, in its fullness as an indwelling power, a love of God to me that leaps back to Him in love and overflows to my fellow men in love—God's love to me and my love to God and my love to my fellow men. The three are one; you cannot separate them.

And how can I learn to love? Never until the Spirit of God fills my heart with God's love and I begin to long for God's love in a very different sense from which I have sought it so selfishly as a comfort and a joy and a happiness and a pleasure to myself. Never until I begin to learn that God is love and to claim it and receive it as an indwelling power for self-sacrifice. Never until I begin to see that my glory, my blessedness, is to be like God and like Christ in giving up everything in myself for my fellow men. May God teach us that! Oh, the divine blessedness of the love with which the Holy Spirit can fill our hearts! "The fruit of the Spirit is love."

Andrew Murray, *Absolute Surrender*

July 26

Let us consider one another.

Hebrews 10:24

The same Spirit that said, "Consider Christ Jesus," says to us, "Consider one another." How many there are whose circumstances are so unfavorable, whose knowledge is so limited, whose whole life is so hopeless that there is but little prospect of their ever attaining the better life. For them there is but one thing to be done: "We that are strong ought to bear the infirmities of the weak, and not to please ourselves." Each one who begins to see what the blessedness is of a life in full surrender to Christ should offer himself to Christ to be made His messenger to the feeble and the weary.

God is love. And all He has done for us in His Son, as revealed in this epistle, is love. And Christ is love. And there can be no real access to God as a union with Him in His holy will, no real communion with Him, but in the Spirit of love. Our entering into the Holiest is mere imagination if we do not yield ourselves to the love of God in Christ to be filled and used for the welfare and joy of our fellow men.

The very essence, the beauty and the glory of Christ's salvation, is that it is for all. He who truly receives it, as the Holy Spirit gives it, receives it as a salvation for all and feels himself impelled to communicate it to others. The baptism of fire is a baptism of redeeming love—but that not as a mere emotion but a power at once to consider and to care for others.

Andrew Murray, *Let Us Draw Near*

July 27

Let us not love in word or in tongue, but in deed and in truth.

1 John 3:18

When the divine Owner takes possession of a property, He has a twofold objective: intense cultivation and abounding fruitfulness. The first acre He put under cultivation in Rees Howells was his prayer life. He was never again to ask God to answer a prayer through others if He could answer it through him.

The first prayer of this kind was for a man named Will Battery. Liquor had a hold on him, and he had gone from bad to worse. He hadn't slept in a bed for two years. He was dirty and unshaven; he wore no socks and never tied his shoelaces. It was for this man that Mr. Howells found the Holy Ghost travailing in him. Rees was to pray him through to sanity and salvation and love him "not in word, neither in tongue; but in deed and in truth."

"It wouldn't have come to my mind to love him," he said, "but when the Holy Ghost comes in, He brings in the love of the Savior. It seemed as if I could lay down my life for this man; there was a love pouring out of me that I never knew before."

In his free hours Rees made this man his friend and spent all his Sundays with him. He even walked about the village with him, although embarrassed once or twice as people turned and stared at them, but "the Lord pulled me up on it," he rejoiced.

But the work was not done in a few weeks or months. Stage by stage Will was lifted, until Rees was able to put him in lodgings and get him to take a job in the mine. The day came when the chapel people were amazed to see Battery sitting in the meetings respectably dressed, but it took three years for the final victory. "In this way," said Mr. Howells, "I started at the bottom and loved just one; and if you love one, you can love many; and if many, you can love all."

Norman Grubb, *Rees Howells: Intercessor*

July 28

As the branch cannot bear fruit of itself,
unless it abides in the vine, neither can you, unless you abide in Me.

John 15:4

After you have confessed your sins, claim the promise Jesus made about the Holy Spirit: "I will send him unto you" (John 16:7). The Holy Spirit is here; Jesus sent Him at Pentecost. Obey the joyful commandment "Be filled with the Spirit" (Eph. 5:18), and then the fruit will come.

What fruit does the Holy Spirit have? He has love, joy, peace, longsuffering, gentleness, goodness, faithfulness, meekness, and self-control. Jesus was all these when He was on earth. I once read somewhere, "The fruit of the Spirit is a perfect portraiture of Christ."

Love is the love of Christ that passes knowledge. Joy is the joy unspeakable and full of glory. Peace is the peace that passes all understanding that Jesus promised when He said, "My peace I give unto you." Longsuffering is forgiving—even your enemies, just as Jesus forgave His when He was on the cross. Gentleness is the reproduction of the gentleness of Jesus. Goodness is Christlikeness—a kindly disposition. The next fruit is faithfulness. The disciples were not always faithful. At the betrayal of Jesus in the garden, they all forsook Him and fled. But when the Holy Spirit came down at Pentecost, they all became faithful unto death. Meekness—that is not the same as weakness. Nor is it a native fruit of the human heart. It is an exotic from heaven. Self-control means mastering the appetites and passions, particularly the sensual.

All this fruit can be seen in you but only when you are in contact with the vine. You are "not good if detached."

Corrie ten Boom, *Not Good If Detached*

July 29

By this we know that we abide in Him,
and He in us, because He has given us of His Spirit.

1 John 4:13

The fruits of the Spirit, so often mentioned in Scripture, are not things different or separate from the Spirit; and if the Spirit be not dwelling and working in us, His fruits must be as absent from us as He is.

If there is not granted by God a divine encounter and the inner realization that the fruits and gifts of the Spirit proceed from His present workings in our hearts, then how could we know that they are of the Spirit? For the fruits of the Spirit are living and can only be living in us as the Spirit manifests Himself through us. And since the "manifestation of the Spirit is given to every man to profit thereby" (1 Cor. 12:7), how can any deny such present workings of the Holy Spirit in the church unless they also deny His presence?

"Hereby we know that he abideth in us, by the Spirit which he hath given us" (1 John 4:13). Here is a sure statement that there is no higher proof of our being indwelt by the risen Christ than the inward working in our hearts and lives of His Holy Spirit as a present reality which can be recognized by every child of God.

William Law, *The Power of the Spirit*

July *30*

Awake, O north wind, and come, O south! Blow upon my garden, that its spices may flow out. Let my beloved come to his garden and eat its pleasant fruits.

Song of Solomon 4:16

"Awake, O north wind"—and how chilling, frosty, and penetrating that can be! "Come, thou south"—and how mild, gentle, and pleasurable that can be! The spouse realizes that in her relation to the King, she was as a garden in which were many spiritual fruits and blessings of grace. She had arrived at a state of grace wherein she recognized that the crux of spiritual prosperity hinged upon the inner man of the heart and not upon external circumstances.

The south wind and the north wind are representative of different circumstances appointed by the sovereign choice of the Holy Spirit to develop the fragrance of her garden, and she acknowledged the right of the Spirit of God in His choice of such. Although pleasant was the south wind and fearful the north wind, yet for one whose abode was in the heavenlies, both winds were of equal value. She had the blessed assurance that in every place and in all things, since circumstances are engineered and controlled by the Holy Spirit, these would release the spiritual grace stored up within.

Her first remark described herself as "my garden"; then almost immediately she changed the expression to "His garden"—"His own garden." In other words, my garden is His garden. The whole garden of her inner life was for Him and so were all its fruits. Thus we see that the very fruits of the Spirit which adorn the lives of the saints, far from being the boast of the believer who bears them, are for the sole pleasure of the Lord and for the sole glory of God.

Watchman Nee, *Song of Songs*

July 31

How long will you neglect to go and possess the land which the Lord God of your fathers has given you?

Joshua 18:3

If we understand the teaching of the epistles aright, there is for each member of the mystical body of Christ a distinct share in the Pentecostal gift. We may describe it as a share in His baptism, or in His fullness. This is immaterial. But there is surely something more than is ordinarily understood by regeneration, or the gift of faith, or the revelation of the living Savior. There is a power, an overflowing love, an assurance, an exuberant joy, a freedom which are not enjoyed by all Christians but which are as evidently their birthright as they are to be desired.

And in addition, there are the bestowments of the Holy Spirit by which we are specially qualified to do Christ's work in the world: tact in leadership; wisdom to win souls; power to help believers into a fuller life; utility to administer or to speak or to teach; sympathy; facility in utterance; power in prayer. These may be named among others. The whole continent of Pentecostal blessing is avoided by many believers as if it were full of swamps, of fever, noisome pestilence; it stands upon their globes as Africa did in the days of our childhood. There is surely in this direction much land to be possessed.

Let us ask our heavenly Joshua to settle us in this good land so that there may be no rill or valley or mountain or tract of territory unpossessed. God has given us in Christ all things which pertain unto life and godliness; let us claim the whole of our inheritance by a living faith so that we may enter on the enjoyment of all that is possible for us on this side of heaven.

F. B. Meyer, *Joshua*

August

Cultivating Christ's Presence

The Testimony of Charles Trumbull

I think I am correct when I say that I have known more than most men know about failure, about betrayals and dishonorings of Christ, about disobedience, about consciously falling short of what I knew Christ was expecting of me.

There were great fluctuations in my spiritual life, in my conscious closeness of fellowship with God. Sometimes I would be on the heights spiritually; sometimes I would be in the depths. A strong, arousing convention; a stirring, searching address; a Spirit-filled book; or the obligation to do a difficult piece of Christian service myself, with the preparation in prayer that it involved, would lift me up, and I would stay up—for a while. But it wouldn't last.

It seemed to me that it ought to be possible for me to live habitually on a high plane of closer fellowship with God as I saw certain other men doing. They seemed to have a consciousness of Christ that I did not have—higher, bigger, deeper. I rebelled at the suggestion when it first came to me. How *could* anyone have a better idea of Christ than I? (I am just laying bare to you the blind, self-satisfied workings of my sin-stunted heart.)

I heard from a preacher of power a sermon on Ephesians 4:12–13—"till we all come to . . . the knowledge of the Son of God, to a perfect man, to the measure of the stature of the fullness of Christ"—and as I followed it, I was amazed, bewildered. He was unfolding Christ in a way that was utterly unknown to me.

I learned from another minister that what he counted his greatest spiritual asset was his habitual consciousness of the actual presence of Jesus. Nothing so bore him up, he said, as the realization that Jesus was always with him in actual presence, independent of his own feelings. Whenever his mind was free from other matters, it would turn to Christ, and he would talk aloud to Christ when he was alone—on the street, anywhere—as easily and naturally as to a human friend. So real to him was Jesus' presence.

I was in Edinburgh attending the World Missionary Conference, and I saw that one whose writings had helped me greatly was to speak on "The Resources of the Christian Life." His opening words made my heart leap with a new joy. What he said was something like this: "The resources of the Christian life, my friends, are just—Jesus Christ."

That was all. But that was enough.

Alone in my room, I prayed it out with God. If there was a conception of Christ that I did not have, I asked God to give it to me. And God, in His long-suffering patience, forgiveness, and love, gave me what I asked for.

I realized for the first time that the many references throughout the New Testament to "Christ in you" and "abiding in Christ" are literal, actual, blessed fact and not figures of speech. I had always known that Christ was my Savior, but I had looked upon Him as an external Savior. Now I knew something better than that. At last I realized that Jesus Christ was actually and literally within me; He had made Himself my very life.

What has the result been? It has meant a revolutionized, fundamentally changed life within and without. There has been a fellowship with God infinitely better than anything I had ever known. There has been an utterly new kind of victory, victory-by-freedom, over certain besetting sins. And the spiritual results in service have given me such a sharing of the joy of heaven as I never knew was possible on earth.

Life is filled with the miracle evidences of what Christ is willing and able to do through anyone who just turns over the keys to His complete indwelling.

CHARLES TRUMBULL, *VICTORY IN CHRIST*

August

As God has distributed to each one,
as the Lord has called each one, so let him walk.

1 Corinthians 7:17

Many, on entering the life of full consecration and devotion, are eager to change the circumstances of their lives for those in which they suppose that they will more readily attain a fully developed character—hence much of the restlessness and fever, the disappointment and willfulness of the early days of Christian experience. Such have yet to learn that out of myriads of circumstances, God has chosen the lot of each as being specially adapted to develop the hidden qualities and idiosyncrasies of the soul He loves. Anything else than the life which you are called to live would fail in giving scope for the evolution of properties of your nature, which are known only to God, as the colors and fragrance which lie enfolded in some tropical seed.

Do not therefore seek to change, by some rash and willful act, the setting and environment of your life. Stay where you are until God as evidently calls you elsewhere as He has put you where you are. Abide for the present in the calling wherein you were called. Throw upon Him the responsibility of indicating to you a change when it is necessary for your further development. In the meanwhile, look deep into the heart of every circumstance for its special message, lesson, or discipline. Upon the way in which you accept or reject these will depend the achievement or marring of the divine purpose.

F. B. Meyer, *Jeremiah*

August 2

I went down to the potter's house, and there he was, making something at the wheel.

JEREMIAH 18:3

The Potter achieves His purpose by means of the wheel. In the discipline of human life, this surely represents the revolution of daily circumstances—often monotonous, commonplace, trivial enough and yet intending to effect ends on which God has set His heart.

You complain of the monotony of your life. "Day in, day out, the same round. Year after year, the same path trodden to and fro, no horizon, no space or width, only the same lane of sky between the high houses on either side. What scope is there here for the evolution of noble character? What opportunity to meditate and achieve great deeds?"

Yet remember that the passive virtues are even dearer to God than the active ones. They take the longest to learn and are the last learned. They consist in patience, submission, endurance, longsuffering, persistence in well doing. They need more courage and evince greater heroism than those qualities which the world admires most. But they can only be acquired in just that monotonous and narrow round of which many complain as offering so scant a chance of acquiring saintliness.

F. B. MEYER, *JEREMIAH*

AUGUST 3

Draw near to God and He will draw near to you.

JAMES 4:8

John R. Mott has said, "Next to receiving Christ as Savior and claiming the filling of the Holy Spirit, we know of no act attended with larger good to ourselves or others than the formation of an undiscourageable resolution to keep the morning watch and spend the first half hour of the day alone with God."

At first that statement may seem to appear too strong. The act of receiving Christ as Savior is one of such infinite consequence for eternity, and the experience of being filled with the Holy Spirit is one that works such a revolution in the Christian life, that such a simple thing as the firm determination to keep the morning watch hardly appears important enough to be placed next to them.

However, when we think how impossible it is to live our daily life in Christ and be kept from sin or to maintain a walk in the leading and power of the Holy Spirit without daily, close fellowship with God, we shall soon see that this statement is not exaggerated.

By this simple daily act, we express that we have a fixed determination that Christ shall have our whole lives and that we will fully obey the Holy Spirit in everything. The morning watch is the key to unceasingly and fully maintaining our surrender to Christ.

ANDREW MURRAY, *THE INNER CHAMBER*

August 4

My Father loves Me.

John 10:17

The Son of God gloried in the glory of His Father. It was His habit to rise early that He might behold His Father's glory and delight in His presence. He rejoiced in the Father's greatness and in the majesty of His power. It is good to go over His affirmations of the Father; the accents of adoring love vibrate in every tone: "God is spirit; and they that worship him must worship him in spirit and in truth: for the Father seeketh such to worship him." "My Father is greater than all. . . . I and the Father are one."

He loved to dwell upon the care and bounty of the Father's love. Nothing is insignificant. Each is to the Infinite as if there were no other. Even the odd sparrow is not forgotten, and man is so much the more the child of His care that even the hairs of his head are numbered.

The Son lived in the sovereign will of the Holy and Righteous Father. He did not pray to subdue the Father's will to His desire but that the will of the Father might be done. The sweat and agony of prayer were in the strong praying of the Father's Son, and it was always in obedience to the Father's will.

Because we pray to our heavenly Father in the secret place of prayer, we may pray with the artless unreserve of little children. There is nothing about which we may not pray. We pray as His children, and we trust Him as our heavenly Father. His answer will transcend our asking.

Samuel Chadwick, *The Path of Prayer*

August 5

The upright shall dwell in Your presence.

Psalm 140:13

Communion with God is meant to be ours during the whole day, whatever our condition or circumstances. But its enjoyment depends upon the reality of the communion we have with God in the inner chamber. The power for maintaining close and glad fellowship with God all day will depend largely upon the intensity with which we seek to secure it in the time of secret prayer. The one essential during the morning watch is *fellowship with God.*

The chief thing to do in secret is to obtain the Father's presence and attention. Know that He sees and hears you. More important than all your urgent requests or your efforts to pray right is the childlike, living assurance that *your Father sees you.* You meet Him there, His eyes are on you and yours on Him, and you are now enjoying actual communion with Him.

Beware of substituting prayer and Bible study for living fellowship with God. You may get so occupied with your needs and their expression, your method of praying and believing, that the light of His face and the joy of His love can't even enter you. Then you go out into the day's work without the power of an abiding fellowship and wonder why you are so weak in your spirit.

What a difference it would make in the lives of many if they looked upon that time of morning watch as a definite engagement with the Father and understood that it grieves Him when it is broken. What strength we miss, what daily control by the Father, what preparedness for anything that might come to us when we do not secure God's presence with us through this daily appointment with God.

Andrew Murray, *The Inner Chamber*

AUGUST 6

The LORD said to Moses, "Behold, I will rain bread from heaven for you. . . ." So they gathered it every morning.

EXODUS 16:4–21

There is no time like the early morning hour for feeding on Christ by communion with Him and pondering His words. Once lose that, and the charm is broken by the intrusion of many things, though it may be they are all useful and necessary. You cannot remake the broken reflections of a lake swept by wind. How different is that day from all others the early prime of which is surrendered to fellowship with Christ! Nor is it possible to live today on the gathered spoils of yesterday. Each man needs all that a new day can yield him of God's grace and comfort. It must be daily bread.

To feed on Christ is the only secret of strength and blessedness. If only believers in Christ would realize and appropriate the lesson so clearly taught in this narrative as well as in the wonderful discourse which our Lord founded upon it (John 6:22–58), they would find themselves the subjects of a marvelous change.

It is almost incredible how great a difference is wrought by the prolonged and loving study of what the Scriptures say concerning Him. To sit down to enjoy them; to read two or three chapters, an epistle, or a book, at a sitting; to let the heart and mind steep in it; to do this before other intruders have noisily entered the heart and distracted its attention—ah, how this transforms us!

F. B. MEYER, *MOSES*

AUGUST 7

They received the word with all readiness, and searched the Scriptures daily.

ACTS 17:11

The Spirit works with and through the Word. If then we neglect the reverent study of Scripture, we cut ourselves off from the very vehicle through which God's Spirit enters human spirits. Christian people will attend conventions, plunge into all kinds of Christian work, read many good books about the Bible and Christian living, but they give the Bible itself the most cursory and superficial heed. And it is for this reason that the Bible does not speak to them.

If you would know all the wondrous beauty of a forest glade, you must not be satisfied with passing through it with hasty foot. No, you must go alone and sit quietly down on the log of some felled tree and wait. Then the mystery of beauty will begin to unfold itself—the fairy bowers, the mossy glens, the interlacing boughs. Presently a note will sound from yonder bough as the signal for the outburst of many sweet-voiced choristers, and the woodland will ring with the music of the birds, while the squirrel runs up some neighboring tree and the rabbits come out to feed and the young foxes play about their holes.

All this is hidden from those who cannot wait. So there are mysteries of glory and beauty in Scripture hidden from the wise and prudent but revealed to babes. There is no book that will so repay time spent over its pages as the Word of God.

A neglected Bible means a starved and strengthless spirit, a comfortless heart, a barren life, and a grieved Holy Ghost. If the people who are now perpetually running to meetings for crumbs of help would only stay home and search their Bibles, there would be more happiness in the church and more blessing on the world.

F. B. MEYER, *ELIJAH*

AUGUST 8

The words that I speak to you are spirit, and they are life.

JOHN 6:63

I am convinced that one chief cause why some do not grow more in grace is that they do not take time to hold inward communion with the Lord. Spiritual truth does not become our possession at once. Although I understand what I read, although I consent heartily to it, although I receive it as truth, it may speedily fade away and be forgotten unless by private meditation I give it time to become fixed and rooted in me, to become united and identified with me. Christians, give your Lord time to transfer His heavenly thoughts to your inner, spiritual life. Take time to remain before Him until He has made His Word living and powerful in your souls.

The Christian must take special care that he does not allow himself to be led away from the Word of God by the many books which in our days are being produced. These books can become a blessing to the reader only when they lead him to that portion of God's Word which is being dealt with in order that he may meditate further upon it himself and receive it for himself as from the mouth of God.

Christians, there is in the Word of God an incredible power. The blessing which lies hidden in it is inconceivable. See to it that when you have read a portion of any book, you always return to that passage of the Scriptures of which an explanation is given. Receive that not as the word of man but, as it is in truth, the Word of God, which works mightily in those who believe. Hold fellowship with God through the Word. Take time to speak with Him about it, to give an answer to Him concerning it. Then shall you increase in prayer and in the life of God.

ANDREW MURRAY, *THE LORD'S TABLE*

AUGUST 9

If you keep My commandments, you will abide in My love.

JOHN 15:10

The scriptural key to abiding is in 1 John 2:6: "He that saith he abideth in him ought himself also so to walk, even as he walked."

The way Mr. Howells maintained this abiding was by spending a set time of waiting upon God every day during the period in which the intercession [that he was making for a certain person] lasted. The Holy Spirit would then speak to him through the Word, revealing any standard that he was to come up to, particularly in "the laws of the kingdom"—the Sermon on the Mount. Any command the Spirit gave him he must fulfill, because the way of abiding is the keeping of His commandments (John 15:10). The Spirit would also search his heart and throw light on his daily life, revealing any motives or actions that needed confession and cleansing in the blood.

The necessity for abiding is seen in that same chapter, John 15. The life is in the vine. As the branch remains united to it by abiding in it, that life of the vine produces the fruit through the branch. In other words, the power is in *Christ.* As the intercessor remains united to Him by abiding in Him, His power operates through the intercessor and accomplishes what needs to be done.

As Mr. Howells would continue in this place of abiding day by day, he would be increasingly conscious that the Spirit was engaging the enemy in battle and overcoming him until finally he would become fully assured of the victory. The Spirit would then tell him that the intercession was finished, the position gained, and he would await the visible deliverance in praise and faith.

NORMAN GRUBB, *REES HOWELLS: INTERCESSOR*

AUGUST 10

*If you abide in Me, and My words abide in you,
you will ask what you desire, and it shall be done for you.*

JOHN 15:7

There is no power in prayer except by the words of Christ becoming wrought into the inner life. The believer must "eat" and "drink" His words in order to have power in prayer. If you cannot pray, go and read God's Word until it burns in your heart—then pray. You need fuel for prayer, God's "words" abiding in you. "Ye shall ask what ye will" is only for those who have the knowledge of God's will as written in His Word wrought into their innermost being. Such souls will ask nothing contrary to His will, for His Word will become assimilated into their very being so that the spirit life is built up upon the Word of God.

"If ye abide in me"—if you will stand where I have put you, in My death, as the graft abides in the tree—"and my words abide in you"—if they are wrought into you and not merely lodged in the mind and memory as texts. If My words become incorporated into your very life by your spiritually feeding upon them, then there will be formed in you a will that is in perfect harmony with My will. My words will strengthen and guide your will and make you to know My will, and then, ah! then, you shall ask "*what ye will*, and it *shall be done.*"

JESSIE PENN-LEWIS, *PRAYER AND EVANGELISM*

AUGUST 11

When you pray, go into your room, and when you have shut your door, pray to your Father who is in the secret place.

MATTHEW 6:6

The heavens cannot contain God our Father, but He dwells in the inner chamber of the soul. He is in secret and seeth in secret. He waits and watches for the opening of the sanctuary door. It is holy ground and must be approached with reverence. The soul must summon all its powers for this its holiest exercise. Here the mind must be at its best that it may think of God and life.

Thought of God is more than thinking of our thoughts about Him. Communion is deeper than theology. Prayer in secret is life finding expression in the realized presence of God our Father. All things are voluntarily laid bare before Him. All pretense is stripped from motive, all hypocrisy from desire, all dissimulation from speech. A season of silence is the best preparation for speech with God. Infinite glory finds new value when interpreted in terms of fatherhood, and prayer finds new horizons in the majesty of our Father in heaven.

SAMUEL CHADWICK, *THE PATH OF PRAYER*

AUGUST 12

Building yourselves up on your most holy faith, praying in the Holy Spirit . . .

JUDE 1:20

When you are in your closet to pray alone, you should always take plenty of silent time before your prayers and in between your prayers. It is a solemn thing to consider that I am going to exercise power in heaven and bring down heavenly blessings upon myself and others, and I ought to be very quiet before God. Think of God, the triune God, while you engage in prayer. Let us always spend a few minutes at least in worship—until my faith realizes that here is the almighty God waiting to bless me; He is longing to fill me with His Holy Spirit. This faith will not come unless we take time to think about it.

It is a solemn thing to pray. I do beseech you, in your prayer every time, learn more and more to yield yourself up to the Holy Spirit. If your inmost being is humbly and patiently made subject to Him, He can take and make you not a prayer machine but a vessel in which He lives and in which He works His prayers down into your desires and will so that you pray in the Spirit and the Spirit prays in you.

ANDREW MURRAY, *THE SPIRITUAL LIFE*

August 13

Let not your heart utter anything hastily before God.

Ecclesiastes 5:2

We grew into a kind of prayer that is, for us at least, very helpful. We ask to be led by the Holy Spirit from point to point, each prayer leading on from the preceding prayer till the particular subject laid on our hearts has been dealt with and we have the assurance that "the Lord will complete all," as Kay translates Psalm 138:8.

This way of prayer is just the opposite to the kaleidoscope kind, which darts hither and thither all over the earth or over a number of scattered interests (often within the limits of a single long prayer), leaving the mind which has tried to follow perhaps dazzled, perhaps tired. It is a much simpler thing. Such prayer is often brief; it is often silent, or it may take the form of song, and we are lifted up as with wings to our Lord's feet. It is possible only when all who are praying together do thoroughly understand that one another are indeed as one instrument under the control of the Spirit of God, who moves on each severally as He will or unites all in silence or in song. Such prayer asks for something not easily defined. Darby's translation of Exodus 23:21, "Be careful in his presence," comes to mind as a word that expresses its quietness and awe, and the jubilant Psalms show its joy.

"Do not be so busy with work for Christ that you have no strength left for praying," said Hudson Taylor once. "True prayer requires strength." To secure even half a day's quiet in a large family like ours needs careful planning beforehand, but it is worth that. Again and again things have happened after such a day that nothing we could have done could have effected, for prayer is truly force.

Amy Carmichael, *Gold Cord*

AUGUST 14

We do not have a High Priest who cannot sympathize with our weaknesses.

HEBREWS 4:15

Sometimes, when some distraction has called us off, we cannot even remember for what we were praying. "Sometimes I find that I had forgot what I was about, but when I began to forget I cannot tell." These words were written nearly two hundred years ago, but they might have been written by some of us yesterday. "I pray giddily and circularly, and returne againe and againe to that I have said before, and perceive not that I do so."

"We have not an high priest which cannot be touched with the feeling of our infirmities," and He has a gentle way of recalling us from these undesired wanderings.

I have found that it is fatal to get into a kind of hot fuss over our elusive thoughts. That is exactly what the adversary wants us to do. The only way is to refuse to chase about: "Be still, and know . . ." (Ps. 46:10). "In quietness and in confidence shall be your strength" (Isa. 30:15), for prayer as for all else. Often by a way so simple that a child can follow it, the tempter may be foiled.

Sometimes nothing helps so much as to turn from trying to pray and instead to read on the knees of the spirit some familiar passage from the Bible, for those words have a power in them to effect that of which they speak. Another sure way into peace is found in a literal obedience to Colossians 3:16. Turn a psalm or a hymn into prayer, read or repeat it aloud, for to speak to oneself deep down in one's heart, using words that one knows and loves, is often a wonderfully quickening thing to do, and nothing more quickly and gently leads one into the place of peace where prayer is born.

AMY CARMICHAEL, *THOU GIVEST . . . THEY GATHER*

August 15

When You said, "Seek My face," my heart said to You,
"Your face, LORD, I will seek."

PSALM 27:8

It is to be feared that despite all the knowledge of today, not all God's children know their God so as to have direct intercourse with Him. There is a fellowship with God which is sight to the eyes of the heart, even though in comparison with the full vision that is yet to come, "we see through a glass, darkly."

There is a face-to-face fellowship with God where we inquire of the Lord, as David did, and get our answer; where we have such communion with Him that He is able to reveal His mind to us; and where we intelligently know and enter into the purposes of our God.

Face-to-face fellowship with God is our birthright as children of God, and if we are but willing to follow on to know the Lord, we shall be led by the Spirit from faith to faith and glory to glory until we are in reality "no longer servants but friends."

Face-to-face fellowship means that anywhere, at any moment, we may have spiritual communion with Him who is invisible and hear His voice in our hearts speaking to us across the blood-sprinkled mercy seat. As we wait before our God, let us cry, "Thy face, LORD, will I seek"; so will He cause His face to shine upon us, and we shall walk habitually in the light of His countenance, see His glory, and speak of Him.

JESSIE PENN-LEWIS, *FACE TO FACE*

AUGUST 16

You received the Spirit of adoption by whom we cry out, "Abba, Father."

ROMANS 8:15

Our Lord bases prayer on personal relationship. He taught us to call God our Father, and the implication of sonship changes the whole aspect of prayer. Whatever difficulties may remain, intercourse must be possible between father and child, and to suggest that a child may not ask of a father would be to empty the terms of all meaning. It is a child's right to ask, and it is a father's responsibility to hear in affectionate sympathy and discerning love.

The wonder is not that God hears prayer but that He is our Father. The greater wonder includes the less. All the teaching of Jesus about the supremacy of the child heart in the kingdom of God is rank blasphemy if God is not our Father. The relationship carries with it accessibility, intimacy, and fearless love. Sons of great men have sometimes remembered their father as an institution rather than as a father, and God is to some of His children little more than an institution. It was not thus that Jesus revealed Him.

I have never forgotten the dread that gripped me when as a youth, I was invited to go for an interview at the manse. I walked past the door several times before I had courage to ring the bell, and as I stood at the door, my heart throbbed in my ears. Imagine my surprise, when shown into the room, to find the great man on all fours, giving a ride to riotously happy children, who turned his long beard into driving reins! He was their father!

There are many such revelations of the divine Glory and Majesty, and it is well to ponder them in adoring worship; but Jesus Christ turned them into terms of filial virtue. He is our Father! That is the crowning fact. Others may cringe in fear, but the child heart is a stranger to terror.

SAMUEL CHADWICK, *THE PATH OF PRAYER*

August 17

Rejoice in the Lord always. . . . Be anxious for nothing,
but in everything by prayer and supplication, with thanksgiving,
let your requests be made known to God.

Philippians 4:4-6

The Christian life, as such, is to be, and may be, a life of "joy in the Lord always." Such is the Lord that He is indeed able to be a perpetual cause of joy. The believer has but to recollect *Him*, to consider *Him*, to converse with *Him*, to make use of *Him* in order to have in himself (not *of* himself) "a well of water, springing up unto eternal life."

The normal Christian life is given here as a life free from care—from that miserable anxiety which blights and withers human happiness far and wide, whether it comes in the form of a weight of large responsibilities or of the most trifling misgivings. "Be careful for nothing"—"care-full" in the antique sense of the word: "burdened with care."

The normal Christian life is a life of perpetual, habitual converse with God about everything. The man who would be unanxious is to cultivate the practice of reverent, worshiping, thankful, *detailed prayer*; so shall he enter into peace.

The all-important thing to remember here is that we are called to pray as the great means to a divine, unanxious peace and that we are called to pray in the sense of "making our requests known *in everything*."

Will we act upon it? More and more, and always more, will we really "in everything" turn to Him and tell Him? Thought is good, but prayer is better; or rather, thought in the form of prayer is, in ten thousand cases, the best thought. Let us make it a rule, God helping, "*in everything*" which calls for pause, for consideration, for judgment, to pray first and then to think.

H. C. G. Moule, *Philippian Studies*

August 18

I have prayed for you, that your faith should not fail.

Luke 22:32

She gave herself to prayer. Streaming through the busy day, flowing far into the night, it was not always in words, for such longings as consumed her cannot wait for words. "I am a prayer" might describe her.

This attitude could not be kept wholly hidden to her world, and one day her brother—he to whom so much had been given—taunted her thus: "Thou thinkest that thou canst pray! From whom hast thou learned? Thou who canst not read!" And he sniffed.

She was only a poor woman, she said humbly to herself; she knew nothing at all. What if this that her learned brother said was true? What if her concept was all a mistake? Sharply and deep the sword entered into her soul.

"Wilt thou be indeed to me as waters that fail?" Did her heart cry that at this hour?

"I have prayed for thee, that thy faith fail not."

She had never heard the words, knew nothing of the truth that reinforces our fainting spirits. But wonderful, wonderful are the ways of the Lord. He is here, sometimes revealed to us, sometimes hidden, but always a God at hand and not a God far off. Near at that moment was the Lover of souls.

"Have I been a wilderness unto thee?"

Then with a warm glow of joy she knew what He had been to her all through the bitter years. No, He had not been a wilderness to her; He had comforted all her waste places. Had He not Himself taught her how to speak to Him, even as a mother teaches her little child?

Amy Carmichael, *Mimosa*

August 19

On You I wait all the day.

Psalm 25:5

The Father in heaven is so interested in His child and so longs to have his life at every step in His will and His love that He is willing to keep the child's guidance entirely in His own hand. He so well knows that we are unable to do what is really holy and heavenly—except as He works it in us—that He intends His very demands to become promises of what He will do in watching over and leading us all day long. Not only in special difficulties and times of perplexity but in the common course of everyday life we may count upon Him to teach us His way and show us His path.

And what is needed in us to receive this guidance? One thing: waiting for instructions, waiting on God. We need in our times of prayer to give clear expression to our sense of need and our faith in His help. We need definitely to become conscious of our ignorance as to what God's way may be and our need of the divine light shining within us. And we need to wait quietly before God in prayer until the deep, restful assurance fills us. It will be given.

As simple as it is for one who has eyes to walk all the day in the light of the sun, so simple and delightful can it become for a soul that has practiced waiting on God to walk all day in the enjoyment of God's light and leading. What is needed to help us to such a life is just one thing: the real knowledge and faith in God as the only source of wisdom and goodness—as ever ready and longing to be to us all that we can possibly require.

Yes, this is the one thing we need! If only we saw our God in His love, if only we believed that He waits to be gracious, that He waits to be our life and to work all in us—how this waiting on God would become our highest joy, the natural and spontaneous response of our hearts to His great love and glory!

Andrew Murray, *Waiting on God*

AUGUST 20

The anointing which you have received from Him abides in you, and . . . teaches you concerning all things.

1 JOHN 2:27

There must be a limit. Presumably God has drawn somewhere a line of demarcation. Stay within the bound of that line, and we will be safe; cross it, and grave danger threatens. But where does it lie?

We are not to be tied by rules but are to remain all the time within bounds of another kind—the bounds of His life. If our Lord had given us a set of rules and regulations to observe, then we could take great care to abide by these. In fact, however, our task is something far more simple and straightforward, namely, to abide in the Lord Himself. We need only keep in fellowship with Him. And the joy of it is that, provided we live in close touch with God, His Holy Spirit within our hearts will always tell us when we reach the limit.

"Ye have an anointing from the Holy One, and ye know all things. . . . As his anointing teacheth you concerning all things, and is true, and is no lie, and even as it taught you, ye abide in him" (1 John 2:20, 27). This is certainly an allusion to the Spirit of truth, who, Jesus promised His disciples, would both convict the world and guide them into all the truth (John 16:8–13).

In any given instance there must be safe limits known to God beyond which we should not go. They are not marked out on the ground for us to see, but one thing is certain: He who is the Comforter will surely know them. Can we not trust Him? If at some point we are about to overstep them, can we not depend on Him at once to make us inwardly aware of the fact?

WATCHMAN NEE, *LOVE NOT THE WORLD*

August 21

Send out Your light and Your truth! Let them lead me.

Psalm 43:3

If the next step is clear, then the one thing to do is to take it. Don't pledge your Lord or yourself about the steps beyond. You don't see them yet.

Once when I was climbing at night in the forest before there was a made path, I learned what the word meant, "Thy word is a lantern to my path" (Ps. 119:105). I had a lantern and had to hold it very low or I should certainly have slipped on those rough rocks. We don't walk spiritually by electric light but by a hand lantern. And a lantern only shows the next step—not several ahead.

There can be only one right way, one right thing to say or do. If you refuse to be hurried and pressed, if you stay your soul on God, nothing can keep you from that clearness of spirit which is life and peace. In that stillness you will know what His will is. Strength and calm will come to do it. You will go on with Him, and you will prove Him in new ways and grow in strength and joy.

Amy Carmichael, *Candles in the Dark*

August 22

Wait on the Lord; be of good courage . . . ; wait, I say, on the Lord!

Psalm 27:14

Is waiting on God a work so difficult that for it such words [as those in Psalm 27:14] are needed? Yes, indeed. The deliverance for which we often have to wait is from enemies in whose presence we are powerless. The blessings for which we plead are spiritual and all unseen—things impossible with men—heavenly, supernatural, divine realities. Our heart may well faint and fail.

Our souls are so little accustomed to hold fellowship with God; the God on whom we wait so often appears to hide Himself. We who have to wait are often tempted to fear that we do not wait properly, that our faith is too weak, that our desire is not as upright or as earnest as it should be, that our surrender is not complete. Amid all these causes of fear or doubt, how blessed to hear the voice of God: "Wait on the Lord: be strong, and let thine heart take courage; *yea, wait thou on the Lord.*"

Let nothing in heaven or earth or hell—let nothing keep you from waiting on your God in full assurance that it *cannot* be in vain.

Andrew Murray, *Waiting on God*

August 23

Those who wait on the Lord *. . . shall mount up with wings like eagles.*

Isaiah 40:31

In the nurture of the soul, the Potter's fingers represent the touch of the Spirit of God working in us to will and to do of His good pleasure. He is in us all, His one purpose being to infill us with Himself and to fulfill through us "all the good pleasure of his goodness, and every work of faith with power: that the name of our Lord Jesus Christ may be glorified in us, and we in him."

God's touch and voice give the meaning of His providences, and His providences enforce the lesson that His tender monitions might not be strong enough to teach. Whenever therefore you are in doubt as to the meaning of certain circumstances through which you are called to pass and which are strange and inexplicable, be still; refrain from murmuring or repining; hush the many voices that would speak within; listen until there is borne in on your soul a persuasion of God's purpose; and let His Spirit within cooperate with the circumstance without.

It is in the equal working of these two—the circumstance supplying the occasion for manifesting a certain grace and the Holy Ghost supplying the grace to be manifested—that the spirit soars, as the bird by the even motion of its two wings.

F. B. Meyer, *Jeremiah*

August 24

It happened after a while that the brook dried up,
because there had been no rain in the land.

1 Kings 17:7

Week after week, with unfaltering and steadfast spirit, Elijah watched that dwindling brook, often tempted to stagger through unbelief but refusing to allow his circumstances to come between himself and God. Unbelief sees God through circumstances, but faith puts God between itself and circumstances and looks at them through Him.

And so the dwindling brook became a silver thread, and the silver thread stood presently in pools at the foot of the largest boulders, and then the pools shrank. The birds fled; the wild creatures of field and forest came no more to drink; the brook was dry. Only then, to his patient and unwavering spirit, "the word of the LORD came unto him, saying, Arise, get thee to Zarephath."

Most of us would have got anxious and worn with planning long before that. We would have ceased our songs as soon as the streamlet caroled less musically over its rocky bed, and with harps swinging on the willows, we would have paced to and fro upon the withering grass, lost in pensive thought. And probably, long before the brook was dry, we would have devised some plan and, asking God's blessing on it, would have started off elsewhere.

Only when we are met by insuperable obstacles do we begin to reflect whether it was God's will or to appeal to Him. Would that we were content to wait for God to unveil His plan so that our life might be simply the working out of His thought, the exemplification of His ideal! Let this be the cry of our hearts: "Lord, show me Thy way; teach me to do Thy will. Show me the way wherein I should walk, for unto Thee do I lift up my soul."

F. B. Meyer, *Elijah*

August 25

The Lord is good to those who wait for Him.

Lamentations 3:25

When we are in doubt or difficulty, when many voices urge this course or the other, when prudence utters one advice and faith another, then let us be still, hushing each intruder, calming ourselves in the sacred hush of God's presence; let us study His Word in the attitude of devout attention; let us lift up our nature into the pure light of His face, eager only to know what God the Lord shall determine—and ere long a very distinct impression will be made, the unmistakable forthtelling of His secret counsel.

It is not wise, in the earlier stages of Christian life, to depend on this alone but to wait for the corroboration of circumstances. But those who have had many dealings with God know well the value of secret fellowship with Him to ascertain His will.

Are you in difficulty about your way? Go to God with your question; get direction from the light of His smile or the cloud of His refusal. If only you will get alone, where the lights and shadows of earth cannot interfere, where the disturbance of self-will does not intrude, where human opinions fail to reach—and if you will dare to wait there silent and expectant, though all around you insist on immediate decision or action—the will of God will be made clear. And you will have a new name in addition, a new conception of God, a deeper insight into His nature and heart of love, which shall be for yourself alone—a rapturous experience to abide as your precious possession forever, the rich reward for those long waiting hours.

F. B. Meyer, *David*

August 26

Fear not, I will help you.

Isaiah 41:13

God's help does not, for the most part, come miraculously or obviously. It steals as gradually into our life as the grass of spring clothes the hills with fresh and verdant robes. Before men can say "Lo, here!" or "Lo, there!" it has suddenly entered into our need and met it.

A smile, a flower, a letter, a burst of music, the picture of a bit of mountain scenery, a book, the coming of a friend—such are the ways in which God comes to our help. Not helping us far in advance but just for one moment at a time. Not giving us a store of strength to make us proud but supplying our need as the occasion comes. Sometimes the Almighty helps us by putting His wisdom and strength and grace into our hearts, sometimes by manipulating circumstances in our behalf, and sometimes by inclining friends or foes to do the very thing we need.

But it matters little as to the channel—only let us rest confidently in the certainty of receiving what we need. It may be delayed to the last moment, but it will come. "God shall help when the morning appeareth" (Ps. 46:5, margin). If the last mail has come in without bringing the expected assistance, then wait up and expect a special messenger. "There is none like unto the God of Jeshurun, who rideth upon the heaven in thy help, and in his excellency on the sky" (Deut. 33:26).

When the godly man ceaseth and the faithful fail, there is no cry that so befits our lips as the brief ejaculation with which the psalmist begins Psalm 12: "Help, Lord." And this is the response attested by old experience and by the spirit of inspiration: "The God of thy father shall help thee."

F. B. Meyer, *Joseph*

August 27

Rest in the Lord, and wait patiently for Him.

Psalm 37:7

Resting in Him is nothing but being silent to Him, still before Him—having our thoughts and wishes, our fears and hopes, hushed into calm and quiet by that great peace of God which passes all understanding. That peace keeps the heart and mind calm when we are anxious about anything, because we have made our request known to Him.

He longs to bless us far more fully than we can desire it. But as the farmer waits in patience till the fruit is ripe, so God bows Himself to our slowness and bears long with us. Let us remember this and wait patiently. Of each promise and every answer to prayer, the statement is true: "I the Lord will hasten it *in his time*" (Isa. 60:22).

Do not seek only the help or the gift; seek *Him*. Wait for *Him*. Give God His glory by resting in Him, by trusting Him fully, by waiting patiently for Him. This patience honors Him greatly; it leaves Him, as God on the throne, to do His work; it yields self wholly into His hands. It lets God be God.

Andrew Murray, *Waiting on God*

August 28

The LORD will wait, that He may be gracious to you; . . .
blessed are all those who wait for Him.

ISAIAH 30:18

Look up and see the great God upon His throne. He is Love—an unceasing and inexpressible desire to communicate His own goodness and blessedness to all His creatures. He longs and delights to bless. He has inconceivably glorious purposes concerning every one of His children: by the power of His Holy Spirit to reveal in them His love and power.

He waits with all the longings of a father's heart. He waits so that He may be gracious unto you. And each time you come to wait upon Him or seek to maintain in daily life the holy habit of waiting, you may look up and see Him ready to meet you, waiting so that He may be gracious unto you. Yes, connect every activity, every breath of the life of waiting with faith's vision of your God waiting for *you*.

"How is it, if He waits to be gracious, that even after I come and wait on Him, He does not give the help I seek but waits on longer and longer?"

God is a wise farmer who "waiteth for the precious fruit of the earth, and hath long patience for it" (James 5:7). He cannot gather the fruit till it is ripe. He knows when we are spiritually ready to receive the blessing to our profit and His glory. Waiting in the sunshine of His love is what will ripen the soul for His blessing. Waiting under the cloud of trial that breaks in showers of blessing is just as needful. Be assured that if God waits longer than you could wish, it is only to make the blessing doubly precious.

ANDREW MURRAY, *WAITING ON GOD*

August 29

Your prayer is heard.

Luke 1:13

Zacharias had prayed through long, lean years for a son. He and Elizabeth had many qualifications for a life of blessing: good ancestry; they "were righteous before the Lord," not merely before men; they walked in all the commandments of the Lord blameless—not faultless but living up to their light.

But there follows the sad statement, "And they had no child." Have you sought to live the blameless life, yet your piety seems to have borne no progeny—you are barren? Remember Zacharias. It was now too late, from the natural viewpoint, to have a son, but Zacharias had not forgotten his altar and his duty. He kept offering incense, a symbol of thanksgiving, when there seemed so little to be thankful for.

Do not forsake your incense, and the angel will yet appear! The herald from heaven announces a son. God often waits until it is too late with us; it is never too late with Him.

Poor Zacharias is doubtful. And doubt leads to dumbness—it always does. When we do not trust, we have no testimony. But God fails not, though Zacharias does.

The baby is born, and when neighbors would name him for his father, Zacharias puts God first and names him by the divine direction. Do not name things after yourself; give God the glory. Then dumbness gives way to delight: Zacharias speaks, and so will you.

How marvelously God's plans work out exactly on schedule!

Vance Havner, *Reflections on the Gospels*

AUGUST 30

As soon as Jesus heard the word that was spoken, He said . . . , "Do not be afraid; only believe."

MARK 5:36

"According to your faith be it unto you," Jesus declared long ago, but still we do not believe it; we try roundabout methods to secure what comes only by believing.

This was made clear in the case of Jairus. He had summoned Jesus to help his daughter, who was at the point of death. Someone came from Jairus's house, saying, "Thy daughter is dead: why troublest thou the Master any further?" Ah, that is always the attitude of this poor world. "My case is hopeless; why pray?" But our Lord answered, "Be not afraid, only believe."

Would that we could hear Him today in the moment when all seems lost, when fondest hopes have perished, when dearest ones lie dead, saying still as He does, "Be not afraid, only believe." No matter what your circumstance, keep your confidence in Him, and He will do what is for the best.

There come so many times when, through the voice of others, the evil one says, "What is the use in calling on the Lord? It is a dead prospect; why trouble Him any further?" But there never was a situation in which faith is not the victory. He may not raise our dead as He did then, but He will raise them one day; and there is no occasion to be afraid, for we know that all things work together for good to them who are His.

VANCE HAVNER, *REFLECTIONS ON THE GOSPELS*

August 31

His desire is toward me.

Song of Solomon 7:10

There is nothing on earth that awakens love and rouses it to activity so powerfully as the thought of being desired and loved. Let me endeavor to conceive how true it is that I am an object of desire to the Son of God. He looks out to see whether I am coming to Him or not. With the deepest interest, He would know whether I come hungering after Him that He may be able to bestow much of His blessing on me. That would be such a joy to His love. Thus does He stir me up to earnest longings. His desire is toward me.

My soul, believe and ponder this wonderful thought until you feel drawn with overmastering force to give yourself over to Jesus for the satisfaction of His desire toward you. Then shall you too be satisfied.

My Savior, it is this especially that I crave at Your hand: unveil to me the love of Your heart that makes You long so much after me. I know that this is one of the secret things that remain for Your dearest friends, and I hardly dare reckon myself among them. And yet, Lord, may I venture to do so. Grant me, I pray, one more glance into Your heart that I may know how earnestly You desire me.

You would have me as Your own possession. You would enter into the deepest communion with me. You would communicate Yourself to me. You would become one with me. You would have me for Yourself. My Jesus, if this be really so, cause me to feel it. Let not my heart remain in darkness. Then shall I turn away from all else, and my life shall be filled with one supreme desire: Jesus, my King and my Friend.

Andrew Murray, *The Lord's Table*

September

Suffering with Christ

The Testimony of Hanmer Webb-Peploe

At Cambridge Hanmer William Webb-Peploe was a youth of enormous zest, jumping and swimming for the university and being one of the very few to have made the famous leap up the wide steps from Trinity Great Court to the doorway of Hall. He had not intended holy orders. Shortly after coming down from Cambridge, he stayed in Derbyshire with a friend called Wright. A talk together under the stars and an incident outside the local racecourse when a stranger thrust a tract into his hands altered the direction of his life, and Webb-Peploe was duly ordained as curate to his father.

By 1874 he had six children and a small stipend. Fourteen years "a faithful preacher of the doctrine of justification," his existence was a "constant watching, waiting, and struggling to do right. . . . I had no joy for every moment, no rest in the midst of trouble, no calm amid the burdens of this life; I was strained and overstrained until I felt I was breaking down."

That year he took his family for a seaside holiday at Saltburn on the Yorkshire coast. Stevenson Blackwood was also on vacation and told him of the Oxford Conference opening that very day: "He said, 'People are coming together there to seek for a blessing, to pray for the life of rest.' He looked me in the face and said, 'Have you rest?'" When Webb-Peploe understood his meaning, he replied, "That is what I long for most."

A friend of Blackwood's sent daily reports from Oxford, and they went into the woods and read them together.

Webb-Peploe's six-month-old son, Edward Alec, died at Saltburn, and he carried the little coffin back alone across England in the train to bury him. His holiday spoiled, his heart sore, an unexpected Sunday ahead in his own church, he tried to prepare a sermon, choosing from the set lesson a text: "My grace is sufficient for thee." He could not concentrate. He resented "all God called upon me to bear. I flung down my pen, threw myself on my knees, and said to God, 'It is not sufficient; it is *not* sufficient! Lord, *let* Thy grace be sufficient. O Lord, do!'"

He opened his eyes and saw on the wall a framed text which his mother had given him the day before he left for holiday and the servant had hung during his absence. In scrolls and squiggles and colored inks it proclaimed, "My grace is sufficient for thee." The word "is" showed up bright green. A voice seemed to say, "You fool, how dare you ask God to make what *is*! Get up and take, and you will find it true. When God says 'is,' it is for you to believe Him." Webb-Peploe got up. "That 'is' changed my life. From that moment I could say, 'O God, whatever Thou dost say in Thy Word, I believe, and please God, I will step out upon it.'"

He took God at His word, he believed the *fact*, and his life was revolutionized. He entered into such an experience of rest and peace, such trust in a sufficient Savior, as he never before had dreamed could be possible. Within a month the governess in the family said to Mrs. Webb-Peploe, "The farmers are remarking how much changed the vicar is: he does not seem fretful any more but seems to be quiet and gentle about everything." And from that day to this, now forty-five years later, many have praised God that the life of this minister of the gospel is a testimony to the sufficiency of the grace which God declares is a fact.

Dr. John Charles Pollock, *The Keswick Story*

September 1

Do not fear or be dismayed; . . . go out against them, for the Lord *is with you.*

2 Chronicles 20:17

There are days so extraordinary for the combination of difficult circumstances, human opposition, and spiritual conflict that they stand out in unique terror from the rest of our lives. Looking back on them, we may almost adopt the language of the sacred writer, "There was no day like that before it or after it."

But these days do not come, if we are living in fellowship with God, intent on doing His will, without there coming also His sweet "Fear them not, for I have delivered them into thy hands!" Our only anxiety should be that nothing divert us from His path or intercept the communication of His grace. Like a wise commander, we must keep open the passage back to our base of operations, which is God. Careful about that, we need have no anxious care beside. The greatness of our difficulties is permitted to elicit the greatness of His grace. We may even be glad to enter the storm that we may make fresh discoveries of the all-sufficiency of Jesus, who is never so near as in these days of special trial.

Moreover, these days may always be full of the realized presence of God. All through the conflict, Joshua's heart was in perpetual fellowship with the mighty Captain of the Lord's host, who rode beside him all the day. So amid all our conflicts, our hearts and minds should thither ascend and there dwell where Christ is seated, drawing from Him grace upon grace as we need.

F. B. Meyer, *Joshua*

September 2

Though our outward man is perishing,
yet the inward man is being renewed day by day.

2 Corinthians 4:16

The apostle Paul's life might be illustrated by that remarkable scene in *Pilgrim's Progress* where the Interpreter, in his house of parables, takes the traveler in to watch the fire which burns on ever brighter under difficulties. Yet in front of it stands one who continually casts water on the heat to put it out. Christian is much perplexed. Then his host leads him round behind the wall, and lo! another agent is at work there, pouring through a secret channel oil into the fire. So the paradox is explained.

Thus it was with Saint Paul's life and the forces which threatened hard to bear it down. Behind it, within it, was "the secret of the Lord." The veil of tired and suffering humanity held concealed below it the life of Jesus. "For this cause" he did "not faint." "The outward man," he admits, was "perishing." But it did not matter. "The inward man," the pulse of the machine, "was renewing day by day."

Let us realize afresh that there is such a "secret of the Lord" and that it is for us today, if indeed we are His disciples. It is a talisman as potent in the twentieth century as in the first. Now as then, the eternal Master claims our whole devotion, in whatever path it is to be shown. Now as then, world, flesh, and devil cross that path at every turn and make the Christian life not only difficult but impossible, if we try to live it of ourselves. But now as then, the oil of heaven is ready to run in from behind the wall.

"The life of Jesus," the living Lord dwelling in the heart, can still prove inexhaustible, victorious "in the mortal flesh," and then that which is impossible with man is, in man, found possible with God.

H. C. G. Moule, *The Second Epistle to the Corinthians*

September 3

Many are they who say of me, "There is no help for him in God."

Psalm 3:2

Have you ever been discouraged and distressed because of something people said or the voices inside you said? Such people and such voices talk most when one is in trouble about something. "Many there be which say of my soul, There is no help for him in God." That was what the many said who were round about poor King David in a dark hour. But he turned to his God and told Him just what they were saying, and then he affirmed his faith: "But thou, O Lord, art a shield for me; my glory, and the lifter up of mine head" (Ps. 3:2–3).

We cannot use these words if we are pleasing ourselves in anything and doing our own will, not our Lord's. In that case what the many say is only too true. There is no help for us in God while we are walking in any way of our own choice. But when all is clear between us and our Father, even if like David we are in trouble because of something we have done wrong in the past, then those words are not true. There is help for us in God. He is our shield, our glory, and the lifter up of our head, and we need not be afraid of ten thousands of people (Ps. 3:6)—ten thousands of voices—for the Lord our God is our very present help.

But David is not confounded. He refuses to be cast down, let the many say what they will. "Lord, lift thou up the light of thy countenance upon us" (Ps. 4:6). If only we can look up and meet His ungrieved countenance, what does anything matter? And we shall experience good. "The Lord is my light and my salvation; whom shall I fear? the Lord is the strength of my life; of whom shall I be afraid?" (Ps. 27:1).

Amy Carmichael, *Thou Givest . . . They Gather*

SEPTEMBER 4

Shall we indeed accept good from God, and shall we not accept adversity?

JOB 2:10

Job's wife seems to have been the only one left to him, and she appears to have followed him to the ash mound outside the village. In her anguish over her husband's sufferings, she unknowingly lends her mouth to the adversary. She did not realize that Satan was keenly watching the effect of his attack upon Job and hoped in this critical hour to force him to the point he desired by his wife's words.

"Renounce God and die," said Job's loving and faithful wife to her afflicted husband. We do not read of any word she said when she saw their earthly goods swept away or of any rebellion over the loss of her children, but now it seems too much to see her husband suffer. But Job again stood the test: "In all this did not Job sin with his lips" (2:10).

It is, alas, true that many of the children of God serve Him for the good they get in this present world and in the world to come rather than for Himself alone. Worldlings too expect what they call "good" from a God who is called Love and misjudge and renounce Him because of the suffering in the world which they cannot reconcile with His love. Both stumble at the mystery of pain and fail to understand what a writer has so truly said: "Pain has other and higher functions than penalty," for "the outer man must be sacrificed *in the interests of the man within*" (W. W. Peyton).

Job was a true man of God! Blow upon blow had come upon him, but his integrity had stood the test. He proved by his surrender and faith the faithfulness of God.

JESSIE PENN-LEWIS, *THE STORY OF JOB*

September 5

I remember You. . . . You have been my help.

Psalm 63:6–7

Why, oh why, were hearts allowed to be so unkind? Nothing that had ever happened to her hurt like this, and the barriers of her self-control, so painfully maintained through the morning and all through the day, having once broken down, left her to the mercy of heavy, sweeping waves of grief. And now, to add to her distress, she was conscious of the working of a new passion within. What about this flaming anger? Was anger right? Should she not forgive? But how could she forgive?

At last, and suddenly, she remembered her Lord.

Remembering Thee, I straight forgot
What otherwhile had troubled me;
It was as if it all were not,
I only was aware of Thee.
Of Thee, of Thee alone aware,
I rested me, I held me still;
The blessed thought of Thee, most Fair,
Banished the brooding sense of ill.
And quietness around me fell.

Oh, it is true, it is true. He who knew what it was to be wounded in the house of His friends; He who turned not His face from a shame which shames our hottest, reddest shame, making it feel cool and pale; He, though of all this she did not know, was with her then. The thought of Him brought Him near; just a thought, and He was there, softening the sharp edges of the pain, soothing, tending, cooling, comforting, till her soul was hushed within her. She took heart to forgive, and she slept.

Amy Carmichael, *Mimosa*

September 6

name of Yahweh, who had spoken unto her, Thou God *of vision! . . . On this account is the well called, The well of the life of vision.*

Genesis 16:13–14, Rotherham

Thou God seest me, Thou God of vision." Those words were spoken by Hagar, who had been utterly discouraged but now was encouraged. Sarah had been very unkind to her, but the angel of the Lord did not say to her, "Poor Hagar!" The sympathy of the Lord our God is never weakening; it is bracing. Hagar had run away, so the angel said, "Return." God's love is always brave love. He never says, "Give way"; He always says, "Return."

He said more. Perhaps Hagar had thought He did not care much about her. He cared for Sarah, of course, but she was only Hagar. So the angel put her right about that and told her how the Lord would bless her, because He had seen and heard her affliction.

Awed and heartened, Hagar called the name of the Lord "Thou God seest me, Thou God of vision." The well nearby was named "The well of Him that liveth and seeth me, the well of the life of vision."

Thank God for that well in the wilderness. If we are discouraged or tired or hurt today, one long drink from that well will give us new life, new courage, new patience to go on running the race set before us—even to the end.

Amy Carmichael, *Whispers of His Power*

SEPTEMBER 7

These things I have spoken to you, that in Me you may have peace.

JOHN 16:33

These words [of John 16:33] have brought peace to me this morning. Sometimes our circumstances are so peaceful that without knowing it we slip into finding our peace in them. Then something happens to disturb them and our peace is disturbed. Sometimes those about us are so dear that our hearts rest in them. And this is good, but it is not enough; for what if one in whose love we trust should disappoint us?

Our Lord did not say, "These things I have spoken unto you, that in your circumstances ye might have peace," or, "These things I have spoken unto you, that in the love of others ye might have peace," but He did say, "These things"—things of wonder, joy, sorrow, preparation—"I have spoken unto you, that in *me* ye might have peace." "Remember the word that I said unto you, The servant is not greater than his lord; . . . if they have kept my saying, they will keep yours also."

Is there any surprise of grief that our dear Lord has not foreseen? Is there any wound to love that His love has not suffered? "These things I have spoken unto you, that *in me ye might have peace.*"

AMY CARMICHAEL, *EDGES OF HIS WAYS*

September 8

In the world you will have tribulation; but be of good cheer,
I have overcome the world.

John 16:33

Sorrow or suffering poses what has probably been in all ages the most serious problem for believers. Suffering is not only the last thing to be considered useful but rather something to be avoided, evaded, and shunned. But according to the Word of God, suffering is not an accident but a gift to be cherished, for when properly received, it works to enhance one's eternal rank, fame, and honor.

In a fallen world, suffering of some kind is universal. There is no permanent release or escape from it, either by rank, holy living, health, or wealth. "Man is born unto trouble, as the sparks fly upward" (Job 5:7). "But of course you know that such troubles are a part of God's plan for us Christians. Even while we were still with you we warned you ahead of time that suffering would soon come—and it did" (1 Thess. 3:3–4, TLB). Trouble therefore comes to all, both saint and sinner.

But *why* should the righteous suffer? Why isn't every believer healed, and healed immediately? Why isn't he "carried to the skies on flowery beds of ease"? It is difficult for most people to understand why sorrow comes to a saint. That is one of the mysteries of the ages. However, regardless of the mystery involved, we know that God is love and that, according to 2 Corinthians 4:17–18, He permits suffering to the saint only to work (create) for him an "eternal weight of glory." No one ever becomes a saint without suffering, because suffering, properly accepted, is the pathway to glory.

Paul Billheimer, *Don't Waste Your Sorrows*

SEPTEMBER 9

If need be, you have been grieved by various trials, that the genuineness of your faith . . . may be found to praise, honor, and glory.

1 PETER 1:6–7

The apparent aimlessness of some kinds of pain is sometimes their sorest ingredient. We can suffer more cheerfully if we can clearly see the end which is being slowly reached. But if we cannot, it is hard to lie still and be at rest. But the believer knows that nothing can come to him save by the permission of God's love. Every trial must reach him through the mystic barriers that engird him and must show a permit signed by the hand of God Himself. Nothing comes by chance or by the will of friend or foe, but all is under law. And each separate calamity has a specific purpose.

As the farmer carefully adjusts his method to various kinds of grain and to accomplish the object he has at heart, so the Almighty varies His method of dealing with us: He ever selects the precise trial that will soonest and best accomplish His purposes, and He only continues it long enough to do all that needs to be done. "Bread corn is bruised: but he will not ever be threshing it, nor break it with the wheel of his cart, nor bruise it with his horsemen." I commend that precious promise to those who think their sorrows past endurance. They will not last forever; they will be suited to our peculiar needs and strength. They will accomplish that on which the great Husbandman has set His heart.

F. B. MEYER, *ISRAEL*

September 10

We do not look at the things which are seen, but at the things which are not seen.

2 Corinthians 4:18

God's victories often look like defeats. Victory occurs in the *unseen* realm while one is, apparently, absolutely down and out in the visible. It was so at Calvary, so in the life of Paul, so in the life of Peter; it is so everywhere and for everyone who can say "Death worketh in me, but life in you"—those who are planted into the death of Christ for a life of fruit bearing.

If we look for a life of continual outward success and desire to look prosperous and pleasing to the world, we have a wrong conception of God's way of working. If, on the other hand, we have the inward vision to see that the life of God in us is only brought to fruition through suffering, then we will learn to live in the unseen spirit life by faith. We will not be disturbed by the conflict, the opposition, the betrayal of friends but will keep our soul in patience and filled with the love of God. We will see that our life course is according to the pattern of the God-Man on earth and the pattern of Paul and say, "Yes, I am in the succession!"

Jessie Penn-Lewis, *Prayer and Evangelism*

September 11

If you have run with the footmen, and they have wearied you, then how can you contend with horses?

Jeremiah 12:5

Does not God ever deal with us thus? He does not put us at once to contend with horses but tests us first with footmen. God graduates the trials of our life; He allows the lesser to precede the greater. He gives us the opportunity of learning to trust Him in slighter difficulties that faith may become muscular and strong and that we may be able to walk to Him amid the surge of the ocean. Whatever your sorrows and troubles are at this hour, God has allowed them to come to afford you an opportunity of preparation for future days. Do not be discouraged or give up the fight or be unfaithful in the very little. Do not say you cannot bear it. You can!

There is sufficient grace in God; appropriate it, use it, rest upon Him. Be very thankful that He has given you this time of discipline and of searching; and now, taking to yourself all that He waits to give—the grace and comfort and assurance—go forward! He cannot fail you. What He is in the lesser, He will be much more in the greater. The grace He gives today is but as a silver thread compared to the river of grace He will give to you tomorrow. If you start back now, you will miss the greater discipline that will surely come, but in missing it you will also miss the greater revelation of Himself that will accompany the discipline.

F. B. Meyer, *Jeremiah*

September 12

I will rather boast in my infirmities, that the power of Christ may rest upon me.

2 Corinthians 12:9

Too ready, too outspoken, too confiding we cannot be in "telling Jesus all." Such crying out will not weaken us; it will only strengthen us. For it is the outgoing of our soul not only to infinite kindness but at the same moment to infinite wisdom and strength. It is taking refuge in the Rock.

So Paul "besought the Lord thrice." He was answered. There was a divine attention and response. The Lord, once Himself driven to "strong crying and tears," Himself once a suppliant in a yet darker hour, quite understood His servant.

It must have been a help to the servant, heartbroken with the struggle, to reflect that he appealed to One who once said Himself, "Reproach hath broken my heart" (Ps. 69:20). Saint Paul could be sure then, as we may be sure now, of that Friend's supreme "acquaintance with grief."

Yet the answer was not a consent. The thorn was not willed away; the "evil angel" was not driven back into the deep. As in Gethsemane, so with the apostle in his dark hour—there came not a consent to the request in detail but the meeting of it with a transcendently higher blessing.

"Thorn" and "angel of Satan" might or might not be ultimately withdrawn. But then and there in all His fullness, in His all-sufficient present Self (for grace is just the Lord of all love and power Himself in action for us), Jesus Christ was given to this saint. In the power of that gift, the saint found that the dread adversity had changed its character and position. It was not upon his head, overwhelming. It was beneath his feet, overcome.

H. C. G. Moule, *The Second Epistle to the Corinthians*

SEPTEMBER 13

No chastening seems to be joyful for the present, but painful; nevertheless, afterward it yields the peaceable fruit of righteousness to those who have been trained by it.

HEBREWS 12:11

There is a utility in every trial. It is intended to reveal the secrets of our hearts; to humble us and prove us; to winnow us as corn is shaken in a sieve; to detach us from the earthly and visible; to create in us an eager desire for the realities which can alone quench our cravings and endure forever.

Christ would not test us if He did not see the precious ore of faith mingled in the rocky matrix of our nature, and it is to bring this out into purity and beauty that He forces us through the fiery ordeal. Be patient, O sufferer; He must love you, or He would not chasten you.

And we shall be more than recompensed for all our trials when we see how they wrought out the far more exceeding and eternal weight of glory. To have one word of God's commendation; to be honored before the holy angels; to be glorified in Christ, so as to be better able to flash back His glory on Himself—ah! this will more than repay for all. Let us live more constantly in that future under the powers of the world to come!

All the blessings which accrue through trial are only possible to us, however, when the heart meekly accepts it from the hand of God and opens to the operation of the Holy Spirit. Trial *alone* may harden. But when trial is accompanied with the gracious influences of the Holy Spirit, it is as precious oil that does not break the head (Ps. 141:5).

F. B. MEYER, *TRIED BY FIRE: EXPOSITION OF 1 PETER*

SEPTEMBER 14

Let those who suffer according to the will of God commit their souls to Him in doing good, as to a faithful Creator.

1 PETER 4:19

All things are yours if you are Christ's. All things serve you. Even those that seem most awry and trying are really promoting your best interests. If you knew as much about them as God does, you would go down on your bended knees and thank Him, with streaming eyes, for the most untoward of your circumstances. The seed buried in the ground may rejoice in the frost as much as in the genial sunshine. And even though some events cut us to the quick, if we believe that the infinite love of God is working in and through them, we may sing as Paul and Silas did—despite the fact that our feet are fast in the stocks.

Look not at the things which are seen but at those which are not seen. Cast into the one scale your sorrows, if you will, but put into the other the glory which shall presently be the outcome of the pain. Consider how splendid it will be when the discipline is over and the lovely shape is acquired and the lesson learned and the pattern fixed forever. Anticipate the time when every vestige of Jacob shall have been laid aside and Israel has become the befitting title for your soul. Will not that repay you—because you will have been brought into a oneness with Christ which shall be heaven in miniature?

Take heart, thou bit of heaven's porcelain; thou must be shaped and fashioned on the rapid wheel; thy fairest hues must be burned in amid the most fiery trials—but thou shalt yet grace the table of thy King and shalt be used of Him for His choicest purposes.

F. B. MEYER, *ISRAEL*

SEPTEMBER 15

May the God of hope fill you with all joy and peace in believing, that you may abound in hope by the power of the Spirit.

ROMANS 15:13

I understand the buffeted days and the days of no small tempest, when neither sun nor stars appear. And it is good to pass through such days, for if we didn't, we could neither prove our God nor help others. If any experience of ours helps to bring others to our Lord, what does any buffeting matter?

But we are not meant to live in a perpetual stormy sea. We are meant to pass through and find harbor and so be at peace. Then we are free from occupation with ourselves and our storms—free to help others.

I want to live in the light of the thought of His coming, His triumph—the end of this present darkness, the glory of His seen Presence. This bathes the present in radiance. You won't be sorry then that you trusted when you couldn't see, when neither sun nor stars in many days appeared and no small tempest lay on you (Acts 27:20). No, you won't be sorry then. So I won't be sorry now. I am believing. "All joy and peace in believing": the words ring like a chime of bells.

AMY CARMICHAEL, *CANDLES IN THE DARK*

SEPTEMBER 16

Though He slay me, yet will I trust Him.

JOB 13:15

It is not unusual that the greatest saints, those who have made the greatest contribution to the kingdom, are those who have suffered the most. The world never would have heard of Madame Guyon and the church never would have been enriched by the fragrance of her life and perhaps eternity would have been poorer if it had not been for her victory over tribulation.

If ever a person could have *wasted her sorrow*, it was she. By the depth of her triumphant submission, her sufferings were transmuted into character which has left an indelible mark upon the spiritual life of succeeding generations and probably, more significantly, enriched heaven. Among those influenced by her life and witness was the sainted Fénelon. Would it have been better for the kingdom, would it have brought more glory to Christ, if Madame Guyon had been healed of smallpox and spared the crushing humiliation and sorrows that followed in its wake?

Madame Guyon's eternal worth and service, her contribution to the eternal kingdom, was enhanced by the way she was enabled to triumph in adversity of every kind. It seems possible that the completeness of her submission and triumphant faith in the wisdom and goodness of her adorable Lord brought more joy and satisfaction to His heart than would have a miracle-working faith for healing and deliverance. The faith that can truly say "Though He slay me, yet will I trust Him" may be more precious in God's sight than faith that moves mountains, because it may arise out of a more self-sacrificial love.

PAUL BILLHEIMER, *DON'T WASTE YOUR SORROWS*

SEPTEMBER 17

I . . . fill up in my flesh what is lacking in the afflictions of Christ.

COLOSSIANS 1:24

The suggestion is this: all ministry for the Master must be possessed by the sacrificial spirit of the Master. If Paul is to help in the redemption of Rome, he must himself incarnate the death of Calvary. If he is to be a minister of life, he must "die daily." Every real lift implies a corresponding strain. The Spirit of Calvary is to be reincarnate in Ephesus and Athens and Rome, the sacrificial succession is to be maintained through the ages, and we are to "fill up that which is behind of the sufferings of Christ."

The gospel of a broken heart demands the ministry of bleeding hearts. As soon as we cease to bleed, we cease to bless. When our sympathy loses its pangs, we can no longer be the servants of the passion.

I do not know how any Christian service is to be fruitful if the servant is not primarily baptized in the spirit of a suffering compassion. We can never heal the needs we do not feel. Tearless hearts can never be the heralds of the passion. We must bleed if we would be the ministers of the saving blood. We must, by our own suffering sympathies, "fill up that which is behind of the sufferings of Christ."

Are we in the succession?

REVEREND J. H. JOWETT IN JESSIE PENN-LEWIS,
THE STORY OF JOB

September 18

Walk in love, as Christ also has loved us and given Himself for us.

Ephesians 5:2

Learning agape love as personified in Christ is the supreme purpose of life on earth. This is the meaning of all that God permits to come to one of His children. God's primary occupation in this age is not regulating the universe by "the mighty power of His command," but it is teaching the members of His bride elect the lessons of agape love in preparation for the throne.

He is doing nothing in the realm of redemption that is not related to this task. Therefore, every single incident—whether of joy or sorrow, bane or blessing, pain or pleasure—without exception, is being utilized by God for the purpose of procuring the members of His bridehood and maturing them in agape love.

There is no love without self-giving. There is no self-giving without pain. Therefore, there is no love without suffering. Suffering is an essential ingredient of agape love and therefore of a moral universe. Even God cannot love without cost. Love that does not accept suffering voluntarily is a misnomer, for the essence of love is decentralization, that is, repudiation of self in behalf of another.

Suffering love is the cornerstone of the universe, because without it there is no decentralization of the self and therefore no agape love. One who has never voluntarily suffered is totally selfish. Only great sufferers are truly benevolent. There is no such thing as a saint who has not suffered.

Paul Billheimer, *Don't Waste Your Sorrows*

SEPTEMBER 19

My peace I give to you; not as the world gives do I give to you.
Let not your heart be troubled, neither let it be afraid.

JOHN 14:27

I do not find that this position, that of unbroken peacefulness and inward song, is one which we can hope to hold unassailed. It is no soft arrangement of pillows, no easy chair. It is a fort in an enemy's country, and the foe is wise in assault and especially in surprise.

And yet there can be nothing to fear, for it is not a place that we must keep but a stronghold in which we are kept, if only, in the moment we are conscious of attack, we look "away unto our faith's Princely leader and perfecter, Jesus, who endured" (Rotherham's rendering of Hebrews 12:2). He who endured can protect and maintain that of which He is Author and Finisher.

The peace of God can keep us steady in the place where we most desire to dwell so that we shall not shadow the lives of those who love us.

If, in the paths of the world,
Stones might have wounded Thy feet,
Toil or dejection have tried
Thy spirit, of that we saw nothing.

Of that we saw nothing—how good if, by His blessed enabling, we should daily so receive His peace that others should see nothing of stone, thorn, toil, dejection but find, when they come, only the gift of a great contentment, the restful peace of God.

AMY CARMICHAEL, *ROSE FROM BRIER*

SEPTEMBER 20

Jesus spoke to them, saying, "Be of good cheer! It is I, do not be afraid."

MATTHEW 14:27

Just now I am reading through the Gospels and marking in the margin every place where suffering is mentioned. It is mentioned very often. The Lord Jesus made it plain from the beginning that there would be trial of many kinds for all who would follow Him, and He Himself led the way in that path. Should we be surprised when we find ourselves following in His footsteps?

There is joy too. He said clearly that sorrow would be turned into joy, joy that would never end. But I think that He wants us all to understand quite definitely that if we follow in the way of the cross, we must be prepared to take up the cross. We must not think of life as a joyride. But there is nothing whatever to be afraid of. "Blessed are they that dwell in thy house: they will be always praising thee" is a shining word for us all.

One thing is sure. He is enough for every difficulty that may arise. He is enough for today's difficulty. Do you sometimes feel like the disciples when they were in the midst of the sea toiling in rowing, for the wind was contrary to them? Then take the lovely words for your comfort: "He cometh unto them and saith unto them, Be of good cheer: it is I; *be not afraid.*"

No matter how much the wind blows, it will be true for us as it was for them, "The wind ceased." So let us be of good cheer and go on our way rejoicing.

AMY CARMICHAEL, *CANDLES IN THE DARK*

SEPTEMBER 21

Let us therefore come boldly to the throne of grace,
that we may obtain mercy and find grace to help in time of need.

HEBREWS 4:16

Why should we fear the attacks of the great adversary of souls so long as the God of all grace is ours? There is no kind of grace we can need which does not reside in Him; yea, grace on grace, so that when one supply is exhausted, there is always more to follow. And the attacks of Satan are, perhaps, permitted that we may be constrained to realize and avail ourselves of the stores of grace which are treasured up in Jesus Christ our Lord. "In him dwelleth all the fullness of the Godhead bodily, and in him ye are made full" (Col. 2:9–10, RV).

How safe and strong then may we be if only we will go again and again to the God of all grace, claiming, with holy boldness, grace to help us in time of need—and believing that it is to us not according to our feeling but our faith! We may not be always conscious of the vast changes which are being gradually effected within us in answer to our faith, but when we approach the bank of some foaming river of difficulty or temptation, our behavior and victory will open the lips of onlookers to exclaim, "Lo, God is here."

Let us give Him glory! Do not hesitate to tell Him what you think of Him. Amid all the hatred and blasphemy and misunderstanding of His foes, let us blend voice and heart in ascribing to Him glory and dominion forever and ever! Let the notes rise higher and higher as life climbs up toward its goal—until they are merged in the ocean of praise, the billows of which smite against His throne, breaking into the spray of a thousand songs! Thus may it be "forever and ever." Amen.

F. B. MEYER, *TRIED BY FIRE: EXPOSITION OF 1 PETER*

SEPTEMBER 22

We know that we are of God, and the whole world lies under the sway of the wicked one.

1 JOHN 5:19

Jesus came "from above." He could claim without fear of challenge, "The prince of this world cometh, and hath nothing in me" (John 14:30). The line of demarcation was drawn not on the ground at His feet but in His own heart. But just as truly, everything in this world that is "from above" is as safe as He is. A life that belongs above is being sustained and provided for down here *by Him.*

"Ye are of God, my little children, and have overcome them: because greater is he that is in you, than he that is in the world" (1 John 4:4). We are of God! Could we possibly discover a more blessed fact to balance against that other ugly fact and to outweigh it? We who believe on Jesus' name "were born, not of blood, nor of the will of the flesh, nor of the will of man, but of God" (John 1:13). And praise Him, because we are begotten of God, the evil one cannot touch us (1 John 5:18).

Put very simply, Satan's power in the world is everywhere. Yet wherever men and women walk in the Spirit, sensitive to the anointing they have from God, that power of his just evaporates. There is a line drawn by God, a boundary where, by virtue of His very presence, Satan's writ does not run. Let God but occupy all the space Himself, and what room is left for the evil one?

WATCHMAN NEE, *LOVE NOT THE WORLD*

September 23

. . . that you may be able to stand against the wiles of the devil.

Ephesians 6:11

How are we to acquit ourselves in the presence of the adversary—His adversary and ours? God's word is "stand"! The Greek verb "stand" with its following preposition "against" in verse 11 [of Ephesians 6] really means "hold your ground." Our task is one of holding, not of attacking. In the person of Jesus Christ, God has already conquered. He has given us His victory to *hold.*

We need not struggle to occupy ground that is already ours. In Christ we *are* conquerors—nay, "more than conquerors" (Rom. 8:37). In Him therefore we *stand.* Thus today we do not fight *for* victory; we fight *from* victory. We do not fight in order to win but because in Christ we have already won. Overcomers are those who rest in the victory already given to them by their God.

Let me ask you: Has defeat been your experience? Have you found yourself hoping that one day you will be strong enough to win? Then my prayer for you can go no further than that of the apostle Paul to his Ephesian readers: it is that God may open your eyes anew to see yourself seated with Him who has Himself been made to sit "far above all rule, and authority, and power, and dominion, and every name that is named" (Eph. 1:21). The difficulties around you may not alter; the lion may roar as loudly as ever; but you need no longer *hope* to overcome. In Christ Jesus you *are* victor in the field.

Watchman Nee, *Sit, Walk, Stand*

SEPTEMBER 24

Your life is hidden with Christ in God.

COLOSSIANS 3:3

God's plans for the victory are perfect. He knows the enemy and the reactions of the enemy—has been aware of them from before the foundation of the world—and He does not need to fear any unexpected attack. He also knows His men. He knows their need for food and clothing. He provides the necessary equipment, and He launches them at the right time and the right place, for He leads them to victory.

Those who fight on our side are greater and stronger than those who stand against us; we have a mighty high priest and legions of angels as well. Jesus came to destroy the works of the devil. At the cross of Calvary, He has already won the victory. There He crushed the head of the serpent. But we need to know *our* position in this battle. The Bible speaks of this position to be hid with Christ in God.

CORRIE TEN BOOM, *MARCHING ORDERS FOR THE END BATTLE*

Mighty, mighty is the Lord;
Mighty is the piercing sword.
Teach us how to use our weapons;
Teach our fingers how to fight.
O unconquerable Captain,
Put the enemy to flight.

AMY CARMICHAEL, *MOUNTAIN BREEZES*

September 25

Take . . . the sword of the Spirit, which is the word of God.

Ephesians 6:17

Do you know how to fight using the Word of God and what to do when the onslaught comes in your private life? Do you know, when heavy oppression comes on your spirit, how to break through it all in spirit by using the truth of God?

Do you understand how to wield the victory texts, such as, "The Son of God was manifested, that he might destroy the works of the devil"; "Through death he might destroy him that had the power of death, that is, the devil"; and, "They overcame him by the blood of the Lamb, and by the word of their testimony; and they loved not their lives even unto death"? Begin then with your texts, and use them until your spirit is free and rejoicing in victory, and you see the conquest of Christ over the foe.

You can live in the darkest place and still live in the light of the Sun of Righteousness. There is *a sphere above the sphere of darkness*, and that is your right place!

When you pray, "Oh, that thou wouldst rend the heavens, and come down," you are asking God to break through the thick and misty air, and by prayer you are making way for Him. He wants a link below. He can rend the heavens; He can rend this thick, misty air in answer to our prayers and come down in melting power among His people.

Jessie Penn-Lewis, *Life in the Spirit*

September 26

They overcame him by the blood of the Lamb and by the word of their testimony.

Revelation 12:11

Let us answer Satan always and only by the blood. It is our wholly sufficient defense.

The precious blood of Christ is our defense; the word of our testimony is our weapon of attack. By this is meant our testimony to man but not to man alone. The victory of Christ, the fact that He reigns, that His kingdom is near, that we have been translated from Satan's kingdom into His—all these are facts to be declared not to men only but to the powers of darkness.

Affirm that God is King, that His Son is Victor, that Satan is defeated, that the kingdoms of this world are shortly to become the kingdom of our God and of His Christ. These are positive divine facts, and they are our shafts of offense. Satan fears such declarations of spiritual fact, for the word of our testimony can move back the gates of hell. Declare that Jesus is Lord, that His name is above every name. Declare it! *Say* it to the enemy. Many a time such testimony brings more results than does prayer.

Watchman Nee, *What Shall This Man Do?*

September 27

The name of the Lord is a strong tower.

Proverbs 18:10

Throughout the Scriptures a name is not simply, as with us, a label; it is a revelation of character. In the history of the early church, "the Name" was a kind of summary of all that Jesus had revealed of the nature and the heart of God. "For the sake of the Name they went forth" (3 John 1:7). There was no need to specify whose name it was—there was none other name by which men could be saved, none other name that could be compared with that or mentioned on the same page.

For a man to speak in the name of England means that England speaks through his lips, that the might of England is ready to enforce his demands. Thus when Jesus bids us ask what we will in His name, He means not that we should simply use that name as an incantation or formula but that we should be so one with Him in His interests, purposes, and aims that it should be as though He were Himself approaching the Father with the petitions we bear.

There is much for us to learn concerning this close identification with God before we shall be able to say, with David, "I come to thee in the name of the Lord of hosts." It is only possible to those who carefully fulfill certain conditions. But it were well worth our while to withdraw ourselves from the activities of our life, to lay aside everything that might hinder the closeness of our union with the divine nature and interests, and to become so absolutely identified with God that His name might be our strong tower, our refuge, our battle cry, our secret of victory.

F. B. Meyer, *David*

SEPTEMBER 28

The LORD your God Himself fights for you.

DEUTERONOMY 3:22

The story is told that in the French Wars our soldiers were very dispirited on the eve of a great battle, owing to the disparity in the number of the English troops. Gathered around a campfire as night fell, a few men were pessimistically discussing the situation; every now and then another and another joined the group, unrecognized in the darkness, but all seemed to agree on the hopelessness of the morrow's fight: they were so heavily outnumbered—their own so few, the enemy's so many.

When out spoke a new voice in the discussion, a voice of one who had come unnoticed in the shadows of the firelight—a voice so well known to them all, a voice whose ringing tones called them instantly out of their despair, a voice that posed one strategic question: "And how many do you count me for?" It was the Iron Duke himself, the great Duke of Wellington, who led them that next morning, in spite of the French big majority, to a brilliant victory.

How much, how many, do you count your Leader for? If you are even standing alone for Him in the fight—in your office, in your workshop, in your factory, in your school, in your company, in your home—remember the blessed truth that "one, with God, is always a majority." Even if there be but two of you, and that surrounded by belligerent forces, 2 Kings 6:16 remains true: "Do not fear, for those who are with us are more than those who are with them." Such, O ye Philippians, O ye my readers, is the Leader under whom this fight of faith is waged to victory.

GUY KING, *PHILIPPIANS: JOY WAY*

September 29

*Put on the whole armor of God. . . . For we . . . wrestle against . . .
the rulers of the darkness of this age.*

Ephesians 6:11–12

The Christian is not only a servant but a soldier; he belongs not only to a home but to a citadel. And to recollect the formidable surroundings is of course vitally necessary if the life lived amid them is not to be swept away in ruin.

If these revelations of an invisible host around us, bent upon our calamity, do nothing else for us, they may at least render the inestimable service of driving us home, as for our very life, to personal dealings with our personal Deliverer. He can indeed face for us the dreadful personalities marshaled in the shadows that surround our life.

To Him the apostle bids us come. For is it not to Him? Reduced to its essence, the "armor" means *Jesus Christ.* The soldier, in other words, is made strong for a victory which is otherwise impossible—by his relation to his Lord. He is safe, he is successful, because he is spiritually right with Christ in God-given truth and righteousness; because he is sure of Christ beneath his feet as "the equipment of the gospel of peace" for his own soul; because he finds Christ the mighty buckler against the fiery volley when he uses Him in faith; because he "covers his head in the day of battle" with Christ as his assured salvation; because Christ speaks through the Word of God and so makes Himself His servant's sword to cut the accuser down; because prayer in the Spirit grasps Him and holds Him fast.

Yes, here, to the last hour of our conflict and our siege, and here only lies our victory. It is *He,* not it. It is the all-sufficient Lord, "objected to the fiend," while the believer stands safe behind Him.

H. C. G. Moule, *Ephesian Studies*

SEPTEMBER 30

To me, to live is Christ, and to die is gain.

PHILIPPIANS 1:21

Bwana [C. T. Studd] came to prayers that night in Ibambi greatly burdened about the condition of things and feeling that somehow there must come an explosion of spiritual dynamite which would clean out hindrances and leave room for the Spirit to work.

There were some eight missionaries gathered with him. They were reading together his favorite chapter on the heroes of faith in Hebrews 11. What was the spirit which caused these mortals so to triumph and to die? The Holy Spirit of God—one of whose chief characteristics is a pluck, a bravery, a lust for sacrifice for God and a joy in it which crucifies all human weakness and the natural desires of the flesh.

The talk turned to the Great War and the heroism of the British Tommy, who went "over the top" at the word of command and did it knowing all the odds were against his coming back alive. But how describe this spirit? The question was asked of some who had been soldiers, and one replied, "Well, that Tommy doesn't care what happens to him so long as he does his duty by his king, his country, his regiment, and himself."

Those words were the spark needed. Bwana arose, raised his arm, and said, "That is what we need, and that is what I want! Oh, Lord, henceforth I won't care what happens to me, life or death, aye, or hell, so long as my Lord Jesus Christ is glorified." One after another, all who were present rose and made the same vow.

It was a new company that left the hut that night. There was a sparkle in their eyes, a joy and a love unspeakable, for each had become a soldier, a devotee to death for the glory of King Jesus his Savior, who Himself had died for him. The joy of battle possessed them, that joy that Peter described as "unspeakable."

NORMAN GRUBB, *C. T. STUDD: CRICKETER AND PIONEER*

October

Prayer and Revival in the Body of Christ

The Testimony of Samuel Chadwick

Samuel Chadwick was born in the industrial north of England in 1860. His father worked long hours in the cotton mill, and when he was only eight, Samuel went to work there too as a means of supporting the impoverished family.

Devout Methodists, they attended chapel three times on Sunday, and as a young boy, Chadwick gave his heart to Christ. Listening to God's Word week by week, he often felt the inner call to serve Christ. It seemed impossible, as he was poor and uneducated, but in faith he made preparations. After a twelve-hour factory shift, he would rush home for five hours of prayer and study.

At the age of twenty-one, he was appointed lay pastor of a chapel at Stacksteads, Lancashire. It was no dream appointment; the congregation was self-satisfied. Yet Chadwick threw himself in with great optimism. He had been trained to prepare well-researched and interesting sermons as the sure way to bring in the crowds. He recalled later, "This led unconsciously to a false aim in my work. I lived and labored for my sermons and was unfortunately more concerned about their excellence and reputation than the repentance of the people."

Soon, however, his sermons were exhausted, and nothing had changed. Staring defeat in the face and sensing his lack of real power, he felt an intense hunger kindled within him for more of God. At this point he heard the testimony of someone who had been revitalized by an experience of the Holy Spirit, so with a few friends he covenanted to pray and search the Scriptures until God sent revival.

One evening, as he was praying over his next sermon, a powerful sense of conviction settled on him. His pride, blindness, and reliance on human methods paraded before his eyes as God humbled him to the dust. Well into the night he wrestled and repented; then he got out his pile of precious sermons and set fire to them! The result was immediate: the Holy Spirit fell upon him. In his own words: "I could not explain what had happened, but it was a bigger thing than I had ever known. There came into my soul a deep peace, a thrilling joy, and a new sense of power. My mind was quickened. I felt I had received a new faculty of understanding. Every power was vitalized. My body was quickened. There was a new sense of spring and vitality, a new power of endurance, and a strong man's exhilaration in big things."

The tide turned. At his next sermon seven souls were converted ("one for each of my barren years"), and he called the whole congregation to a week of prayer. The following weekend most of the church was baptized in the Holy Spirit, and revival began to spread through the valleys. In the space of a few months, hundreds were converted to Jesus, among them some of the most notorious sinners in the area.

In his famous book *The Way to Pentecost*, which was being printed when he died in 1932, we read, "I owe everything to the gift of Pentecost. For fifty days the facts of the gospel were complete, but no conversions were recorded. Pentecost registered three thousand souls. It is by fire that a holy passion is kindled in the soul whereby we live the life of God. The soul's safety is in its heat. Truth without enthusiasm, morality without emotion, ritual without soul make for a church without power."

> Destitute of the fire of God, nothing else counts;
> Possessing fire, nothing else matters.
>
> SAMUEL CHADWICK, *THE PATH OF PRAYER*

October 1

Men ought always to pray and not lose heart.

Luke 18:1

There is no way to learn to pray but by praying. No reasoned philosophy of prayer ever taught a soul to pray. The subject is beset with problems, but there are no problems of prayer to the man who prays! They are all met in the fact of answered prayer and the joy of fellowship with God. We know not what we should pray for as we ought, and if prayer waits for understanding, it will never begin. We live by faith. We walk by faith. Edison wrote in 1921:

> We don't know the millionth part of 1 percent about anything. We don't know what water is. We don't know what light is. We don't know what gravitation is. We don't know what enables us to keep on our feet when we stand up. We don't know what electricity is. We don't know what heat is. We don't know anything about magnetism. We have a lot of hypotheses about these things, but that is all. But we do not let our ignorance about all these things deprive us of their use.

We discover by using. We learn by practice. Though a man should have all knowledge about prayer and though he understand all mysteries about prayer, unless he prays, he will never learn to pray.

Samuel Chadwick, *The Path of Prayer*

OCTOBER 2

Do you not know that those who run in a race all run, but one receives the prize? Run in such a way that you may obtain it.

1 CORINTHIANS 9:24

Learning to pray is no light undertaking. If prayer is the greatest achievement on earth, we may be sure it will call for a discipline that corresponds to its power. The school of prayer has its conditions and demands. It is a forbidden place to all but those of set purpose and resolute heart. Strong men often break down under the strain of study. Concentration here is a heavier task than handling a hammer or guiding a plow. The discipline curbs freedom and drills the mind to attention. Understanding is more taxing than doing, and meditation is a severer tax than service.

The reason so many people do not pray is because of its cost. The cost is not so much in the sweat of agonizing supplication as in the daily fidelity to the life of prayer. It is the acid test of devotion. Nothing in the life of faith is so difficult to maintain.

There are those who resent the association of discipline and intensity with prayer. They do not pray like that, and certainly they would not like their children to entreat and plead for anything they wanted with "strong crying and tears." This aversion to tears is quite understandable—but then no one suspects them of praying like that, and the analogy of their children may not be the whole truth. Nothing can be further from the truth than a false analogy. The school of prayer is for those who really want to learn to pray.

SAMUEL CHADWICK, *THE PATH OF PRAYER*

October 3

Because of his persistence he will rise and give him as many as he needs.

Luke 11:8

Prayer is, in its essence—when it is inspired by faith—an openness toward God, a receptiveness, a faculty of apprehending with open hand what He would impart. Standing upon God's promises, the suppliant cries to the heavens to drop down their blessings—while heart and hands and mouth are open wide to be filled with good.

Prayer is measured not by length but by strength. The divine gauge of the worth of prayer is its pressure on the heart of God. The lock of prayer sometimes turns hard and calls for strength of purpose. The kingdom of heaven has to be taken by force. There is such a thing as laboring and striving in prayer. Thus Jesus prayed in the garden, and Daniel in Babylon, and Epaphras in Paul's hired house. Such were the prayers offered of old in the catacombs as the torchlight flickered; in alpine caves where Waldenses cowered; on hillsides where the Covenanters sheltered under the cliffs.

Let us pray so that our prayers may reverberate with repeated blows on the gates of God's presence chamber—"Praying always with all prayer and supplication in the Spirit, and watching thereunto with all perseverance and supplication for all saints" (Eph. 6:18). Let us pray remembering that everything depends on the gracious promise of God but as if the answer depended on the strength and tenacity of our entreaty.

F. B. Meyer, *Christ in Isaiah*

OCTOBER 4

You have kept what You promised Your servant.

2 CHRONICLES 6:15

God's promises are given not to restrain but to incite to prayer. They show the direction in which we may ask and the extent to which we may expect an answer. They are the mold into which we may pour our fervid spirits without fear. They are the signed check, made payable to order, which we must endorse and present for payment.

Though the Bible be crowded with golden promises from cover to cover, yet will they be inoperative until we turn them into prayer. It is not our province to argue the reasonableness of this; it is enough to accentuate and enforce it. Why should it not be sufficient to silence all questions by saying that we have here reached one of the primal laws of the spiritual world as simple, as certain, as universal as any in the world of nature?

As we know more of God through His promises, we are stayed from asking what He cannot give and are led to set our hearts on things which lie on His open palm waiting to be taken by the hand of an appropriating faith. This is why all prayer, like Elijah's, should be based on promise. We stand on an immovable foundation and have a ready avenue of influence with God when we can put our finger on His own promise and say, "Do, as thou hast said."

F. B. MEYER, *ELIJAH*

October 5

I know the thoughts that I think toward you, says the Lord, thoughts of peace and not of evil, to give you a future and a hope.

Jeremiah 29:11

Rotherham understands God's thoughts to mean His plans: "*I know the plans which I am planning for you.*" Thoughts of peace for our prayers: for our intercessions for others which seem to be ineffective; a future and a hope for the prayers that we feared were covered by the snow; and for those others that appeared to fall to earth like the falling stars that break and scatter into nothingness as we watch them—even those prayers are folded up in the thoughts of peace that He thinks toward us.

These words are for us. We may take them though they were spoken to another people in another age. All the green fields of the Scriptures are for all the sheep of His pasture; none are fenced off from us. Our Lord and Savior, that great Shepherd of the sheep, Himself led the way into these fields, as a study of His use of the Old Testament shows. His servants, the writers of the New Testament, followed Him there, and so may we. The words of the Lord about His thoughts of peace are for us as well as for His ancient people Israel.

The pledged word of God to man is no puffball to break at a touch and scatter into dust. It is iron. It is gold, that most malleable of all metals. It is more golden than gold. It abideth imperishable forever. If we wait till we have clear enough vision to see the expected end before we stay our mind upon Him who is our strength, we shall miss an opportunity that will never come again: we shall never know the blessing of the unoffended. Now is the time to say, "My heart is fixed, O God, my heart is fixed: I will sing and give praise."

Amy Carmichael, *Gold by Moonlight*

OCTOBER 6

Whatever we ask we receive from Him, because we keep His commandments and do those things that are pleasing in His sight.

1 JOHN 3:22

That [the statement that God will give us whatever we ask] is a sweeping assertion, but nevertheless, let us be quite confident that the *receiving* is all right if the *asking* is all right. Let us mark at this point that there is a stage of spiritual development in the experience of the true Spirit-guided intercessor in which he may be sure that his prayers shall be answered.

It is a truism that God always keeps His promises; we may put our finger—indeed our whole being—on it and rest upon His fidelity to His pledged word. But wait! Before you are in a position to do that, you must remember that almost, if not quite, without exception, the promises of God are not unconditional, and their fulfillment is dependent upon such conditions.

Promise and proviso go in pairs—if we keep the second, He will keep the first. There are several conditions attaching to God's gracious undertaking to answer our petitions. What is perhaps the chiefest of them is the one that is enunciated here—the all-important "because"! It all depends upon our attitude toward Him: an obedient conduct and a pleasing behavior. A prayer that is acceptable and answered is dependent not on diligence or on eloquence but, quite simply, on obedience.

GUY KING, *I JOHN: THE FELLOWSHIP*

OCTOBER 7

Whatever you ask the Father in My name He will give you.

JOHN 16:23

Prayer is the present exercising of my will in God's favor—declaring that His will shall be done. For this is true prayer: what God makes known, we express. Man wills something that God has already willed and gives it utterance. The will of God is the starting point; we voice it; God does it. And if we do not voice it, it will not be done.

Our prayers thus lay down the track on which God's power can come. Like some mighty locomotive, His power is irresistible, but it cannot reach us without rails. When men cease to pray, God ceases to work, for without their prayer He will do nothing. It is they who direct heaven's power to the place of need.

"What things soever"—these are precious words. There is always more power in heaven than the measure of our asking. The children of God today are taken up with far too small things, whereas their prayer is intended for the release of heaven's mighty acts. Prayer for myself or my own immediate concerns must lead on to prayer for the kingdom.

The church is to be heaven's outlet, the channel of release for heaven's power, the medium of accomplishment of God's purpose. How is God to get this? Only by every one of us remembering, in the solemn conditions of today, that this ministry of being God's outlet is our greatest possible work. God shows what He wants, we stand and ask, and God acts from heaven. This is true prayer.

WATCHMAN NEE, *WHAT SHALL THIS MAN DO?*

October 8

Shall God not avenge His own elect who cry out day and night to Him?

Luke 18:7

The parables of the friend at midnight and the unjust judge are not like Jesus' other parables, for they teach by contrast and not by comparison. God is not like the reluctant friend or the unjust judge. Then why tell the stories? The point in common between them and prayer is that in both, *importunity prevails.* But if God be Father, knowing what we need, waiting to be asked, why should there be supplication and pleading?

There is a grip and grappling that calls for vigilance and concentration. It is quite clear that prayer is not the easy thing that seems to be implied in the simplicity of asking our heavenly Father for what we want and getting it. There is travail in it. There is work in it. There is entreaty in it. There is importunity in it. Maybe Coleridge was not far wrong when he spoke of prayer as the highest energy of which the human heart is capable and the greatest achievement of the Christian's warfare on earth.

Intensity is a law of prayer. God is found by those who seek Him with all their heart. Wrestling prayer prevails. The fervent effectual prayer of the righteous is of great force.

We must never try to work up an emotion of intensity. Avoid all that is mechanical and perfunctory. Shun the casual and flippant. When alone with God, be alone with Him. Begin in silence. Speak with simplicity. Listen in meekness. Never leave without a conscious season of real communion. We have not to persuade God, but He has to discipline and prepare us. In all moods and at all seasons, pour out the soul in prayer and supplication with thanksgiving, and if the Spirit groans in intercession, do not be afraid of the agony of prayer. There are blessings of the kingdom that are only yielded to the violence of the vehement soul.

Samuel Chadwick, *The Path of Prayer*

October 9

When you pray, say: . . . Your will be done on earth as it is in heaven.

Luke 11:2

The effectiveness of prayer does not depend so much on quantity as on quality. One condition of prevailing prayer is asking according to the revealed will of God. This plainly implies asking not only for such things as God is willing to grant but also asking in such a state of mind as God can accept. I fear it is common for professed Christians to overlook the state of mind which God requires as a condition of answering their prayers.

In the petition "Thy will be done on earth as it is in heaven," it is plain that sincerity is a condition of prevailing with God. But *sincerity* implies a state of mind that accepts the whole revealed will of God, so far as we understand it, as they accept it in heaven. It implies a loving, confiding, universal obedience to the whole *known* will of God, whether that will is revealed in His Word, by His Spirit, or in His providence. It implies that we hold ourselves and all that we have and are as absolutely and cordially at God's disposal as do the inhabitants of heaven. If we fall short of this and withhold anything whatsoever, we "regard iniquity in our hearts," and God will not hear us.

What is true of offering this petition is true of *all* prayer. Do Christians lay this to heart? Do they consider that all professed prayer is an abomination if it is not offered in a state of entire consecration to God? If we do not offer ourselves with and in our prayers, our prayer is an abomination.

Who that has witnessed real revivals of religion has not been struck with the change that comes over the whole spirit and manner of the prayers of really revived Christians?

Charles Finney, *Power from On High*

October 10

If My people who are called by My name will humble themselves, and pray and seek My face, and turn from their wicked ways, then will I hear, . . . forgive . . . and heal.

2 Chronicles 7:14

If God has foreseen and predicted a tendency on the part of the church in the latter days to decline in faith and devotion, He has not forewarned us of it that we may apathetically await its fulfillment but that we may be forearmed and strive together to avert it. There is no more effective way of achieving this than by preparing our hearts and pleading with God for genuine revival. There is nothing more calculated to arrest the downward spiritual trend and set a lukewarm church on fire than a mighty awakening of the Holy Spirit.

God's dealings with Israel, "written for our admonition" (1 Cor. 10:11), both illustrate and confirm the argument. When spiritual decay set in with the death of Solomon and the division of the kingdom, God constantly warned His people of the consequences of departure and predicted coming judgment, which was ultimately fulfilled.

We find nevertheless that the history of decline is punctuated by some outstanding spiritual revivals through godly kings and fearless prophets who turned the people back to God. These men did not argue, as some Christians do today, that departure and judgment were prophesied and could not be averted and that therefore a widespread turning to God was not to be contemplated. God had not revoked His promises. He was still the God of revival, if they would fulfill the conditions.

Arthur Wallis, *In the Day of Thy Power*

October 11

"Because your heart was tender, and you humbled yourself before God . . . , I also have heard you," says the Lord.

2 Chronicles 34:27

There are indeed now ever-expanding beachheads of revival in many hearts, in many fellowships, and in various lands. It is for those in whose hearts Jesus has established such beachheads to hold fast the vision and to know that God's establishment of such beachheads is surely but the prelude for His invasion in mighty and wide-ranging power into our situations of need.

If God is to bless you, you must have a deep hunger of heart. You must be possessed with a dissatisfaction of the state of the church in general and of yourself in particular. You must be willing for God to begin His work in you first rather than in the other man. You must moreover be possessed with the holy expectancy that God can and will meet your need.

If you are in any sense a Christian leader, the urgency of the matter is intensified many times over. Your willingness to admit your need and be blessed will determine the degree to which God can bless the people to whom you minister. Above all, you must realize that you must be the first to humble yourself at the cross. If a new honesty with regard to sin is needed among your people, you must begin with yourself. It was when the king of Nineveh arose from his throne, covered himself with sackcloth, and sat in ashes as a sign of his repentance that his people repented.

Let not, however, those readers who are not leaders be tempted to look at those who are and wait for them. God wants to begin with each one of us. He wants to begin with *you*.

Roy Hession, *The Calvary Road*

October 12

I pray, Lord God of heaven . . . that You may hear the prayer of Your servant.

Nehemiah 1:5–6

When Nehemiah commenced to seek God, he may have had little idea how his prayers were to be answered and the situation recovered. Of one thing he could be certain: God would be faithful to His promises.

But as he continued to press his case in the courts of heaven, there was borne in upon him by the Spirit the conviction that he himself was to be the instrument in the fulfillment of his own prayers and that God had given him this place of influence in the Persian palace that he might use it for the good of Jerusalem. A new note comes into his praying: "Prosper, I pray thee, thy servant this day, and grant him mercy in the sight of this man" (Neh. 1:11).

An intercessor cannot expect to prevail unless willing to be the instrument, if God should require it, in the fulfillment of the prayer. Let all who would intercede for revival face up to the possible implications of their praying. Many a cherished ambition may be shattered. Many a smooth pathway of ease and safety may have to be exchanged for a thorny track, encompassed with dangers, afflictions, and reproaches.

Do not pray for the outpouring of the Spirit unless, like Nehemiah, you mean to go through with God. Perhaps if some knew what was involved, they would be imploring God *not* to send revival. "But the people that know their God [and can therefore trust Him] shall be strong, and do exploits" (Dan. 11:32).

Arthur Wallis, *In the Day of Thy Power*

OCTOBER 13

Repent, . . . and you shall receive the gift of the Holy Spirit. For the promise is to . . . as many as the Lord our God will call.

ACTS 2:38–39

Rees's return to Wales was in a strategic year. It was in 1904, the time of the great revival, and his own recent experience just fitted him to take part in it. "In a short while the whole of the country was aflame," he said. "Every church was stirred to its depths. Strong men were in tears of penitence, and women moved with a new fervor. People were overpowered by the Spirit as on the Day of Pentecost and were counted as drunken men. In the services they were praying, singing, and testifying. It was a church revival, turning Christians everywhere into witnesses: 'Certainly we cannot but speak the things which we have seen and heard.'"

The presence and power of the Holy Ghost in the church has always been a fact recognized by true believers, so it was not so much a case of asking Him to come as acknowledging His presence and very soon realizing His power. But often they had first to pray out the hindrances to blessing; disobedience and unforgiving hearts were two sins that were constantly dealt with. On the other hand, obedience to the promptings of the Spirit and open confession of Christ brought down the blessing.

The revival proved what the Holy Ghost could do through a company of believers who were of one spirit and of one mind as on the Day of Pentecost. The church had seen over and over again what the Lord could do through a yielded evangelist or pastor, such as Moody or Finney, but in the Welsh revival it was a divine power manifested through the church. The keynote was "Bend the church, and save the world."

NORMAN GRUBB, *REES HOWELLS: INTERCESSOR*

October 14

. . . that you also may have fellowship with us;
and truly our fellowship is with the Father and with His Son Jesus Christ.

1 John 1:3

There is something so joyous about real love! Those who had been in physical contact with the Lord had been drawn together and bound together in a bond of mutual love. Like the spokes of a wheel, being so close to the axle, they were thus near to one another.

It was this quality in the relationship between these early believers that so impressed the onlookers in that rather hard world: "See how these Christians love one another!" Oh, that in place of bickering and backbiting the church at large were to receive a new baptism of love as in the first days of power. The world would still be impressed by such a practical evidence of the reality and joy of our fellowship.

Higher and happier still is the love of divine fellowship. How amazing it is that we receive a welcome into fellowship with Him—the atom consorting with the Almighty; the Holy One and the unholy conversing together through the appointed media of Bible and prayer. Such godly friendship has always been open to those who, whatever their circumstances, have been willing to pay the price of utter fidelity to Him.

These two fellowships hang together—the one with Him cementing the other; the one with them reflecting the other. God sets great store by the fellowship and warns us against doing any hurt or harm to it—a Christian, a church member, failing in love toward a fellow believer, acting or speaking in an unloving way. That is a very serious thing, for it is not only the victim that we hurt but the Lord Himself, who died for us both.

Guy King, *I John: The Fellowship*

OCTOBER 15

Without ceasing I remember you in my prayers day and night.

2 TIMOTHY 1:3

If only we could come to a practical realization of the fact that we cannot do anything greater for one another than to pray! Paul is so thankful to God that in spite of everything, it still remains possible for him to help his young protégé by praying for him "without ceasing."

It is good to notice, in passing, that to "pray without ceasing" was the very thing he told his converts to do (1 Thess. 5:17). So here is a preacher who practices what he preaches. All too many of us, alas, are somewhat like the scribes and Pharisees of Matthew 23:3 in that we "say, and do not do."

To do anything, even to pray, "without ceasing"—with the exception of breathing—seems an impossibility, but an old papyrus letter dug up from ancient Eastern sands helps us to get the meaning. These excavations have, through an inspired discovery of the late Professor Deissmann, thrown a flood of light upon the nature and meaning of the New Testament Greek. In one such, the writer complains of an "incessant cough"—meaning, of course, not that the poor man barked without stopping but with constant recurrence. It is the same word as Paul uses and which indicates not that he is continually at it without interruption but that he is constantly at it whenever he gets the chance.

GUY KING, *II TIMOTHY: TO MY SON*

OCTOBER 16

In everything by prayer and supplication, with thanksgiving, let your requests be made known to God.

PHILIPPIANS 4:6

What a persistent practitioner of prayer Paul was. Over and over again does he touch upon the subject of prayer. He frequently tells us of his own habit of intercession and occasionally includes in his letters some of the very petitions that he offered on behalf of his friends and of his children in the faith.

Of course there are some who will say that prayer can take no real part in affairs at all: it may be a comfort to the one who prays; it may even have a beneficent influence on his character; but it can have no outside, objective effect on the circumstance or the person for whom he prays. And this they would say for a very simple and conclusive reason—that the universe is governed by laws, and no prayer can alter them.

Our answer is that of course the universe is ruled by laws, and it is by a combination of laws that things happen, but, but, but—prayer itself is one of the laws! The history of such an institution as Dr. Müller's orphanage is an imperishable textbook on that theme; and so is the story of the China Inland Mission; and so is the testimony of a myriad Christians who have, in personal experience, proved the truth and force of the law of intercession when the proper conditions are observed.

Oh, how much opposition might be overcome, how much backsliding might be nipped in the bud, how much Christian progress might be furthered, how much earnest service might be prospered—if only we would pray, and keep on praying, for the persons concerned.

GUY KING, *I TIMOTHY: A LEADER LED*

October 17

Above all things have fervent love for one another,
for "love will cover a multitude of sins."

1 Peter 4:8

Most controversies in local congregations are produced not primarily by differences over essentials but by unsanctified human ambitions, jealousy, and personality clashes. The real root of many such situations is spiritual dearth in individual believers, revealing lamentable immaturity in love. Therefore, the local congregation is one of the very best laboratories in which individual believers may discover their real spiritual emptiness and begin to grow in agape love.

This is done by true repentance, humbly confessing the sins of jealousy, envy, resentment, etc. and begging forgiveness from one another. This approach will result in real growth in *the love that covers.* It will release the Holy Spirit to heal wounds and quicken revival fires.

This is why the apostle Paul exhorts the Ephesian church to "keep the unity of the Spirit in the bond of peace," noting that there is "one body, one Spirit, . . . one Lord, one faith, one baptism, one God and Father of all, who is . . . in you all" (Eph. 4:3–6). Therefore, nothing short of heresy or open sin, which affects relationship with the Father, should be permitted to bring schism in the professed body of Christ.

Paul Billheimer, *Love Covers*

October 18

Break up your fallow ground.

Hosea 10:12

What is fallow ground? It is simply ground which has in the past yielded fruit but has now become largely unproductive through lack of cultivation—land that is lying idle. Seed may be sown upon it in abundance, the heavens might pour out a copious rain—but what would be the good of either so long as the ground is in this uncultivated state? As we look out upon the state of the church today, as we look within at the condition of our own hearts, we cannot but admit the accuracy of Hosea's figure. Vast tracts of fallow ground in the hearts of professing Christians surely constitute the greatest barrier to the rain of revival.

In this state believers may diligently attend the ministry of God's Word, the heart may be sown continually with the incorruptible seed, but there is no fruit unto holiness; for like the wayside ground in the parable, the seed lies upon the surface and is quickly devoured by the agents of the evil one (Matt. 13:4). Perhaps this is the main reason why there appears to be so little effectual result from so much ministry of the Word.

It is time to cease excusing our sins by calling them shortcomings or natural weakness or by attributing them to temperament or environment. We must face our sins honestly in the light of God's Word, view them as He does, and deal with them as before Him.

The fruit that God expects the believer to bring forth is not religious activity or even zealous Christian service so much as Christlike character as set forth in Galatians: "The fruit of the Spirit is love, joy, peace, longsuffering, kindness, goodness, faithfulness, meekness, self-control" (Gal. 5:22, RV, margin).

Arthur Wallis, *In the Day of Thy Power*

OCTOBER 19

The sacrifices of God are a broken spirit, a broken and a contrite heart—these, O God, You will not despise.

PSALM 51:17

Here is the first great condition of revival—that brokenness of heart that is sensitive to the least touch of the Spirit and that has only to know the will of God to do it. One may cross fallow ground and not see where the feet have trod—no impression has been made. But when the plough and the harrow have done their work and the soil is soft and brittle, then the print of the foot is clearly seen.

When our hearts are sensitive, responsive, and impressionable to the movements of God across our lives, we may be sure that the fallow ground is broken. My reader, have you come to this point? Are you willing for God to bring you there? If so, the first step is with you. There must be, in the words of saintly Robert Chapman, "a looking back and a dealing afresh with God respecting past iniquities." This is the way to a humble and contrite heart.

Having faced what is implied in this command to break up the fallow ground, let us nevertheless remember that ploughing is not reaping, that breaking up the fallow ground is not the coming of the showers, that repentance is not revival. The one is but the pathway to the other.

ARTHUR WALLIS, *IN THE DAY OF THY POWER*

October 20

He said to me, "Son of man, can these bones live?" . . . Breath came into them, and they lived, and stood upon their feet, an exceedingly great army.

Ezekiel 37:3–10

The outward forms of revivals differ considerably, but the inward and permanent content of them all is always the same: a new experience of conviction of sin among the saints; a new vision of the cross of Jesus and of redemption; a new willingness on man's part for brokenness, repentance, confession, and restitution; a joyful experience of the power of the blood of Jesus to cleanse fully from sin and to restore and heal all that sin has lost and broken; a new entering into the fullness of the Holy Spirit and of His power to do His own work through His people; and a new gathering in of the lost ones to Jesus.

Revival is not a green valley getting greener but a valley of dry bones being made to live again and stand up "an exceeding great army" (Ezek. 37). It is not good Christians becoming better Christians—as God sees us, there are not any good Christians—but rather Christians honestly confessing that their Christian life is a valley of dry bones and by that very confession qualifying for the grace that flows from the cross and makes all things new.

Roy Hession, *The Calvary Road*

OCTOBER 21

The water that I shall give him will become in him a fountain of water springing up into everlasting life.

JOHN 4:14

If we were asked this moment if we were filled with the Holy Spirit, how many of us would dare to answer yes? Revival is when we can say yes at any moment of the day. It is not egotistic to say so, for filling to overflowing is utterly and completely God's work—it is all of grace. All we have to do is to present our empty, broken self and let Him fill and keep filled.

Andrew Murray says, "Just as water ever seeks and fills the lowest place, so the moment God finds you abased and empty, His glory and power flow in." The picture that has made things simple and clear to so many of us is that of the human heart as a cup which we hold out to Jesus, longing that He might fill it with the Water of Life. Jesus is pictured as bearing the golden water pot with the Water of Life. As He passes by, He looks into our cup, and if it is clean, He fills it to overflowing. And as Jesus is always passing by, the cup can be always running over. That is something of what David meant when he said, "My cup runneth over."

This is revival—the constant peace of God ruling in our hearts, because we are full to overflowing ourselves, and sharing it with others. People imagine that dying to self makes one miserable. But it is just the opposite. It is the refusal to die to self that makes one miserable. The more we know of death with Him, the more we shall know of His life in us and so the more of real peace and joy.

ROY HESSION, *THE CALVARY ROAD*

October 22

Humble yourselves in the sight of the Lord.

James 4:10

We want to be very simple in this matter of revival. Revival is just the life of the Lord Jesus poured into human hearts. Jesus is always victorious. In heaven they are praising Him all the time for His victory. Whatever may be our experience of failure and barrenness, He is never defeated. His power is boundless. And we, on our part, have only to get into a right relationship with Him, and we shall see His power being demonstrated in our hearts and lives and service, and His victorious life will fill us and overflow through us to others.

If, however, we are to come into this right relationship with Him, the first thing we must learn is that our wills must be broken to His will. To be broken is the beginning of revival. The Lord Jesus cannot live in us fully and reveal Himself through us until the proud self within us is broken.

Being broken is both God's work and ours. He brings His pressure to bear, but we have to make the choice. If we are really open to conviction as we seek fellowship with God, God will show us the expressions of this proud, hard self that cause Him pain. This can be very costly.

For this reason we are not likely to be broken except at the cross of Jesus. The willingness of Jesus to be broken for us is the all-compelling motive in our being broken too. We see Him who is in the form of God counting not equality with God a prize to be grasped at and hung on to but letting it go for us and taking upon Himself the form of a servant.

Only the vision of the Love that was willing to be broken for us can constrain us to be willing for that.

Roy Hession, *The Calvary Road*

OCTOBER 23

None of these things move me; nor do I count my life dear to myself, so that I may finish my race with joy, and the ministry which I received from the Lord Jesus.

ACTS 20:24

Everywhere we see evidence of the bitter enmity which Satan bears to the Son who gave His blood for the life of the world. This age, blinded by its god, has not revoked the tragic decree, "We will not that this man reign over us" (Luke 19:14); nor has it ceased to ask, whether in fear or in scorn, the question, "What have we to do with thee, thou Jesus of Nazareth?" (Mark 1:24).

Nevertheless, the promise still stands: "He shall see of the travail of his soul, and shall be satisfied" (Isa. 53:11). In that word "satisfied" there are depths eternal and consolations that outweigh even the agonies of Gethsemane and Golgotha. This was "the joy that was set before him" when He "endured the cross, despising the shame" (Heb. 12:2).

Nearly two millennia have passed, and still He waits. Is it not strange that many who profess so much seem to care so little? Where are those with Paul's passion for the glory of Christ who can say with that apostle, "I hold not my life of any account, as dear unto myself, so that I may accomplish my course . . . to testify the gospel of the grace of God" (Acts 20:24)? Where are those with an intense longing that the Savior may be satisfied with the fruit of His suffering?

You may expect to find them praying for revival, for that is a time when multitudes bow the knee before Him and clamor to confess Him Lord. It is a precious foretaste of that final harvest when "a great multitude, which no man could number," shall stand before the throne (Rev. 7:9).

ARTHUR WALLIS, *IN THE DAY OF THY POWER*

OCTOBER 24

The effective, fervent prayer of a righteous man avails much.

JAMES 5:16

Prayer preceded the first Pentecost, and prayer must precede the wider outpouring of the Spirit. The extent of the one will govern the extent of the other, for prayer prepares the channels for the Holy Spirit to fill—through which He will flow out into the world. To obtain a wide vision, let us in heart and mind watch the movings of His Spirit among His people.

We will go in thought back to the year 1898 or 1899 and, glancing into a Bible institute in America, see gathered there three to four hundred children of God meeting every Saturday night to pray for a "worldwide revival."

Rapidly we cross to another faraway land and in Australia find a band of ministers and laymen who have met for eleven years, pleading with God for a "big revival."

We come again back to Great Britain and look in at the meetings of five thousand Christians gathered at Keswick in July 1902.

Just one month earlier, in faraway India, the divine Spirit laid the same burden upon the servants of God and guided them—without any conscious connection with the prayer movement in other lands—to form a prayer circle of those who would unite to plead for the outpoured Spirit upon that dark and needy land.

Manifestly the Spirit of God was simultaneously moving the people of God in various parts of the world to pray, creating the cry for that which He was preparing to do.

In 1902 the Holy Spirit had drawn His people to pray for a worldwide revival, and in 1903 the eternal Spirit broke forth upon the people of God gathered from the ends of the earth. Yes, truly *prayer* must prepare God's people for the moving forth of the Spirit.

JESSIE PENN-LEWIS, *THE AWAKENING IN WALES*

October 25

They raised their voice to God with one accord. . . .
And when they had prayed, the place where they were assembled together was shaken; and they were all filled with the Holy Spirit.

Acts 4:24–31

The early church was without doubt a praying church, and what tremendous things they accomplished through prayer alone: prison doors were opened, fanatical opponents were struck down and converted to Christ, signs and wonders were done. But the open secret was that the early church knew the presence and power of the Holy Spirit not theoretically but experientially. Those first believers were mighty in prayer because they were mighty in the Spirit.

We have only to scan the pages of Acts to discover that the early church met and overcame every great crisis in their early history with the weapon of "all prayer." Read in Acts 4 that account of the first recorded prayer meeting of the young Jerusalem church for an example of anointed praying. What boldness! What power! What authority! Little wonder the place where they were assembled was shaken and they were all filled anew with the Holy Spirit. So the enduement of the Spirit was both the cause and the consequence of their effectual praying. They prayed because they were filled, and they were filled because they prayed. A victorious circle!

Arthur Wallis, *Pray in the Spirit*

OCTOBER 26

*Do not cast away your confidence, which has great reward.
For you have need of endurance, so that after you have done the will of God,
you may receive the promise.*

HEBREWS 10:35-36

Believe that ye have received," is the Savior's word to us, "and ye shall have." It is clear that during the waiting time, Abraham believed that he had received, for the simple reason that he was "giving glory to God" in confident anticipation of the blessing. While still praying and waiting, he was brought to the point of faith where he was as sure of the son that was to be given as if he held the babe in his arms. To reach the same point should be our goal as we pray for revival.

Referring to the outbreak of the awakening in Kilsyth, July 23, 1839, William Burns wrote, "Some of the people of God who had been longing and wrestling for a time of refreshing from the Lord's presence and who had, during much of the previous night, been travailing in birth for souls came to the meeting not only with the hope but with well-nigh the certain anticipation of God's glorious appearing." We cannot expect to reach this point without perseverance and patience.

You may have prayed long and earnestly for revival. Your faith may have been sorely tried and tested. You may have been tempted to give up in despair. Hold on! Hold on! For He is faithful that promised. The very testing is effecting in you the will of God and preparing you for the blessing.

ARTHUR WALLIS, *IN THE DAY OF THY POWER*

October 27

Will You not revive us again?

Psalm 85:6

We should not be surprised to discover that it has been in times of spiritual revival that most of the forward movements of the church have been born. The great missionary advance of the last century derived its momentum from the widespread revivals that blessed America and Britain during those years. Ever since the light was almost eclipsed in medieval times, God has been working to recover the situation and to restore to the church the light, the purity, and the power which are her birthright and which characterized her in the first century.

The affairs of God's house must be reestablished as He instituted them at the beginning. The ways of apostolic Christianity must be recovered, or the church of the latter days will never ride the storms that already threaten to engulf her. God has used revivals to this end.

During such times new light has broken from the sacred page, and out of such times new expressions of the church have evolved, recovering in most cases something more of the mind of God. Although the revivals of the future will surely reveal that there is yet more land to be possessed in this respect, let us never forget what we owe to the spiritual momentum derived from the movements of the past, and let us be ready to walk in whatever new light may break forth when once again God is pleased to manifest His power and glory.

Arthur Wallis, *In the Day of Thy Power*

OCTOBER 28

Do not quench the Spirit. Do not despise prophecies.

1 THESSALONIANS 5:19–20

We quench a fire when we pour water upon it, and we can quench the fire of the Holy Spirit's working in another, in a fellowship, or in a meeting by "pouring cold water upon it"—by discouraging or actually forbidding it.

The Holy Spirit demands to have right of way in the assemblies of God's people and in their fellowship. But so often we have a mental picture of the way in which He must work, and we forbid all forms of His working which do not conform exactly to our ideas—especially those forms that would seem to bypass our own pet methods and would seem to make nothing of our own special position. How prone we are to think that if revival is to come, it must come through the minister or the missionary or only through those who have a special training. The Spirit, however, often brings revival through the back door, through someone of no account at all and of little official position.

How often has the Lord Jesus come knocking at the door of a situation, a church, or a mission station but the door has been bolted against Him because He did not come through the proper channels or along normal lines, and thus He had sadly to turn away from a situation that needed Him so desperately?

ROY HESSION, *BE FILLED NOW*

October 29

*I exhort first of all that supplications, prayers, intercessions . . .
be made for all men, for kings and all who are in authority,
that we may lead a quiet and peaceable life in all godliness and reverence.*

1 Timothy 2:1–2

Paul is speaking here [in 1 Timothy 2:1–2] not of individual but of national wellbeing. Note that "quiet" is tranquility from without—there is no disturbance from outward circumstances; "peaceable" is tranquility from within—a nation's heart at rest. This is to be enjoyed and demonstrated "in all godliness and reverence. For this is good and acceptable in the sight of God our Savior."

This is a lesson that our country needs desperately to learn afresh—for she once knew it—that "righteousness exalts a nation" (Prov. 14:34). Many voices are bemoaning these days the wave of moral delinquency that seems to be sweeping through the length and breadth of our beloved land—it isn't only the church that is disturbed but the police, the magistrates, the scholastic profession as well. Serious-minded people the country through are reluctantly confessing that all is not well with our land. Where lies the remedy?

Oh, that the Christians would wake up to the situation and that the wave of crime might be matched by a great wave of prayer—that we might see again the part prayer plays in national life. We saw it so recently as the last war in the mighty deliverances that God wrought for us in answer to His people's cry; may we not see it now in a mighty turning back of the nation's heart to God? Such a burden of intercession would secure for us all that guidance, that grit, that gumption, and that grace that are so sorely needed in this hour of the nation's perplexity.

Guy King, *I Timothy: A Leader Led*

OCTOBER 30

Righteousness exalts a nation.

PROVERBS 14:34

Here is the primary effect of revival—the church awakes, casts off the works of darkness that have blanketed her in her slumber, and puts on the armor of light. The assertion that we cannot have an awakening in these days is but the devil's lullaby to hush the church to sleep.

Conversions take place without any appeals and tend to be clear-cut and decisive. As in the early church, many born again in revival are at once filled with the Spirit and become effective for God. Whether in meetings or out of them, whether through personal dealing or without it, men and women broken over their sin find their way to Christ.

When God thus moves in power, He wrests the initiative from Satan. Sin no longer stalks the land in triumph but hides its head in shame. It is not unusual for social evils to be swept away and industrial problems to be solved overnight. Drink saloons, places of amusement, and dens of iniquity have often had to close through lack of patronage. Magistrates have been known to take a holiday and the jails to be nearly empty. Everywhere there seems to be one topic of conversation: the things of eternity. On the faces of the people, there is a spirit of inquiry or of concern. They are asking, "What meaneth this?" or "What shall we do?" Every stratum of society has been affected, and the widespread indifference of the masses is a thing of the past.

Such are the effects upon sinners—and are they not sufficient justification for revival? Do they not provide a powerful reason, if we have any concern for the souls of men, why we should all be thirsting for revival?

ARTHUR WALLIS, *IN THE DAY OF THY POWER*

October 31

Pursue . . . holiness, without which no one will see the Lord.

Hebrews 12:14

Do you ask, "How is the church to be lifted up to the abundant life in Christ, to that expanded vitality which will fit her for the work that God is putting before I her?" Without hesitation many will say, "Nothing will help but a revival."

Yes, all will agree, nothing less than a mighty revival is needed to rouse and fit the church for the work to which God calls her. And yet there may be a great difference in what we understand by revival. Many will think of the power of God as it has been manifested in the work of evangelists like Moody and Torrey. They feel sure that what God has done in the past He can do again. They will perhaps hardly understand us when we say that we need a different and a mightier revival than those were. In them the chief object was the conversion of sinners and in connection with that, incidentally, the stirring up of believers. But the revival that we need calls for a deeper and more entire upheaval of the church itself.

The great defect of those earlier revivals was that converts were received into a church that was not living on a high level of consecration and holiness. Speedily they sank down to the average standard of ordinary religious life. Even the believers who had taken part in the work and had been roused by it also gradually returned to their former life of clouded fellowship and lack of power to testify for Christ.

The revival we need is the revival of *holiness* in which the consecration of the whole being is to the service of Christ. For this there will be needed a new style of preaching in which the promises of God to dwell in His people and to sanctify them for Himself will take a place which they do not now have.

Andrew Murray, *The State of the Church*

November

Serving in the Power of Christ

The Testimony of Roy Hession

In 1947 I had been doing full-time evangelistic work in Great Britain for a number of years but had come into a state of great spiritual need. I had somehow lost the power of the Holy Spirit which I once had known in the work of the Lord, and yet I had to continue to conduct evangelistic campaigns without His power—a terrible experience! Ignorant of what had really happened, I redoubled my efforts and became increasingly tense and forceful, all of which was a poor substitute for the Spirit's gentle, penetrating power.

In April 1947 I invited several missionaries from East Africa to come as speakers to an Easter conference which I was organizing. I had heard that they had been experiencing revival in their field, and as an evangelist, I was interested in revival. What they had to say was very different from much of what I had associated with that word. It was very simple and very quiet. As they unfolded their message and gave their testimonies, I discovered that I was the neediest person in the conference and was far more in need of being revived than I had ever realized.

That discovery, however, came only slowly to me. Being myself one of the speakers, I suppose I was more concerned about others' needs than my own. As my wife and others humbled themselves before God and experienced the cleansing of the blood of Jesus, I found myself left somewhat high and dry—dry just because I was high. I was humbled by the simplicity of what I had to do to be revived and filled with the Spirit. When others at the end of the conference testified as to how Jesus had broken them at His cross and filled their hearts to overflowing with His Spirit, I had no such testimony.

It was only afterward that I was enabled to give up trying to fit things into my doctrinal scheme and come humbly to the cross for cleansing from my own personal sins. It was like beginning my Christian life all over again. It has been an altogether new chapter in life since then. It has meant, however, that I have had to choose constantly to die to the big "I" that Jesus might be all and constantly to come to Him for cleansing in His precious blood. But that is why it is a new chapter.

Roy Hession, *The Calvary Road*

November 1

In a great house there are not only vessels of gold and silver, but also of wood and clay.

2 Timothy 2:20

In that "great house" we are expected to be of use. To each of us is allotted a task—not the same task for all but some task for each. The vessels were not intended to be just beautiful but useful. Perhaps you have at some time attended a great banquet at the City of London's old Guildhall. You may have got a view of the city's "plate"—exquisitely beautiful, immensely valuable but serving no useful purpose at the feast, bringing no nourishment or refreshment to any; there to be looked at and admired; not to be in any practical way employed. That is not the kind of vessel that we are meant to be.

There are some of us Christians whom God cannot employ in higher service—our poor character, our humdrum quality preclude us from better engagement unless some means be found of changing us completely. What a step up it would be if we became as silver vessels—yet even this is only second best. Let me then urge myself, and you, to "earnestly desire the best" (1 Cor. 12:31)—that is, not silver but gold.

Look at some interesting and impressive words in Isaiah 60:17: "Instead of bronze I will bring gold, instead of iron I will bring silver, instead of wood, bronze." Oh, blessed transmutation. Notice it says "I will" do this—it is beyond *our* doing. We have just to bring our wooden old selves to His hands and ask Him to make us golden, and He will assuredly find a way of doing it.

Guy King, *II Timothy: To My Son*

NOVEMBER 2

Every branch that bears fruit He prunes, that it may bear more fruit.

JOHN 15:2

The fruitfulness of the vine largely depends on the care with which it is pruned. There is no tree pruned so mercilessly and incessantly, first with the sharp knife and then with scissors. The Lord has many such implements. There is the *golden* pruning knife of His Word by which He would prune us if we would let Him (John 15:3), so escaping the rougher and more terrible discipline of the *iron* pruning knife of affliction. Our Lord uses that knife with sharp, clean strokes which cut deep into our nature and leave scars which may take years to heal, or even to conceal. And there are the scissors also in His hand—cross events, daily circumstances which appear contrary to each other but which nevertheless work together in the end for good.

So great are the spring prunings that more branches are taken out than left in, and the cuttings which litter the ground are said to be utterly worthless and fit only for the fire. What a comfort it is that the Vinedresser leaves the pruning to no apprentice's hand! No hand but the most skilled may handle the knife. "My Father is the husbandman" (John 15:1).

It is a recognized rule that no shoot should have more than one bunch of grapes. All but that one are nipped off. And I am told that the vinedresser will obtain a greater weight of better grapes in that one bunch than he would by permitting two or three clusters to form. It is thus that we are sometimes shut away from one after another of our chosen directions of Christian activity—not that our Father would diminish our fruit bearing but that the strength of our life may be saved from dissipation and conducted by one channel to a better and richer fruitage.

F. B. MEYER, *JOSEPH*

November 3

Moses . . . looked this way and that way, and . . .
he killed the Egyptian and hid him in the sand.

EXODUS 2:11–12

God meant to save Israel by the hand of Moses but *not* in Moses' way. Moses himself was the greatest difficulty; it would take time and patient training to make this fiery man a polished shaft.

God had to teach Moses first by failure. Moses supposed that his brethren would have understood that God was giving them deliverance! Probably they would have understood if the means had been of God; but this was not God's way, so how could God bear witness to it!

We are amazed when the souls we want to help do not accept us. We know that God has called us and told us that He will give deliverance to souls by our hands. With hearts full of our secret dealings with Him and of all that He has said to us, we go out and suppose that others will understand that God is working through us, when as yet it is not God at all! It is God in so far as that He permits our efforts to be made but only that we may fail and know ourselves.

Does it not dawn upon us that in spite of all our "defending and avenging," souls are yet in bondage to sin and the world and that our puny efforts to free them are like an attempt to empty the ocean with a spoon? Some know it and are almost crushed. They say, "Are we then to do nothing when we see the burdens of the oppressed?" In God's name, yes; but let us *first* get into line with God so as to work with Him and not apart from Him.

Let us thank God for our failures and our rude awakenings. Far, far better to have them now than to live in self-delusion and awaken too late—to find at the judgment seat that we must suffer loss because we could not bear the truth.

JESSIE PENN-LEWIS, *FACE TO FACE*

November 4

Those who wait on the Lord, they shall inherit the earth.

Psalm 37:9

We are too feverish, too hasty, too impatient. It is a great mistake. Everything comes only to those who can wait. You may have had what Joseph had when still a lad—a vision of power and usefulness and blessedness. But you cannot realize it in fact. All your plans miscarry. Every door seems shut. The years are passing over you with the depressing sense that you have not done anything significant in this life.

Now turn your heart to God. Accept His will. Tell Him that you leave to Him the realization of your dream. "Wait on the Lord, and keep his way, and he shall exalt thee to inherit the land: when the wicked are cut off, thou shalt see it" (Ps. 37:34). He may keep you waiting a little longer, but you shall find Him verifying the words of one who knew by experience His trustworthiness: "The salvation of the righteous is of the Lord; he is their strength in the time of trouble. And the Lord shall help them, and deliver them: he shall deliver them from the wicked, and save them, because they trust in him" (Ps. 37:39–40).

F. B. Meyer, *Joseph*

November 5

Unless a grain of wheat falls into the ground and dies, it remains alone; but if it dies, it produces much grain.

John 12:24

Joined to the Lord—one spirit—the grain of wheat awakens to the law of its being and yields itself to the Son of God for sowing in the earth. It cries to God to make it fruitful at any cost. The purpose of its life begins to dawn upon it. The heavenly Husbandman hears the cry and silently begins to prepare it for the answer to its prayer.

It may appear as if He had not heeded the cry, and the little grain wonders why He does not answer; but the air and sunshine are doing their silent work. The corn is ripening unconsciously to itself, until suddenly it finds itself loosened from its old ties; a hand takes hold of it; it is caught away and dropped down into some spot of earth—dark, lonely, strange. What has happened?

The little grain of wheat asked for *fruit* but not for *this* strange path. Where are the sunshine, the old companions, the old happy experience? "Where am I? What does it mean?" cries the lonely grain. "This dark spot of earth, so repulsive, seems to be injuring my nice coat." Presently it is shocked to find its covering going to pieces. This is worse than all.

Poor little grain! Trampled upon in the dark earth, buried out of sight. This little grain of wheat that was once so admired. Now it feels forgotten as it passes into solitude.

Buried grain, say yes to God. He is answering your prayers!

The life of God in you could not break forth into fruitfulness until you had been broken by God's own hand. The earthly surroundings and testings, the loneliness and humiliation, were permitted by Him so that He might release into life abundant the life that had come from God.

Jessie Penn-Lewis, *Fruitful Living*

November 6

Whoever loses his life for My sake will find it.

Matthew 16:25

At last the grain of wheat is willing to be hidden away from the eyes of men. Willing to be trampled upon and lie in silence in some lonely corner chosen of God. Willing to appear what others would call a failure. Willing to live in the will of God apart from glorious experiences. Willing to dwell in solitude and isolation, away from happy fellowship with the other grains of wheat.

The little grain has learned something of the meaning of fellowship with Christ in His death, and silently, surely the divine life breaks forth into fruitfulness. The grain has given itself; it has parted with its own life, yet it still lives—*lives now in the life of its Lord.*

A buried seed grain, it is content to be forgotten! For who thinks of the *grain* and of all the sorrow and suffering that it underwent while sown in the dark when they see the harvest field? But the grain of wheat is satisfied, because the law of its being is fulfilled. It has *sunk itself and its own getting* and now lives in others, not even desiring to have it known that from it the hundredfold has sprung.

So the Christ Himself poured out His soul unto death that He might "see his seed." See the travail of His soul and be satisfied as He lives again in His redeemed ones. Thus in God's wondrous law—the law of nature repeated in the spiritual world—the first Grain of wheat, sown by God Himself, is reproduced in other grains, having the same characteristics and law of being. "*If it die, . . . much fruit.*"

Jessie Penn-Lewis, *Fruitful Living*

NOVEMBER 7

What profit is it to a man if he gains the whole world, and loses his own soul?

MATTHEW 16:26

I wanted to know what my life's work for the Lord Jesus Christ was to be, and I prayed God to show me. But here I made a mistake, for instead of trusting entirely to God to show me, I went to my friends. Thus I tried to find out the Lord's guidance by common sense, and instead of getting into the light, I got into darkness. I became very restless and anxious, my health gave way, and I had to go into the country to recuperate. Having spent three months in reading my Bible and praying to God for guidance, I came back much better but still not knowing what I was to do. About this time I came upon a tract written by an atheist:

> Did I firmly believe, as millions say they do, that the knowledge and practice of religion in this life influences destiny in another, religion would mean to me everything. I would cast away earthly enjoyments as dross, earthly cares as follies, and earthly thoughts and feelings as vanity. Religion would be my first waking thought and my last image before sleep sank me into unconsciousness. I would strive to look upon eternity alone and on the immortal souls around me, soon to be everlastingly happy or everlastingly miserable. I would go forth to the world and preach to it in season and out of season, and my text would be, "What shall it profit a man if he gain the whole world and lose his own soul?"

I at once saw that this was the truly consistent Christian life. When I looked back upon my own life, I saw how inconsistent it had been. I therefore determined that from that time forth, my life would be consistent, and I set myself to know what was God's will for me. But this time I determined not to consult with flesh and blood but just wait until God would show me.

C. T. STUDD IN NORMAN GRUBB,
C. T. STUDD: CRICKETER AND PIONEER

November 8

As they ministered to the Lord and fasted, the Holy Spirit said,
"Now separate to Me Barnabas and Saul for the work to which I have called them."

ACTS 13:2

"As they ministered *to the Lord*, and fasted" is the record given of that gathering of Christians in the early church when "the Holy Ghost said, Separate me Barnabas and Saul for the work whereunto I have called them" (Acts 13:2). It is this waiting upon God until *God speaks* that we twentieth-century Christians know so little about.

If the workers of today gathered together in this way to seek the mind of the Spirit of God, how different would the work be, and how quiet and restful would preparation for any meeting be, sure of its being in God's hands. There would be no making programs and plans without certainty of their being "according to the pattern." Oh, that God's people might know the ministry to the Lord that will bring the personal direction of the Holy Spirit to those who seek and wait for it.

JESSIE PENN-LEWIS, *FRUITFUL LIVING*

November 9

Cause me to know the way in which I should walk, for I lift up my soul to You.

Psalm 143:8

We pray for the call, the thrusting forth. Should any read this who are at the parting of the ways, I want to say very earnestly, *Be sure of your call.* Our Lord deals variously with souls, but the soul must be sure that He and He alone is the Chooser of its path.

Do not feel the call of God is always, as it were, audible. It is more the quiet sense of peace that comes when one is on one's knees before Him and as one goes about one's daily work; peace, but also outward attack. Has anyone come to us unattacked? I do not know of any. Certainly all who are to bear the burden of leadership know it.

"I am not here because of choice"—to be able to say that, unshaken by all that will happen after the field is reached and the pressure of life comes on, is rest of heart. Anything less is torture. A call is a quiet, steady pressure upon the spirit from which there is no escape. It is an assurance, a conviction.

Then there is the leading of God at the other end. If both coincide and the way is opened, let the soul go on in peace. If it be otherwise, then "the meek will he guide in judgment: and the meek will he teach his way" (Ps. 25:9). There is something else in His mind for that life, something better. He will not waste its offer of love if only it is willing that He should choose how it is to be outpoured.

Amy Carmichael, *Fragments That Remain*

NOVEMBER 10

The God of glory appeared to our father Abraham . . . and said to him, "Get out of your country . . . , and come to a land that I shall show you."

ACTS 7:2–3

Not thus does God now appear to us [as He did to Abraham]; and yet it is certain that He still speaks in the silence of the waiting spirit, impressing His will and saying, "Get thee out." Listen for that voice in the inner shrine of thine heart.

This same voice has often spoken since. It called Elijah from Thisbe and Amos from Tekoa; Peter from his fishing nets and Matthew from his toll booth; Cromwell from his farm in Huntingdon and Luther from his cloister at Erfurt. Has it not come to you? If it has, let nothing hinder your obedience; strike your tents, and follow where the God of glory beckons. If you would have His companionship, you must follow.

This call involved hardship. And so must it always be. The summons of God will ever involve a wrench from much that nature holds dear. We must be prepared to take up our cross daily if we would follow where He points the way. Each step of real advance in the divine life will involve an altar on which some dear fragment of the self-life has been offered or a cairn beneath which some cherished idol has been buried.

It is true that the blessedness which awaits us will more than compensate us for the sacrifices which we may have to make; but still, when it comes to the point, there is certain anguish as the last link is broken, the last farewell said, and the last look taken of the receding home of past happy years. Count the cost clearly indeed; but having done so, go forward in the name and by the strength of Him in whom all things are possible and easy and safe. And in doing so, you will approve yourself worthy to stand with Christ in the regeneration.

F. B. MEYER, *ABRAHAM*

November 11

. . . that you may be filled with the knowledge of His will.

Colossians 1:9

Oh, how restive we are in ourselves! How we dislike being still, especially when everything around us seems to be moving at greatest speed. Yes, the church of God has caught the fever of the world! But God has yet His hidden ones, the "quiet in the land" (Ps. 35:20).

Maybe, child of God, you have found your desert training in some workroom or kitchen, at some lonely post on the mission field, or in some worldly home in your own country. You have been agonizing, struggling, wondering when God will set you free. You once thought He meant to do great things by you, but you have been so hedged in that all hope has died away, all plans and schemes are gone.

"Alas! Here am I, occupied with nothing but the things of earth, and God's world seems to be needing me. Am I never to be among those privileged to undo the bands of the yoke and let the oppressed go free?"

Oh child of God, your Father never forgets, and His clocks are never behind time. Wait!

"But I have waited many years!"

Your Father knows; lie down in His will, and be at rest. Don't you know that His will is more than His work and that your Lord has said, "Whosoever shall do the will of my Father . . . is my brother, and my sister, and mother"? The waiting must needs be. The aim and the end of all His work in us is to teach us to "prove what is that good, and acceptable, and perfect, will of God."

Jessie Penn-Lewis, *Face to Face*

NOVEMBER 12

The hand of the LORD was upon me there, and He said to me, "Arise. . . ."
So I arose and went.

EZEKIEL 3:22–23

It may be that we who speak of full surrender to God are too little prepared for giving up ourselves in reality to God to be under the hand of the Holy Spirit. We are too rigid, whereas He must have us pliable. We are so fettered by our "machinery" and say, "I cannot do my work unless I do it in this way!" and so He has to deal with us to get us out of our ruts. There is no freedom for the Spirit of God in cast-iron machinery.

Are we willing to yield ourselves to the Holy Spirit? Do we realize that we are not ready for service till we have met with God so really that we know we have received our commission from Him? There is, alas, a vast amount of "Christian work" today that is not God's work—that is, work carried on by God Himself through human vessels. Take care that *God* sends you, and then, whatever the apparent results are, it will be all right.

God was able to work in Ezekiel so mightily because he was pliable and instantly obedient to the Holy Spirit of God. See all through the story, from this chapter [Ezekiel 3] onward, not the smallest resistance to the revealed will of God or hesitation in obedience. God could count upon him to fulfill His will.

What a blessed picture of a surrendered life!

JESSIE PENN-LEWIS, *FRUITFUL LIVING*

NOVEMBER 13

He counted me faithful, putting me into the ministry.

1 TIMOTHY 1:12

Salvation is to be followed by service. How grandly so in Paul's case. In whatever sort of work we are employed for Him, it is always to be a "ministry of reconciliation" in the sense of 2 Corinthians 5:18–19.

God had counted him "faithful"—that is, trustworthy, and so He had trusted him with this blessed ministry. May He find us also to be as those that He can rely on to do whatever service He may, in His wisdom and grace, appoint us.

Let no timid or hesitant Christian hold back from service from a sense of insufficiency—truly, "our sufficiency is from God" (2 Cor. 3:5). Never does He bid us go upon His errands without supplying us with all we need for the discharging of the commission; never does He send us to engage the foe without providing us with all the equipment that we require for the battle and the victory—"Who ever goes to war at his own expense?" says 1 Corinthians 9:7. Let the earnest believer take comfort and courage from the plain statement of Exodus 18:23: "If . . . God so commands you, then you will be able to." It is in this sense that Augustine said, "Command what Thou wilt; then give what Thou commandest."

GUY KING, *I TIMOTHY: A LEADER LED*

NOVEMBER 14

Those who are Christ's have crucified the flesh.

GALATIANS 5:24

There is no greater enemy than the presence of the flesh in our activities. There is no department of life or service into which its subtle, deadly influence does not penetrate.

We have to encounter it in our unregenerate life, when its passions reveal themselves, brooking no restraint. We meet it after we have entered upon the new life, striving against the Spirit and restraining His gracious energy. We are most baffled when we find it prompting to holy resolutions and efforts after a consecrated life. And lastly, it confronts us in Christian work. In our quiet moments we are bound to trace it to a desire for notoriety, to a passion to excel, and to the restlessness of a nature which evades the deeper life by flinging itself into every avenue through which it may exert its activities.

There is only one solution to these difficulties. By the way of the cross and the grave alone, we can become disentangled and discharged from the insidious domination of this evil principle which is accursed by God and hurtful to holy living.

In the cross of Jesus, when He died in the likeness of sinful flesh, God wrote His curse upon every manifestation of selfish and fleshly energy; and now it remains for each of us to appropriate that cross, to accept the divine sentence, to lie in the grave where the voices of human ambition and adulation cannot follow us. Not, however, to stay there but to pass up by the grace of the Holy Ghost into the pure resurrection air and light where no face is visible but that of the risen Savior; where no voice is audible save His; and where, in the hush of perfect fellowship, the spirit becomes able to discern the wish of its Lord.

F. B. MEYER, *JEREMIAH*

November 15

No one engaged in warfare entangles himself with the affairs of this life, that he may please him who enlisted him as a soldier.

2 Timothy 2:4

There is the entanglement of *overwork*. Who has not known it? The more we love our work, the keener we are to do it well; the more the burden of souls unreached weighs upon our hearts, the greater our joy in reaching them. How very subtle the form this entangling peril takes, and we are most likely to slip into it before we are aware.

And there is another. I would not touch upon it were it not that it is so terribly familiar, so deadly in its entangling: the unconfessed, perhaps unrealized, awakening of *ambition*, the love of the praise of man that bringeth a snare.

Oh, those bonds, invisible cords—why do they hold one so? "As a thread of tow is broken when it toucheth the fire"—we think of that and call upon the God of fire to burn the bonds and set us free to fight this fight for that soul, to enable us to stand ourselves peaceful and strong in heavenly places in Christ Jesus.

Amy Carmichael, *God's Missionary*

November 16

I saw the Lord sitting on a throne, high and lifted up.

Isaiah 6:1

What a terrible possibility for us to be very busy in our service for God but without a new personal vision of Him. The work, as a result, becomes heavy. There is little outcome from it. And the worker himself becomes utterly discouraged. But he knows nothing better, and he plods on, not seeing that he does not see. But there came a day when Isaiah did see, when God granted him a new vision of Himself. Wonderful day for Isaiah!

What did Isaiah see? He saw the Lord, high and lifted up, sitting on a throne. It was, however, the action of the awesome seraphim that seems to have broken him down especially. God was so holy that they were veiling themselves before Him. As Isaiah looked upon all that was happening before the throne of God, he came under terrible conviction of sin, the realization that his service was inspired; and in complete brokenness he cried out, "Woe is me, for I am undone!"

This is the conviction of sin God desires to give us as we see Him in His holiness—that our service has been done in the flesh. Self has intruded even into holy things, and so much of what has been done has been only in the power of the self-life rather than in the power of the Holy Spirit.

The Holy Spirit comes to us when we say, "Woe is me," and points us back to the cross. We cannot be more right with God than what the blood makes us when we call sin, *sin*. We are now fully restored and able to respond to the call, "Whom shall I send, and who will go for Us?" and hear the Lord say to us, "Go!" But this time how different!

Roy Hession, *When I Saw Him*

November 17

Not that we are sufficient of ourselves, . . . but our sufficiency is from God, who also made us sufficient as ministers.

2 Corinthians 3:5–6

When I compared the small results of my service with the fruit given to the apostles at Pentecost, I could not but own that I did not know the Holy Spirit in the fullness of His power. My weekly Bible class was a great trouble to me, for I had no power of utterance. Self-consciousness almost paralyzed me, and no practice ever made speaking less difficult. "Others might have the gift of speech, but it was clearly not given to me," I said.

How I taught the girls in my Bible class! How *full* my Bible was of notes, and how carefully I prepared a dish of spiritual food for them! Food all obtained secondhand, from other books. But they did not change much in their lives.

I thought it was the fault of the girls, until the Lord spoke to me and said, "*It is yourself!*" And then He began to break me, and there came to me the terrible revelation that every bit of this activity, this energy, this indomitable perseverance was *myself* after all, though it was hidden under the name of "consecration."

Calvary precedes Pentecost. Death with Christ precedes the fullness of the Holy Spirit. Power! Yes, God's children need power, but God does not give power to the old creation or to the uncrucified soul.

My Bible became like a living thing and was flooded with light. Christ suddenly became to me a real person. When I went to my Bible class, I found myself able to speak with liberty of utterance, with the conviction of the Spirit at the back of it, until souls were convicted of sin on every side. The secret of a fruitful life is to pour out to others and want nothing for yourself—to leave yourself utterly in the hands of God.

J. C. Metcalfe, *Molded by the Cross*

November 18

. . . with the Holy Spirit and with power.

Acts 10:38

The power of the Spirit is inseparable from His person. God does not let out His attributes. His power cannot be rented. He is not simply the *giver* of power; He wields it. No one else can. It is His power working in us that makes us all-powerful for all the will of God. Is it not in this we so often fail? Is there not often in our praying for power more desire for *it* than for *Him*?

We want visible results, dramatic wonders, mighty works—and it is not always for these that the Spirit of power is given. Power may be as necessary for silence as for speech and as mighty in obscurity as in high places. He comes to make us effective in all the will of God. In the one Spirit there are diversities both of function and manifestation.

The work of the Spirit depends upon the power of the Spirit. No other power will do. The energy of the flesh cannot do the work of the Spirit. When Zion covets Babylonish gold, envies Babylonish garments, copies Babylonish ways, adopts Babylonish altars, and fights with Babylonish weapons, her strength fails, because the Spirit of power is lost.

The work of the church is supernatural. It cannot be done in the strength of the natural man. It is "not by might, nor by power, but by my Spirit, saith the Lord." There is no excuse for failure, no justification for ineffectiveness, for the Spirit of God is the Spirit of power, and the gift of the Spirit is the inheritance of every believer in Christ Jesus our Lord. "He that is feeble among them at that day shall be as David; and the house of David shall be as God, as the angel of the Lord before them."

Samuel Chadwick, *The Way to Pentecost*

NOVEMBER 19

. . . in the spirit and power of Elijah.

LUKE 1:17

What may not one man do in one brief life if he is willing to be simply a living conduit pipe through which the power of God may descend to men? There is no limit to the possible usefulness of such a life. There on the one hand is the oceanic fullness of God; here on the other are the awful need and desolation of man—guilty, weak, bankrupt, diseased. All that is required is a channel of communication between the two, and when that channel is made and opened and kept free from the silting sand, there will ensue one great, plenteous, and equable flow of power carrying the fullness of God to the weary emptiness of man. Why should you not be such a channel?

If I may venture so to put it, God is in extremity for those who, thoughtless for themselves, will desire only to be receivers and channels of His power. He will take young men and women, old men and children, servants and handmaidens and will fill them with the selfsame Spirit whose power was once reserved for a favored few. Besides all this, the positive command has never been repealed which bids us be "filled with the Spirit" (Eph. 5:18).

Moreover, what God commands, He is prepared to do all that is needful on His side to effect. Then when, like John the Baptist, we are filled with the Holy Ghost, like John the Baptist we shall go "before his face in the spirit and power of Elijah, to turn the hearts of the fathers to the children, and the disobedient to walk in the wisdom of the just; to make ready for the Lord a people prepared for him."

F. B. MEYER, *ELIJAH*

November 20

You shall be baptized with the Holy Spirit not many days from now.

Acts 1:5

Before His crucifixion Christ carefully explained to His disciples the necessity of His outward teaching and guidance being changed into the inspiration and operation of His Spirit resident within their souls. He commanded them not to bear witness to the world of what they humanly knew of His birth, life, teachings, death, resurrection, but to wait at Jerusalem until they were endued with power from on high.

"John truly baptized with water," said Christ, "but ye shall be baptized with the Holy Ghost not many days hence" (Acts 1:5). "And in that day," He had said earlier, "ye shall know that I am in you" (John 14:20). Only then could they be His witnesses and gospel ambassadors.

As salvation is in its whole nature the inward birth and life of Christ in the believer, so nothing but this "new creature in Christ" (2 Cor. 5:17) can bear true witness to the realities of redemption. Therefore a man, however expert in all Scripture learning, can only talk about the gospel as of any tale he has been told until the life of Christ has been brought forth, verified, fulfilled, and enjoyed through the power of the Holy Spirit in his soul.

No one can know salvation by a mere rational consent to that which is historically said of Christ. Only by an inward experience of His cross, death, and resurrection can the saving power of the gospel be known. For the reality of Christ's redemption is not in fleshly, finite, outward things—much less in verbal descriptions of them—but is a birth, a life, a spiritual operation which as truly belongs to God alone as does His creative power.

William Law, *The Power of the Spirit*

November 21

You shall receive power when the Holy Spirit has come upon you; and you shall be witnesses to Me.

Acts 1:8

When Jesus promised the disciples that they would receive power from the Holy Spirit, in the same breath He foretold its use. The great work of the Christian is to spread the gospel—to tell the story of the cross.

But remember this: *it is not only that.* That would be the story of a dead Savior. Thank God, we have a *living* Savior who continually intercedes for us. The story of the resurrection and ascension must be added to the story of the crucifixion and burial.

But remember this: *it is not that alone either.* That would be the story of an absent Savior. We have a *present* Savior, mighty to save, able to deliver us from the power of the world, the flesh, and the devil. The story of Pentecost must be added to the crucifixion and resurrection. It is the story of the return of Jesus in omnipresence and omnipotence, in the person of the Holy Spirit, to be with all His disciples everywhere till the end of the age.

We can witness for Jesus, but our testimony cannot go beyond our experience. Like the apostles, we can speak of "the things which we have seen and heard" (Acts 4:20), but we can't speak convincingly about things we have not seen or heard. The Holy Spirit must first witness to us before we can witness to others. Only those who have found the way of sanctification by faith can point to Jesus as the deliverer from sin.

William Boardman, *The Higher Christian Life*

NOVEMBER 22

Be . . . fervent in spirit, serving the Lord.

ROMANS 12:10-11

Perhaps this may speak to someone who is thinking of offering for India—or for anywhere. It is from the *Regions Beyond* magazine, May 1887. "It seems to me, if I had come to India at all skeptical about the truth of the doctrine of the baptism or filling of the Holy Ghost for service, all doubt would have been removed. There must needs have been made such a provision as this for the man sent to work in a field like India. The man who does not know from actual experience what it is to be filled—up to his present capacity—with the Holy Spirit *had far better* not come to India to work."

I have been thinking much of late of those words in Romans 12:11 "*fervent in spirit.*" The Tamil gives a word which means heat as of fever, warmth, glow, fire. His ministers "a flame of fire" (Heb. 1:7)! Let us ask it for each other, this divine soul fervor, the gift of the Holy Spirit: no mere fleshly earnestness but the Spirit's energy. "The flashes thereof are flashes of fire—a very flame of the Lord."

If any missionaries on the face of the earth need to believe in the Holy Spirit, we Indian missionaries do. Pray that we may know that Power as we do not yet and that we will *believe to see* Him conquering.

AMY CARMICHAEL, *FRAGMENTS THAT REMAIN*

NOVEMBER 23

With great power the apostles gave witness.

ACTS 4:33

The atmosphere of the apostolic church is charged with divine power. Their word was with power. Conviction accompanied their speech. Signs and wonders confirmed their testimony. They uncovered the hearts of evildoers, and heaven put its seal upon their judgments. Rulers trembled in their presence. Disease fled at their touch. Demons were subject to their word.

The presence of the Spirit endued men with divine authority and power. They were sure of the mind of God; they asked and received; they wrought mighty works—for they were strengthened in the might of the Spirit. The church was filled, inspired, and empowered in the fullness of the Spirit of the living God.

The study of Pentecost reveals a startling contrast between the promise of power and its absence in the church of today. Judged by its own standards of power, the church is not effectively doing its own proper work. This is the conviction of devout and thoughtful men in all the churches. Why? Where is now the Lord God of Elijah?

So far as external conditions can be judged, they are more favorable to the work of the Spirit than they have been for many years. There is a revolt against materialism and rationalism. There is an intense belief in the reality of the spiritual world. All these things have opened a great and effectual door to the witness of the Holy Spirit of God—and yet the church has less power than in the days of aggressive antagonism. Why? Is the Spirit of the Lord straitened?

There is no substitute for the Holy Ghost. The sufficiency of the church is not of men but of God. The one vital cause of failure in the church is in the poverty of the spiritual life of its people.

SAMUEL CHADWICK, *THE WAY TO PENTECOST*

November 24

. . . by the power of the Spirit of God.

Romans 15:19

Our Lord promised that the indwelling presence of the Spirit of God would be in men the all-prevailing source of power. The Spirit of God is always associated with energy and vitality. During the period recorded in the Old Testament Scriptures, the Spirit was given to men chosen for special tasks. The prophets foresaw an age in which He would be poured forth upon all flesh and spoke of His coming. Jesus manifested the Spirit as He revealed the Father. By His promise the Spirit was to succeed the Son with increased effectiveness and enlarged dominion. For that reason it was better that He should go away.

The gift of the Spirit is God's gift of power for effective witnessing, holiness of life, and consecrated service. It gives authority, aptness, and force in speech. On the Day of Pentecost, men spoke as the Spirit of God gave them utterance. They spoke with authority, certainty, and power because they spoke out of an experience of revealed truth interpreted by the Holy Ghost.

No man has a right to speak for God who has no personal, firsthand knowledge of Him; he certainly will not speak with power. The Spirit of power sanctifies, vitalizes, energizes the natural faculties and makes possible things beyond their most perfect development. God's man becomes mighty in the power of the Almighty. Personality is the seat of power, and the Pentecostal gift of the Spirit is the gift of a God-possessed personality.

Samuel Chadwick, *The Way to Pentecost*

November 25

To this end I also labor, striving according to His working which works in me mightily.

Colossians 1:29

"Labor" is the word he uses. Among the ranks of the Christians, there are workers and shirkers. There is no doubt of the category to which Paul belonged. He was so imbued with the Holy Spirit that he could do no other. Notice his explanation: "striving according to His working which works in me mightily." After all, it is always the inner that governs the outer—and it little avails us to try to whip our energy to work harder for God. That may succeed for a moment, but it will soon exhaust itself, and we shall revert to "tepid" again.

Paul's enthusiasm abides and abounds. Why? Listen to him: "I labored more abundantly than they all, yet not I, but the grace of God which was with me" (1 Cor. 15:10). Listen again: "The love of Christ constrains us" (2 Cor. 5:14). And here in our passage, "His working . . . in me." All this is the motive power—inward and Godward—and therefore is available for us all. Let us then be up and doing. "Son, go, work today in My vineyard" (Matt. 21:28). "Be strong, . . . and work; for I am with you" (Hag. 2:4). Thus for all the service expected of us, we can rely upon the uttermost of His grace.

Guy King, *Colossians: True Life in Christ*

NOVEMBER 26

How much more will your heavenly Father give the Holy Spirit to those who ask Him!

LUKE 11:13

The Reverend Jonathan Goforth, missionary to China, bore testimony that the results of the different evangelistic missions there were just in proportion to the extent that the missionaries and the Chinese Christian leaders yielded themselves to God and sought the power of the Holy Spirit. He expressed the conviction that "if the church of Christ would humble herself under the hand of God, the Holy Spirit would confirm the preaching of the Word with unmistakable signs of His presence and power. I have the strongest of convictions that it would pay many times over for the church at home and abroad to cease its busy round of activities for a while and seek for the Holy Spirit's power as if for hidden treasure. If we want to evangelize the world in our day, we must get back to the Pentecostal factor."

Our faith in the Holy Spirit is, to a great extent, simply intellectual. Were it otherwise, it would be impossible that we should not count it as our greatest privilege to ask and to receive the Holy Spirit in doing God's work.

Oh, take time, children of God, to fall down in adoration and be moved by these four great mysteries: the gift of the Holy Spirit, the infinite willingness of the Father to give Him, the blessed Son who is the channel, and the inconceivable power of the prayer of faith! Let each of us ask and receive for himself. Let us believe with our whole heart that God gives His blessed Spirit, gives Him every day afresh, in increasing power to every child that asks.

ANDREW MURRAY, *THE STATE OF THE CHURCH*

NOVEMBER 27

I will pour out My Spirit on all flesh.

JOEL 2:28

This power of the Holy Spirit is for us all. Of course, we could not believe in Jesus in the remission of sin or the quickening of our spiritual life apart from the work of the Holy Spirit, but there is something more than this: there is a power, an anointing, a gracious endowment of fitness for service—which are the privilege of every believer.

The Holy Spirit is prepared not only to be within us for the renewal and sanctification of character. He waits to empower us to witness for Jesus, to endure the persecution and trial which are inevitable to the exercise of a God-given ministry, and to bring other men to God.

Cease from your work for a little and wait upon the ascended, glorified Redeemer in whom the Spirit of God dwells. Ask Him to impart to you that which He received on your behalf. Never rest until you are sure that the Spirit dwells in you fully and exercises through you the plenitude of His gracious power. We cannot seek Him at the hand of Christ in vain. Dare to believe this: dare to believe that if your heart is pure and your motives holy and your whole desire fervent—and if you have dared to breathe in a deep, long breath of the Holy Spirit—that according to your faith so it has been done to you.

The power of His grace is not passed away with the primitive times, as fond and faithless men imagine; but His kingdom is now at hand, and Christ waits to lead His church to greater triumphs than she has ever known.

F. B. MEYER, *JOHN THE BAPTIST*

NOVEMBER 28

My speech and my preaching were not with persuasive words of human wisdom, but in demonstration of the Spirit and of power.

1 CORINTHIANS 2:4

The commonest bush ablaze with the presence of God becomes a miracle of glory. Under its influence the feeble become as David, and the choice mighty "as the angel of the LORD." The ministry energized by the Holy Ghost is marked by aggressive evangelism, social revolution, and persecution. Holy Ghost preaching led to the burning of the books of the magic art, and it stirred up the opposition of those who trafficked in the ruin of the people.

Indifference to religion is impossible where the preacher is a flame of fire. To the church Pentecost brought light, power, joy. There came to each illumination of mind, assurance of heart, intensity of love, fullness of power, exuberance of joy. No one needed to ask if they had received the Holy Ghost. Fire is self-evident.

So is power! Even demons know the difference between the power of inspiration and the correctness of instruction. Secondhand gospels work no miracles. Uninspired devices end in defeat and shame. The only power that is adequate for Christian life and Christian work is the power of the Holy Ghost.

The work of God is not by might of man or by the power of men but by His Spirit. It is by Him that the truth convicts and converts, sanctifies and saves. The philosophies of men fail, but the Word of God in the demonstration of the Spirit prevails. Our wants are many and our faults innumerable, but they are all comprehended in our lack of the Holy Ghost. We need nothing but the fire.

SAMUEL CHADWICK, *THE WAY TO PENTECOST*

NOVEMBER 29

Epaphras . . . always laboring fervently for you in prayers . . .

COLOSSIANS 4:12

Christian people are too accustomed to look upon prayer as an occasional outward flow or burst of feeling and desire, but in Colossians 4:12 prayer is called work. After conveying the salutations of Epaphras, Paul describes him as "laboring fervently in prayer." The apostle James, evidently speaking from experience, also writes, "The effectual fervent prayer of a righteous man availeth much in its working." If the supplication of a righteous man avails much in its working, then prayer is a work, and a work which, in its accomplishment, is the expression of the will of God.

We find in the book of the Acts of the apostles that prayer was the practice of the early church. In the midst of all the blessing of the days following Pentecost, with their unction upon the spoken word, the apostles said, "We will give ourselves to prayer, and the ministry of the word." Prayer first, preaching second. They knew so well what the work of prayer meant in preparing the way for the utterance of the Word that they said, "We will give ourselves to prayer first"; and by this abandonment to prayer, the Word of the Lord ran and was glorified.

The temptation is to say, "There is so much to be done!" But can you find someone else to do your part in prayer? Your prayer is needed for the church, and if "we give ourselves to prayer," how great will be the work of binding the evil and loosing the good!

JESSIE PENN-LEWIS, *PRAYER AND EVANGELISM*

November 30

You are the branches.

John 15:5

What a simple thing it is to be a branch. The branch grows out of the vine or out of the tree, and there it lives and in due time bears fruit. It has no responsibility except just to receive nourishment. And if we only by the Holy Spirit knew our relationship to Jesus Christ, our work would be changed into the brightest and most heavenly thing upon earth. Instead of there ever being soul weariness or exhaustion, our work would be like a new experience, linking us to Jesus as nothing else can.

This blessed branch life is a life of absolute dependence. The branch has nothing; it depends upon the vine for everything. That is exactly what Christ wants you to understand. Christ wants that in all your work, the very foundation should be the simple, blessed consciousness: Christ must care for all.

And how does He fulfill the trust of that dependence? He does it by sending down the Holy Spirit—not now and then only as a special gift. The relation between the vine and the branches is such that hourly, daily, unceasingly there is the living connection maintained. The sap does not flow and then stop and then flow again; but from moment to moment, the sap flows from the vine to the branches.

Just so my Lord Jesus wants me to take that blessed position as a worker and, morning by morning and day by day and hour by hour and step by step, in every work I have to go out to, just to abide before Him in the simple, utter helplessness of one who knows nothing and is nothing and can do nothing.

Absolute dependence upon God is the secret of all power in work. The branch has nothing but what it gets from the vine, and you and I can have nothing but what we get from Jesus.

Andrew Murray, *Divine Healing*

December

Sharing Christ with the World

The Testimony of C. T. Studd

For six years C. T. Studd had been a backslider. He gave the reason himself: "Instead of going and telling others of the love of Christ, I was selfish and kept the knowledge to myself. The result was that gradually my love began to grow cold, and the love of the world began to come in. I spent six years in that unhappy backslidden state."

But as he rose to prominence in the cricket world, and especially while touring with the Test Team in Australia, there were two old ladies who set themselves to pray that he would be brought back to God. The answer came suddenly.

His brother G. B., to whom he was especially attached, was thought to be dying. C. T. was constantly at his bedside, and while sitting there, watching as he hovered between life and death, these thoughts came welling up in his mind: "Now what is all the popularity of the world worth to George? What is all the fame and flattery worth? What is it worth to possess all the riches in the world when a man comes to face eternity?" And a voice seemed to answer, "Vanity of vanities, all is vanity."

"All those things [C. T. went on] had become as nothing to my brother. He only cared about the Bible and the Lord Jesus Christ, and God taught me the same lesson. In His love and goodness He restored my brother to health, and as soon as I could get away I went to hear Mr. Moody. There the Lord met me again and restored to me the joy of His salvation. Still further, and what was better than all, He set me to work for Him; and I began to try and persuade my friends to read the gospel and to speak to them individually about their souls.

"I cannot tell you what joy it gave me to bring the first soul to the Lord Jesus Christ. I have tasted almost all the pleasures that this world can give. I do not suppose there is one that I have not experienced, but I can tell you that those pleasures were as nothing compared to the joy that the saving of that one soul gave me.

"I went on working for some time, and then the cricket season came round, and I thought I must go into the cricket field and get the men there to know the Lord Jesus. Formerly I had as much love for cricket as any man could have, but when the Lord Jesus came into my heart, I found that I had something infinitely better than cricket. My heart was no longer in the game; I wanted to win souls for the Lord. I knew that cricket would not last, and honor would not last, and nothing in this world would last—but it was worthwhile living for the world to come."

NORMAN GRUBB, *C. T. STUDD: CRICKETER AND PIONEER*

December 1

. . . to the end of the earth.

Acts 1:8

When our Lord ascended to heaven, He left us with His three last words. The very last was, "Ye shall be my witnesses unto the ends of the earth," or, as He had said a little before, "Go into all the world, and preach the gospel to every creature." With that one word in His heart, He sat down upon the throne expecting, longing that every child of man should learn to know Him and His love.

He has one thought—*the ends of the earth*—ever in His heart, and He is ever listening to the song of the redeemed from every people and nation and tongue. How Christ waits and longs for the time when His love can reach every soul in the world for which He Himself gave His blood and His life!

Shall we not take these last words of Christ afresh into our hearts? Do they not have a new meaning now? Has not the terrible indictment against the home churches—as to their not being fit or willing to undertake the glorious Christlike task of bringing God's love to every creature—pierced some hearts at least? The state of the church—its ignorance and its neglect and its rejection of the cross; its lack of the sense of holiness and crucifixion to the world; its neglect of the blessed truth of the Holy Spirit; its lack of loyalty to the Lord Jesus; its terrible weakness in prayer—do these not give some of us a burden that we cannot bear?

And shall we not turn away from all our own human devices and efforts to pay attention with new wholehearted devotion to the last words of the ascending Lord which the church has too long neglected? To take the words that live in Christ's heart and let them live in ours will be the secret of wonderful happiness and irresistible power.

Andrew Murray, *The State of the Church*

DECEMBER 2

If God so loved us, we also ought to love one another.

1 JOHN 4:11

The ends of the earth. All the world. Every creature. Is it possible for the ordinary Christian, in everyday life, to be so possessed by these words that, without effort or strain, they shall be the spontaneous expression of his inmost life? Thank God, it is possible—where the love of God and of Christ is shed abroad in the heart. Ordinary men and women have proved it by the intense devotion with which they could sacrifice everything to make the love of Jesus known to their fellow men.

The love with which Christ loves *us* is a love that takes in *the whole world.* We cannot take just enough of that love to suit ourselves and be indifferent to the needs of all others. That is the selfishness which results in the weak and unhappy life which so many Christians live. It is essential, if we truly wish to possess Christ and to fully enjoy Him, that we take in His love in all its fullness and that we commit ourselves to sharing that love and find our happiness in making that love known to those who are still ignorant of it.

When the church is stirred up into some measure of the experience of the abundant life in Christ Jesus, "the ends of the earth" will become its watchword.

ANDREW MURRAY, *THE STATE OF THE CHURCH*

December 3

Jesus Christ . . . gave Himself for us, that He might . . .
purify for Himself His own special people, zealous for good works.

Titus 2:13–14

In connection with the indifference to mission work that prevails today, it is often said that it is because of Christians being utterly oblivious to the claim Christ has upon them. At conversion the attention was directed to the one desire of salvation from punishment—and to God's grace to help them live a better personal life. The thought that Christ had purchased them as a people of His own to be zealous in good works was little realized.

It had never entered their minds that through them Christ might, from heaven, continue to carry on the work He had begun on earth. They knew that they ought to do good works in proof of their love, but few ever understood that these good works were service that Christ actually needed for the extension of His kingdom. They were not taught early that their whole life, with all their powers, was to be at His disposal for that purpose.

If there is to be any deep missionary revival, it will have to begin here. God's children who are striving to serve Him must get new and far deeper insight into the blessedness of this claim of Christ. Only thus can they tell of it and testify what it is that is the moving spring of their life. From them there can then pass on a power that will rouse Christians who have been living the selfish life to the new thought of the real blessedness of belonging to Christ. Only in this way will the world know that the love of God, in heavenly measure and power, dwells in them.

Andrew Murray, *The State of the Church*

December 4

Bondservants, be obedient to those who are your masters.

Ephesians 6:5

We Christians are called to bring to a hungry world the bread of life: the message of salvation, love, eternal life, riches immeasurable, and a peace that passes all understanding—God's plenty. But how can the world believe this message if they do not hear it, and how can they hear it if we do not tell them?

Peter said, "No, my Lord," but he had to learn that he could not say "no" if he said "my Lord" or "my Lord" if he said "no." We must be obedient and go where God tells us, whether it be a call to the mission field or a call to work for Him at home. He can use us only when we are in the place where He wants us to be. We dare not hoard the gospel secret but must herald forth His story to all.

When we look at ourselves, we are sure that we are unable to be used by the Lord; but when we look to Jesus, we become His mirrors. It is true that of itself a mirror does not do much; but when it is hung or placed in the right position, it does its job properly. It is very important, therefore, that we should be in the right position. And that position, for a Christian, is "looking unto Jesus, the author and finisher of our faith" (Heb. 12:2), for we have no light of ourselves.

A branch cannot bring forth fruit of itself; but however strong or weak it may be, it will bring forth much fruit if it is connected to the vine. We can storm the enemy's territory and win souls for Jesus—but only if we obey. "Follow Me"; then His promise takes effect: "I will make you fishers of men."

Corrie ten Boom, *Plenty for Everyone*

December 5

Go into all the world and preach the gospel to every creature.

Mark 16:15

It is of supreme importance that all Christians understand that this commission to convert the world is given to them by Christ individually. Everyone has been given the great responsibility to win as many souls as possible to Christ. This is the great privilege and the great duty of all the disciples of Christ.

There are many ways we can be a part of this work. But every one of us ought to possess this power so that whether we preach or pray or write or print or trade or travel or take care of children or administer the government of the state or whatever we do, our whole life and influence should be permeated with this power.

Christ says, "If any man believe in Me, out of his inmost being shall flow rivers of living water"—that is, a Christian influence having in it the element of power to impress the truth of Christ upon the hearts of men shall proceed from him. The great need of the church at present is the clear conviction that this commission to convert the world is given to each of Christ's disciples as his lifework.

Oh, for a conviction of the necessity of this gift of power and faith in the promise of Christ!

Charles Finney, *Power from On High*

December 6

Those who were scattered went everywhere preaching the word.

Acts 8:4

"Whole-time service"—the phrase has become common of late. But when was a Christian's work not whole-time service? Weaving or preaching (to mention no other way of using his days and nights), was not Saint Paul always in whole-time service?

Many have forgotten that unofficial witness bearing used to be the chief way by which the good news went around the world. I tell you, and you believe and receive and tell somebody else, and he tells others.

Frank, vital telling in ordinary language that the Lord Jesus Christ lives and loves, and can save and keep, and can be known like a real friend, and is a Master who gives real orders and strength to carry them out—think of the power that is in that! Can you wonder that the devil detests it?

Amy Carmichael, *Fragments That Remain*

DECEMBER 7

It is God who works in you.

PHILIPPIANS 2:13

I was converted at a young age and was a church member for forty years—and yet, as far as I know, I had never been the means by which a single soul had come into the kingdom.

I kept the Sabbath, prayed, read my Bible, took Communion, fasted, and often enjoyed the communion of the Spirit and the fellowship of Christians. I had spent forty years in the church and in nominal service and had not won a soul to Jesus. The realization of the years I had wasted was too much to bear. I decided to make up for it by devoting my life to doing good.

Now, however, was when the real struggle began! In my first attempt to share Christ with others, my own desire, or lack of desire, was revealed to me. In my second attempt, I had an even deeper feeling of how completely unfit I was to do this. Then came the temptation to stop and say, "I can't do anything for God; I have lived so long without using my gifts that they have grown rusty." Satan taunted me with the idea that I was too old to change and a fool to even try.

Then one day, for the first time in my life, I saw that it was Christ's job, not mine, to make my heart right and keep it right in the power of the Holy Spirit. Christ's job was to save; mine was to trust and to serve.

From then on I left the Savior's work to Him, in complete confidence that He would do it. I rejoiced that it was in good hands—so trustworthy, loving, and true—and I was not disappointed. I found it easy to wear the yoke and bear the cross, and God, in His love, has blessed me in the work He has given me to do.

ANONYMOUS CHRISTIAN IN WILLIAM BOARDMAN,
THE HIGHER CHRISTIAN LIFE

December 8

Not by might nor by power, but by My Spirit.

Zechariah 4:6

One thing for the missionary is inevitable. If he is to go forward in the face of seemingly insuperable obstacles which beset him, ushering in a new day for enslaved souls, there are definite spiritual requirements.

If he is to do what God expects of him and the church expects of him and what the heart-rending need of these to whom he is an ambassador of light requires of him, then *he must himself appropriate in an ever-deeper and fuller way the power of Christ.* He must himself be bound to that unconquerable Christ who all down the centuries has through His disciples achieved the impossible. He must get beyond a mere intellectual knowledge of the historical Christ and so entwine the tendrils of his spiritual nature in the eternal Christ that he imbibes a *divine life*!

The job he is attempting to do requires of him superhuman force. The merely human, however noble and strong and cultivated, will prove as insufficient and as inadequate as a handful of glowing coals would be for the dissipation of an arctic blizzard. He must transcend the purely natural and immerse himself in the supernatural. He must experience the power of the indwelling Christ and, dispossessed of his own life, become in an ever-fuller measure possessed of a divine life.

Only rivers of living water flowing from his innermost being—the promise which the Savior has made to His own—can make possible the renewal of life in those to whom he is sent.

F. J. Huegel, *Bone of His Bone*

December 9

I labored more abundantly than they all,
yet not I, but the grace of God which was with me.

1 Corinthians 15:10

It was not Paul but the grace of God that was with him and the power of God which worked through him. He worked, yet not he but Christ worked in him. Anything other than what Christ accomplished in him was wood, hay, and stubble of which he dared not take account.

He did not work *for* Christ but offered himself *to* Him without reserve that Christ might penetrate and irradiate the inmost recesses of his being and then, through its cleansed panes, go forth to illuminate the hearts of men. All his care was to purify himself that he might at all times be meet for the Master's use. His one desire was to yield himself to God and that his members might be used as weapons in the great conflict against the powers of hell.

This is, after all, the first and last lesson for the Christian worker. Let there be no thought of what you can do for God but all thought of what God can do through you. Nothing will make you so intense and ceaseless in your activity as this.

In all such there is the certainty of the gracious cooperation of the Holy Spirit. Whenever they stand up to speak, the Spirit of God bears witness to their words so that they come with His demonstration to prepared hearts. Wherever they bear witness, whether by lip or life, the results that accrue testify to the presence and power of a mightier than they. And whenever they cross the threshold of some new soul or home or land, men become aware that the gospel has come unto them not in word only but also in power and in the Holy Ghost and in much assurance. Be it ours so to live, testify, and minister that we may be workmen not needing to be ashamed, ambassadors through whom God Himself may beseech men to be reconciled.

F. B. Meyer, *Paul*

December 10

Without Me you can do nothing.

John 15:5

What? A church service on my ship? It would be the first in my life!" Then I reply with a smile, "It is high time you began, sir."

At the appointed time nobody appears. The cabin boy brings me a cup of coffee. "I don't want to hear that nonsense," he says. I never saw so empty a church—just a cup of coffee and myself. I am not at all on fire for the Lord; I go to my cabin and am very seasick. That is the only thing I can do during the whole week.

Sunday comes round again. I am feeling discouraged and ashamed. "Lord, I have now been on this ship for almost ten days, and I have done nothing to bring the gospel to all these men who may lose their souls for eternity. I am not worthy to do Your work." At that moment I find in my Bible a little piece of paper. On it is written,

> Cowardly, wayward, and weak, I change with the changing sky,
> Today so eager and strong, tomorrow not caring to try.
> But He never gives in, and we two shall win,
> Jesus and I.

Instantly I see it! Indeed, I am not worthy at all. The branch without the vine cannot produce fruit, but I can do all things through Christ who gives me strength. The strongest and the weakest branches are worth nothing without the vine.

I go up to the bridge. "Captain, it is Sunday. Can we have a church service?

"Again? In a church as empty as last week?" he asks teasingly.

"No, Captain. Not empty but full; and you must help me."

He does, and there are ten men in the mess room. When my sermon is finished, the cabin boy says, "It was not boring at all!"

Corrie ten Boom, *Not Good If Detached*

DECEMBER 11

I have you in my heart.

PHILIPPIANS 1:7

Oh, for a great outpouring of love from the church upon this poor, chilly world. We must learn to walk after the secret of Romans 5:5: "The love of God has been poured out in our hearts by the Holy Spirit who was given to us."

See this true warm affection: "I have you in my heart." This is better than having people on our *minds*—for our thoughts about them might be either full of assurance or full of anxiety, might be glad or sad. In the Philippians' case, Paul says, "It is right for me to think [well] of you"; but it would not be so in every instance. Again, this is better than merely having people on our *lips*—to be constantly talking about them, whether for praise or blame. Paul never tired of talking about his beloved converts; but then he did not stop at talking of them to others but talked about them to God.

It was Paul's habit, as it should be ours, to have people on our *hearts*. If so, then their weaknesses and shortcomings will be allowed for; then their daily needs will be provided for; then their constant welfare will be sought for; then their deepest blessings will be prayed for. There are some ministrations that are not possible to everybody, but the ministry of kindness, so fruitful for the harvest of the kingdom, is open to all.

GUY KING, *PHILIPPIANS: JOY WAY*

December 12

My food is to do the will of Him who sent Me.

John 4:34

Our Lord must needs go through Samaria. Our byway ministries often are more fruitful than our service on the main road. "Being wearied with his journey," our Lord sat on the well. It is a precious human touch.

Then follows a masterpiece of personal work. This woman, coming at noon to draw water, was a bad character. But our Lord saw a soul to save. We love to preach, but do we love the people to whom we preach? We still snub the Samaritans and need to read James 2:1–9.

Our Lord was found by the disciples in the midst of this strong interview, which was astounding to them. Our meat, like His, should be to *do the will of God.* The world says, "Four months, and then cometh harvest." We are not concerned for the lost. The Samaritans were likely coming across the fields even as our Lord spoke the words: "Lift up your eyes, and look on the fields; for they are white already to harvest." Oh, that we might see the lost today with the urgency desired by our Lord! Remember, "he that gathereth not with me scattereth abroad."

Vance Havner, *Reflections on the Gospels*

DECEMBER 13

He shall see the labor of His soul, and be satisfied.

ISAIAH 53:11

At the turn of the twentieth century, Dr. John R. Mott declared, "The most striking example of achievement on the home field, in the interest of foreign missions, is that of the Moravians. They have done more, in proportion to their numbers, than any other body of Christians." What was the incentive for foreign missionary work which has produced such results?

While acknowledging the supreme authority of the Great Commission, the Moravian brethren have always emphasized as their chief incentive the inspiring truth from Isaiah 53:10–12: making our Lord's suffering the spur to all their activity. From that prophecy they drew their missionary battle cry: *"To win for the Lamb that was slain the reward of His sufferings."*

In no other way can we so effectively bring the suffering Savior the reward of His passion as by missionary labor, whether we go ourselves or enable others to go. Get this burning thought of "personal love for the Savior who redeemed me" into the hearts of all Christians, and you have the most powerful incentive for missionary effort.

ANDREW MURRAY, *THE KEY TO THE MISSIONARY PROBLEM*

December 14

The love of Christ compels us.

2 Corinthians 5:14

If we consider Zinzendorf, whom God had so wonderfully prepared to train and guide the young Moravian church in the path of missions, we see at once what the great moving power was. What marked him above everything was a *tender, childlike, passionate love to our Lord Jesus.* Jesus Christ, the originator and inspirer of all mission work, possessed him. The dying love of the Lamb of God had won and filled his heart; the love which had brought Christ to die for sinners had come into his life; he could live for nothing else but to live and, if need be, die for them too.

When he took charge of the Moravians, that love, as his teaching and his hymns testify, was the one motive to which he appealed, the one power he trusted, the one object for which he sought to win their lives. The love of Christ did what teaching and argument and discipline, however necessary and fruitful, never could have done. It melted all into one body; it made all willing to be corrected and instructed; it made all long to put away everything that was sin; it inspired all with the desire to testify of Jesus; it made many ready to sacrifice all in making that love known to others and so make the heart of Jesus glad.

If the dying love of Christ were to take the place in our churches, in our own hearts and fellowship with each other which it had in theirs, which it has in God's heart and in Christ's redemption, would it not work a mighty change in our mission work?

Andrew Murray, *The Key to the Missionary Problem*

DECEMBER 15

All the days of his separation he shall be holy to the LORD.

NUMBERS 6:8

God's true missionary is a Nazirite, who has "made a special vow, the vow of one separated, to separate himself unto the LORD." This "special vow" meant total abstinence from certain things which were not wrong in themselves and which, to others, might be beneficial.

Let Dr. Roberts of Tientsin speak. He recognized it as his clear duty to give necessary time to every case so that he might do the best possible for each patient. "But then," he said, "I might easily go a step beyond that and yield to the temptation that comes to me as a professional man to study closely cases rarely seen in England, with a view to special proficiency. If, to do this, I must neglect Chinese study and spiritual work in the wards, life is not long enough for everything." So he preferred to fill up his time with work which seemed most likely to hasten the coming of his Master's kingdom, laying these possibilities of greater professional efficiency at the Lord's feet as freewill offerings of love.

He said he thought all Christians felt at times a longing to let others see that the followers of Jesus could successfully compete with others in various spheres of work. There was nothing absolutely wrong in this desire; yet he thought if we were only willing to give up for the Lord's sake possibilities of success in other fields than those which tended directly to the advancement of His kingdom, He would give us a very real sense of His approval and acceptance of such freewill offerings.

And so he "narrowed down" his life, bent the whole force of it to what "tended directly" to soul winning. But was earth the poorer to him, and is heaven the emptier to him, because he did so?

AMY CARMICHAEL, *GOD'S MISSIONARY*

December 16

I determined not to know anything among you except Jesus Christ and Him crucified.

1 Corinthians 2:2

Some years ago three missionaries in India, in three different mission stations, were, unknown to each other, seeking light upon the question of separation to God for service. They had been trained in various schools of thought, but each had learned that to show out the life of our Lord Jesus and to be a soul winner, one must live close to the Master, and each came to the mission field longing to win souls.

But they felt themselves befogged, for the traditions of the stations to which they had been appointed did not lean toward separation to the Lord and to His work as they, at least, understood it. There were things crowded into the life for which there had been no room before; there were things crowded out for which much room had been made in the days of earnest preparation for this very service—and they were bewildered and distressed.

Of the three, two gradually gave in, but they lost ground, and went on losing ground, till, startled at finding how much they had lost, they went back to the point from which they had started—the position they had been taught to take at home of simple untrammeled separation unto God.

We are to know *nothing* among any save Jesus Christ and Him crucified. For our calling, by its very nature, calls us apart from everything else; it has for its object nothing less than this: the showing of Christ, the living of Christ among those who do not know Him. The love of our God must shine through us unhindered if we would live to Him here. Surely whatever makes for holiness of life, for the clearing of the glass through which the light shines, *this is for us and nothing else.*

Amy Carmichael, *God's Missionary*

DECEMBER 17

He saved others; Himself He cannot save.

MARK 15:31

In saving others, we cannot save ourselves. I speak of saving others in the sense of winning them to Christ and God. If we are to rescue others, we must expect to spend and be spent. So long as life revolves around self—self-advancement, self-promotion, self-satisfaction—we are wretched and miserable. In service, we Christians must lose ourselves with the spirit of Paul: "Neither count I my life dear unto myself" (Acts 20:24).

Then there is the other side of the paradox: in losing our lives to save others, we most truly save ourselves. I am not here speaking of saving our souls; no good works can save the soul but faith in Christ only. But we can save our lives, our time, our talents as we spend them in saving others. The only time you ever save is the time you spend for others. The only money you ever save is the money you spend for others. Paul has it in mind when he bids the Ephesians redeem the time. Jesus has it in mind when He says to lay up treasure in heaven. Bread cast on the waters of service returns, even if after many days.

How slow men are to learn that in saving life, they lose it, but in losing it for Christ's sake, they save it. Mind you, Jesus said, "Whosoever will lose his life for my sake . . ."—not for one's own sake, not to be called a hero, not for conscience's sake—but for Christ's sake.

We do not save our lives *while* we save others but *because* we save others. We often lose our money, our health, our temporal fortunes. But if we leave all for His sake, we shall be compensated in this world—and in the world to come, receive eternal life.

VANCE HAVNER, *REFLECTIONS ON THE GOSPELS*

December 18

These all continued with one accord in prayer and supplication.

Acts 1:14

It was prayer that brought Pentecost—intense, continued, united prayer. That prayer did not cease until it was answered. Such prayer is not an easy thing.

Hudson Taylor said, "Redemptive work, soul-saving work, cannot be carried on without suffering. If we are simply to pray as a pleasant and enjoyable exercise and know nothing of watching in prayer and weariness in prayer, we shall not draw down the available blessing. We shall not sustain our missionaries, who are overwhelmed with the appalling darkness of heathenism; we shall not even sufficiently maintain the spiritual life of our own souls. We must serve God even to the point of suffering; each one must ask himself, 'To what degree, at what point, am I extending, by personal suffering, by personal self-denial even to the point of pain, the kingdom of Christ?'"

What was it that started those humble fishermen and women praying like that? It was this one thing: Jesus Christ had their whole heart. They had forsaken everything for Him. His love filled them and made them one with Him and with each other. The fellowship of love strengthened them. Their ascended Lord was everything to them; they couldn't help praying.

Let us pray in secret. Let us unite in love with others and pray without ceasing and watch unto prayer that, for the sake of His Son and a perishing world, God will restore His people to their first estate in the devotion and power and joy of Pentecost.

Andrew Murray, *The Key to the Missionary Problem*

DECEMBER 19

Stand fast in one spirit, with one mind striving together for the faith of the gospel.

PHILIPPIANS 1:27

It is a strategic operation when you and I seek to capture one soul by the gospel of Jesus Christ, for who but God Himself can tell what that one may be or do? Truly, Christian history justifies us in applying to this case the words of Isaiah 60:22: "A little one shall become a thousand." Besiege that one, strive for that one—that the gospel flag may be thus far advanced.

No one who has ever engaged in this godly maneuver will deny that it is *a strenuous front*—this work of soul-winning is no easy matter, for the enemy will concentrate all his forces to prevent, if he can, our taking the city. All that is implied in that word "striving" [in Philippians 1:27] will be required from us; all that lies behind the exhortation to "stand fast"—to stand your ground, in face of the foe's counterattacks—may be called for.

Such battles are not normally won simply by the happy little handing of a tract and the putting up of a simple little prayer—though God forbid that I should belittle the immense possibilities of a tract and a prayer. It is only the careless and almost flippant manner in which this is sometimes done that I am warning myself and you about. Do you remember that verse of Horatius Bonar's?

Go, labor on while it is day:
The world's dark night is hastening on;
Speed, speed thy work; cast sloth away;
It is not thus that souls are won.

All the modern hymnbooks have that last line thus; but in an earlier day we used to sing it differently, and as I feel sure was Dr. Bonar's original wording:

With strong, great wrestlings souls are won.

GUY KING, *PHILIPPIANS: JOY WAY*

December 20

When they saw the boldness of Peter and John . . . ,
they marveled. And they realized that they had been with Jesus.

Acts 4:13

The evangelist must be a man of God and not a child of man. He is not the salaried servant of the committee. He is a servant of Jesus Christ, with whom he has settled terms of agreement already. He knows no other Master. If death overtakes him on the battlefield, he knows such to be a special mark of Christ's favor, who has thus honored and promoted him sooner than he had any right to expect.

Too long have we been waiting for one another to begin! The time for waiting is past! The hour of God has struck! War is declared! In God's holy name let us arise and build! "The God of heaven, He will fight for us," as we for Him. We will not build on the sand but on the bedrock of the sayings of Christ, and the gates and minions of hell shall not prevail against us.

Should such men as we fear? Before the whole world, aye, before the sleepy, lukewarm, faithless, namby-pamby Christian world, we will dare to trust our God, we will venture our all for Him, we will live and we will die for Him; and we will do it with His joy unspeakable singing aloud in our hearts. We will a thousand times sooner die trusting only in our God than live trusting in man.

And when we come to this position, the battle is already won and the end of the glorious campaign in sight. We will have the real holiness of God, not the sickly stuff of talk and dainty words and pretty thoughts; we will have a masculine holiness, one of daring faith and works for Jesus Christ.

C. T. Studd in Norman Grubb,
C. T. Studd: Cricketer and Pioneer

DECEMBER 21

The message of the cross . . . is the power of God.

1 CORINTHIANS 1:18

Separation unto God in its true sense does not mean narrowness. Saint Paul seemed to think that being separated should have quite the opposite effect. "You find no narrowness in my love, but the narrowness is in your own" (2 Cor. 6:12, CH). And in order to get rid of their narrowness, he advises the Corinthian Christians to come out and be separate—to come out from the unclean ways of the world.

He strikes another note as well: "Where the Spirit of the Lord is, there is liberty." Liberty for what? Liberty to reflect as in a mirror the glory of the Lord. Here is the positive corollary to the "negativeness" of separation.

"But to win the world, we must meet it halfway," some may object. Must we? Who says so?

How can we most effectively touch our world for Christ? *The cross is the attraction.* Over and over again it has been proved that to those who will go straight on, unswerved by any argument or inducement to turn aside to more roundabout ways of access, opportunities no strategy or plan could have created are most freely and wonderfully given. Our only responsibility is not to miss them as they pass. To speak for our Lord then is not to write on sand. Blessed be the Lord our strength, strong to allure, mighty to save, who uses the very cross of shame to attract the wandering souls of men!

AMY CARMICHAEL, *GOD'S MISSIONARY*

December 22

Jesus . . . for the joy that was set before Him endured.

Hebrews 12:2

These days are full of thoughts of Him "who for the joy that was set before him endured." To the children, the manger is the chief thought; to us who are older (though we are children together at Christmastime), the cross always stands near the manger. It is the background to every picture—invisible but there.

In a book on early French life in Canada, I found a heroic story. It is that of a French missionary to the Indians of the dense forests of Huron who, inspired by the life of another, made a "vow of perpetual stability," which meant the giving of his whole life to those to whom he had been sent.

In speaking of this to one who found it hard to understand, he said—and the words are unforgettable—"Listen, my friend, no man can give himself heart and soul to *one thing* while in the back of his mind he cherishes a desire, a secret hope, for something very different. You know that even in worldly affairs nothing worthwhile is accomplished except by that last sacrifice, the giving of oneself altogether and finally."

Christ my Master beckoneth,
Christ my Lord, the Crucified;
He thus calléd reckoneth
All the world as nought beside.
Show me not imagined loss—
I see His Cross.

Amy Carmichael, *Edges of His Ways*

December 23

. . . that the love with which You loved Me may be in them.

John 17:26

O Father, help, lest our poor love refuse
For our beloved the life that they would choose,
And in our fear of loss for them, or pain,
Forget eternal gain.

Teach us to pray. O Thou who didst not spare
Thine Own Belovéd, lead us on in prayer;
Purge from the earthly; give us love divine,
Father, like Thine, like Thine.

Last night, as I read in Saint John, I felt the force of our Lord's prayer that the love wherewith His Father loved Him may be in us. "O Father, help, lest our poor love refuse" puts that prayer into words, and I have often found it difficult to reach even that. This prayer of our Lord for us reaches infinitely further, for the love wherewith the Father loved Him caused Him to give that beloved One to suffering for the salvation of a lost world. This is very different from, and far surpasses, the love that only does not refuse that a beloved one shall suffer.

Christmastime is full of thoughts of the Father's giving; this thought will deepen all our thinking about it. What do we know of such love? What do I know of it? Am I prepared to give one whom I love to pain or to loss, as the Father gave, if only others may be blessed? This, nothing less, was what the love wherewith the Father loved the Son caused Him to do. It was this love and no other that our Lord prayed should be in us. Is it not a searching thought, a searching prayer?

Amy Carmichael, *Edges of His Ways*

DECEMBER 24

They . . . fell down and worshiped Him. And when they had opened their treasures, they presented gifts to Him: gold, frankincense, and myrrh.

MATTHEW 2:11

Matthew's is the Gospel of the King. "We are come to worship him," the wise men said, and thereby at the outset established what was His right. For worship is everything. The more we worship, the more reason will God give us to do so. Before we pray let us worship; in preaching let us worship; in everything lift up adoring hearts to Him. This is the church's work on earth today—to establish God's worship.

Unless we give it to Him, God will have no worship here in this world. Of course we must not neglect other service, but let us always give to worship the first place. The wise men opened to Him their treasures. How can we hold back anything? And what we offer must be incense, not perfume—incense that has to be wholly consumed on the altar of incense before its fragrance is released. That is true worship, and ours is the day when the Father seeks true worshipers.

WATCHMAN NEE, *A TABLE IN THE WILDERNESS*

DECEMBER 25

There was no room for them in the inn.

LUKE 2:7

As Christmas day brings us around to the blessed story of the Savior's birth, it reminds us of a circumstance connected with that event which still is timely in its application. When Joseph and Mary came to Bethlehem, they were forced to put up in a stable, "because there was no room for them in the inn."

Today amid this commercialized Christmas, this overworked headache of expensive giving, God's great gift—the first Christmas gift—stands often unrecognized. It is easy enough to sing Christmas carols and put on pageants, the tribute of our lips, but how many of us honestly face Christ Himself and His challenge of discipleship at any cost? There is room for many things today, room even for much *about* Jesus—but is there room for *Him*?

Let it be observed that so far as we know, this innkeeper may not have been unkind or discourteous to Joseph and Mary. I don't read that he drove them away when they came to him. He may have been very polite and even expressed his regrets—but just the same, there was no room for them. So today most people turn down the Lord because they are preoccupied. They have nothing against Him; they may even speak well of Him. But there is no room—their hearts and homes are filled with other things.

What other guests do you have in your heart and home that shut out Jesus? For certainly the reason there is no room is because there are others in His place. Is there anybody or anything in all this universe important enough to take His place? I beg of you, on this Christmas day, do not make of it a hollow mockery by paying a wordy tribute to the Christ while you refuse Him your heart.

VANCE HAVNER, *REFLECTIONS ON THE GOSPELS*

DECEMBER 26

As the Father loved Me, I also have loved you; abide in My love.

JOHN 15:9

There is nothing that more deeply searches a man than the habit of speaking to individuals about the love of God. We cannot do it unless we are in living union with Him. Nothing so tests the soul. It is easy to preach a sermon when the inner life is out of fellowship with God, because you can preach your ideals or avenge on others the sins of which you are inwardly conscious. But to speak to another about Christ involves that there should be an absolutely clear sky between the speaker and the Lord of whom he speaks.

Does it seem difficult to have always a full heart? Verily, it is difficult—and impossible, unless the secret has been acquired of abiding always in the love of God, of keeping the entire nature open to the Holy Spirit, and of nourishing the inward strength by daily meditation on the truth. We must close our senses to the sounds and sights around us that our soul may open to the unseen and eternal. We must have deep and personal fellowship with the Father and the Son by the Holy Ghost. We must live at first hand on the great essentials of our faith.

Then, as the vine sap arises from the root, its throb and pulse will be irresistible in our behavior and testimony. We shall speak true things about Jesus Christ. Our theme will be evermore the inexhaustible one of Christ—Christ, only Christ—not primarily the doctrine about Him or the benefits accruing from fellowship with Him but Himself.

F. B. MEYER, *JOHN THE BAPTIST*

DECEMBER 27

It pleased God . . . to reveal His Son in me, that I might preach Him.

GALATIANS 1:15-16

Missionary advance depends upon spiritual life. Evangelical orthodoxy is powerless in itself to spread the gospel. Unimpeachable Protestant teaching in the pulpit and the plainest of gospel declaration in the church services may be seen in combination with entire neglect of the Lord's Great Commission. But if the Holy Ghost Himself stirs the hearts and enlightens the eyes, then the conversion of the unconverted becomes a matter of anxious concern.

The new experience of what Christ has done for *oneself* leads to a larger trust in what He can do for *others*. This gives a point and a courage in testifying of Him, which brings a new tone into a person's preaching or speaking. Christ becomes more distinctly the center of all thought and all work and at the same time the source, the subject, the strength of all our witness. With this the claim of Christ and His service upon our devotion and loyalty and entire surrender becomes clearer. It is seen that entire consecration, which at conversion was hardly understood, is both our simple duty and our highest privilege. And work for Christ, or rather a life wholly given up to live for Him and for the souls He loves, becomes the unceasing aim of the liberated soul.

Lead men to the deliverance there is in Christ. Lead them from the half-hearted, worldly life in which they have lived back to the "first love" of a personal attachment and devotion to the living, loving Christ. Then they will see that there is no life worth living but of devotion to His kingdom.

ANDREW MURRAY, *THE KEY TO THE MISSIONARY PROBLEM*

December 28

How beautiful are the feet of those who preach the gospel of peace, who bring glad tidings of good things!

Romans 10:15

From the viewpoint of heaven, there is nothing on the earth more lovely than the bearing of the name of Jesus Christ into the needy world when the bearer is one "who loves and knows." The work may have, and probably will have, very little of the rainbow of romance about it. It will often lead the worker into the most difficult and trying circumstances. He will often be tempted to think the journey too great for him and long to let his tired and heavy feet rest forever. But his Lord is saying of him all the while, "How fair the feet!"

Man is to be saved through a personal "calling upon His name." And for that "calling" there is need of personal believing. And for that believing there is need of personal hearing. And for that hearing God does not speak from the sky or send visible angels up and down the earth but commands His church, His children, to go and tell.

Nothing can be stronger and surer than the practical logic of this passage. The need of the world, it says to us, is not mere relief or social progress. It is salvation. It is pardon, acceptance, holiness, and heaven. It is God; it is Christ. The work is to be done now, in the name of Jesus Christ and *by* His name. And His name, in order to be known, has to be announced and explained. And that work is to be done by those who already know it, or it will not be done at all. There is no other method of evangelization.

H. C. G. Moule, *The Epistle to the Romans*

December 29

We are ambassadors for Christ, as though God were pleading through us.

2 Corinthians 5:20

The Lord Jesus Christ is the author and leader of missions. Whoever stands right with Him and abides in Him will be ready to know and do His will. It is simply a matter of *being near enough to Him to hear His voice and so devoted to Him and His love as to be ready to do all His will.* Christ's whole relation to each of us is an intensely personal one. He loved me and gave Himself for me. My relation to Him is an entirely personal one. He gave Himself a ransom for me, and I am His, to live for Him and His glory.

You have been redeemed to be the witnesses and messengers of Christ's love. To fit you for it, His love has been given you and shed abroad in your heart. As He loves you, He loves the whole world. He wants those who know it to tell those who don't know it. His love to you and to them, your love to Him and to them, call you to do it. It is your highest privilege; it will be your highest happiness and perfection.

Andrew Murray, *The Key to the Missionary Problem*

December 30

. . . not as pleasing men, but God who tests our hearts.

1 Thessalonians 2:4

Paul bent his strength to save men, and for this he was prepared to make any sacrifice. He was equally careful to the very last to institute and organize little Christian communities, which were absolutely necessary to conserve and develop the life that had been implanted. But all such purposes were subordinated to that which he announced in his earliest epistle: "not as pleasing men, but God, who tests our hearts" (1 Thess. 2:4). It mattered comparatively little what were the outward results of his endeavors or what men might say or do so long as he had the testimony shed through his heart that it pleased God.

We cannot forget that the passion of Christ's heart, during His earthly ministry, was to glorify His Father; and there was a similar passion in the heart of Paul to glorify the Son. To the end of his ministry, that purpose grew even stronger. It was always his earnest expectation and hope that in nothing he should be ashamed but that as always, so then, Christ should be magnified in his body, whether by life or death.

Would that this also were our single aim! We are apt to set ourselves on the accomplishment of purposes which, though good in themselves, fall short of the best; and when we do not succeed in them—when the revival does not ensue or hosts of souls are not converted or the church does not heed—we are apt to write hard things against ourselves and God; whereas if we simply sought the good pleasure and glory of our Master, we should discover that we succeed amid apparent failure and are more than conquerors when fleeing for our lives.

F. B. Meyer, *Paul*

December 31

Why was this fragrant oil wasted?

Mark 14:4

When once our eyes have been opened to the real worth of our Lord Jesus, nothing is too good for Him.

I believe that in that Day we shall all love Him as we have never done now but yet that it will be more blessed for those who have poured out their all upon the Lord today. When we see Him face to face, I trust that we shall all break and pour out everything for Him. But for us the question above all questions is, what am I doing to the Lord *today*?

Have our eyes been opened to see the preciousness of the One whom we are serving? Have we come to see that nothing less than the dearest, the costliest, the most precious is fit for Him? Have we recognized that working for the poor, working for the benefit of the world, working for the souls of men and for the eternal good of the sinner—all these so necessary and valuable things—are right only if they are in their place? In themselves, as things apart, they are as nothing compared with work that is done to the Lord.

The idea of waste only comes when we underestimate the worth of our Lord. The whole question is, how precious is He to us now? When He is really precious to our souls, nothing will be too good, nothing too costly for Him. Everything we have, our dearest, our most priceless treasure we shall pour out upon Him.

Of Mary the Lord said, "She hath done what she could." She had lavished on Him all she had. And the Lord will not be satisfied with anything less from us than that we too should have done "what we could."

Watchman Nee, *The Normal Christian Life*

BIOGRAPHICAL SKETCHES AND DEVOTIONAL INDEX

Paul Billheimer (1897-1984)

Paul E. Billheimer attended Houghton College in Houghton, New York, and Taylor University in Upland, Indiana, and he graduated from Marion College in Marion, Indiana, in 1923. He and his wife were married for sixty-three years and raised three children. They began a tent ministry in Anderson, Indiana, in 1936 that grew to include a Bible institute, a Christian high school, a Christian day school and, in 1957, a Christian television station. Billheimer wrote a number of books, including *Don't Waste Your Sorrows*, *Love Covers*, *Destined to Overcome*, and *Destined for the Throne*. He believed that the greatest tragedy in the history of the church was the sin of disunity. While holding fast to historic Christian doctrine, he reminded Christians that fellowship is based on common spiritual parentage and that unity of heart must take precedence over secondary matters. The thesis of most of his books is that the bride of Christ is in on-the-job training for her eternal destiny through prayer and overcoming.

William Boardman (1810-1886)

After a period of skepticism as a young man, William E. Boardman was dramatically saved. He began studying for the ministry, but the temptation of riches soon drew him back to his business career. A series of financial setbacks and the influence of his godly wife led him to recommit his life to Christ. The realization that Christ could be trusted for his sanctification as well as his salvation led him to write *The Higher Christian*

Life in 1858, which became an immediate bestseller. He went on to write several other books and began an international speaking ministry. His meetings in England were the beginnings of the well-known Keswick Convention, and he became a leader of that movement. Boardman's ministry continued until his death.

January testimony	*The Higher Christian Life*, 45–46
February testimony	*The Higher Christian Life*, 21–24
February 13	*The Higher Christian Life*, 121–23
May 5	*The Higher Christian Life*, 78, 82
May 6	*The Higher Christian Life*, 86
May 23	*The Higher Christian Life*, 66–67
June 12	*The Higher Christian Life*, 76–77
November 21	*The Higher Christian Life*, 134
December 7	*The Higher Christian Life*, 137–39

Amy Carmichael (1867–1951)
Amy Wilson Carmichael was the eldest daughter of a large Christ-centered family in Millisle, Ireland. She was impressed at an early age that "nothing is important but that which is eternal." This understanding proved to be a foundation for her service to the Lord, which began among the mill workers of Ireland while she was still in her teen years. Moving to England in 1889, Amy ministered to women in the Manchester slums and also became involved with the Keswick Convention. During these years "came a word [she] could not escape and dared not resist," and in 1892 Amy became Keswick's first missionary appointee. Although leaving her family was painful, she followed God's call and served briefly in Japan and then in Ceylon, finally settling in India, where she began her ministry to children in 1895. The Dohnavur Fellowship, the family that developed from her work, was devoted to saving children from lives of temple service. Amy wrote over thirty biographical and devotional books, many of which are considered classics. Injured and bedridden for the last twenty years of her life, she remained in India until her death.

January 9	*Whispers of His Power*, 10
March 6	*Thou Givest . . . They Gather*, 201–2
March 13	*Candles in the Dark*, 91 and *Mountain Breezes*, 232

Samuel Chadwick (1840–1932)
As the young pastor of a self-satisfied English congregation in the 1880s, Samuel Chadwick was so frustrated over his lack of power in the pulpit that he collected his sermons in a pile and set fire to them. The result was immediate: the Holy Spirit fell on him. The new vitality in his preaching was evident in his very next sermon, at which seven people came to Christ. Within a few years his reputation had grown to the point that the chapel was full a half hour before the service, and police had to be called in to control the crowds. He served as editor of the *Joyful News* magazine for twenty-seven years, and in his forties he became a tutor in biblical and theological studies at Cliff College, a Wesleyan-Methodist

training school for preachers. In his final years as principal of Cliff College, he wrote his most well-known book, *The Way to Pentecost*, which was being printed when he died.

June 8	*The Way to Pentecost*, 113–15
June 29	*The Way to Pentecost*, 115–17
July 23	*The Way to Pentecost*, 124
July 24	*The Way to Pentecost*, 98–99
August 4	*The Path of Prayer*, 67–68
August 11	*The Path of Prayer*, 65–66
August 16	*The Path of Prayer*, 63–64
October testimony	*The Path of Prayer*, 7–10
October 1	*The Path of Prayer*, 21–22
October 2	*The Path of Prayer*, 27–28
October 8	*The Path of Prayer*, 70–72, 74
November 18	*The Way to Pentecost*, 89–91
November 23	*The Way to Pentecost*, 91–92
November 24	*The Way to Pentecost*, 86–87
November 28	*The Way to Pentecost*, 27

Leona Choy (1925–present)
Leona Choy was born in Cedar Rapids, Iowa, and in her early teens surrendered her life to Christ and began to prepare for full-time Christian service. A graduate of Wheaton College in Illinois, Leona served with her late husband, Ted Choy, in mission, church, and educational work in Hong Kong, Singapore, China, and the United States. Cofounder of Ambassadors for Christ, Inc., a campus ministry among Chinese university students and scholars, her quarter century of work was administrative and editorial. Leona has authored, edited, or collaborated on more than thirty books. Her profound interest in and extensive research into Andrew Murray and his ministry has given her a unique ability to present a faithful and readable contemporizing of Murray's writings. Leona lives in the Shenandoah Valley and continues to write both books and blog posts, which you can find on her website at leonachoy.com.

July 5	*Andrew Murray: The Authorized Biography*, 183–84
July 16	*Andrew Murray: The Authorized Biography*, 181–82

Charles Finney (1792–1875)

Often called America's foremost revivalist, Charles Grandison Finney was a major leader of the Second Great Awakening in America, which had a great impact on the social history of the United States. Born in Warren, Connecticut, to a family of farmers, Finney never attended college, but his six-foot, three-inch stature; piercing eyes; musical skill; and leadership abilities gained him recognition in his community. He studied to become a lawyer, but after a dramatic conversion experience and baptism in the Holy Spirit, he resigned from his law office to preach the gospel. He moved to New York City in 1832, where he pastored the Chatham Street Chapel, and he later founded and pastored the Broadway Tabernacle. In addition to becoming a popular Christian evangelist, Finney was involved with the abolitionist movement and frequently denounced slavery from the pulpit. In 1835 he moved to Ohio, where he would become a professor at and later the president of Oberlin College. Finney died in Oberlin due to a heart ailment.

Norman Grubb (1895–1993)

Norman Page Grubb was born in London, the son of an Anglican vicar. He joined the British Army as a lieutenant in World War I. After the war he went to Trinity College, Cambridge, where he had the vision for Inter-Varsity Fellowship (now UCCF: The Christian Unions), whose goal was the sharing of the Christian message with other students. Later he married Pauline Studd, daughter of the famous British cricketer and missionary to Africa C. T. Studd. Grubb left for the Belgian Congo with Pauline in 1920 to follow in the footsteps of his father-in-law. While there he was struck by the words of Galatians 2:20:

"I am crucified with Christ: nevertheless, I live; yet not I, but Christ liveth in me" (KJV). This message was to become central to his philosophy. Before C. T. Studd's death in 1931, Norman and Pauline returned to England, where they ran the mission from its London headquarters. Under Norman's leadership and direction, the mission flourished and became known as the Worldwide Evangelization Crusade (now WEC International). Retiring in 1965, Grubb moved to the U.S. and spent his remaining years traveling and sharing the message of "Christ in me." He died at WEC's U.S. headquarters in Fort Washington, Pennsylvania, at the age of ninety-eight.

January 6	*Rees Howells: Intercessor*, 29–30
February 21	*Continuous Revival*, 30–33
May testimony	*C. T. Studd: Cricketer and Pioneer*, 45–46
June 10	*Rees Howells: Intercessor*, 124
June 16	*Continuous Revival*, 25–27
July 14	*Continuous Revival*, 11, 13–15
July 27	*Rees Howells: Intercessor*, 47–50
August 9	*Rees Howells: Intercessor*, 70–71
September 30	*C. T. Studd: Cricketer and Pioneer*, 184–86
October 13	*Rees Howells: Intercessor*, 33–34
November 7	*C. T. Studd: Cricketer and Pioneer*, 35–36
December testimony	*C. T. Studd: Cricketer and Pioneer*, 33–34
December 20	*C. T. Studd: Cricketer and Pioneer*, 120–21

Vance Havner (1901–1986)
Dr. Vance Havner was a pastor, itinerant evangelist, conference speaker, and revivalist. Born in Jugtown, North Carolina, his upbringing and early education were rural. He later attended Catawba College, Wake Forest University, and Moody Bible Institute but in many ways was largely self-taught. Havner authored nearly forty books during his ministry. One of his best known, *Though I Walk Through the Valley*, was written after the death of his wife, Sara, and has brought comfort to many. His unique style has impacted thousands of God's people through the years. Known for his pithy one-liners that have found their way into thousands of books and sermons, he is considered by many to be the most-quoted preacher of the twentieth century.

Roy Hession (1908–1992)

Dr. Roy Hession was one of the most effective Christian evangelists in post-World War II Britain, especially among young people. Born in London, he was educated at Aldenham School, where his introduction to religion led him to expect "anything but boredom" from God. He accepted Jesus in 1926 while on a Christian holiday camp. After working for Barings, the merchant bank, for ten years, he committed himself to full-time preaching. In later years Roy, together with Dr. Joe Church, ministered to many churches and conferences in Europe, Brazil, Indonesia, North America, and Africa. He was also involved for more than forty years in organizing Christian holiday conferences for family groups in the United Kingdom. In 1967 he lost his first wife, Revel, in a tragic road accident. He later married Pamela. Roy Hession is remembered for his infectious enthusiasm and humor but above all for his unwavering stand on the principles of repentance and grace that were so precious to him.

March 25	*Our Nearest Kinsman*, 33–34, 48–49
March 27	*Our Nearest Kinsman*, 84–85
March 28	*Our Nearest Kinsman*, 16
July 7	*Be Filled Now*, 37–40
October 11	*The Calvary Road*, 16–17
October 20	*The Calvary Road*, 11–12
October 21	*The Calvary Road*, 25–26
October 22	*The Calvary Road*, 19–22
October 28	*Be Filled Now*, 39
November testimony	*The Calvary Road*, 12–14
November 16	*When I Saw Him*, 15–16, 18–20, 22, 29

Evan Hopkins (1837–1918)
Evan Henry Hopkins was born in Colombia, South America (then called New Grenada), where his father was working as a civil engineer. In 1848 his family returned to England, moving again several years later to Melbourne, Australia. Hopkins attended the College of Chemistry in Melbourne and later the Government School of Mines, intending to pursue a scientific career. But while conducting geological research in south England, he was brought to Christ through the witness of a coastguardsman. His salvation changed the course of his life's purpose, and Hopkins left science to prepare for ministry at King's College, London. During his years of training he became involved in evangelistic work. At age twenty-eight he was ordained a deacon in St. Paul's Cathedral and a year later received his priest's orders. In 1870, following his marriage to Isabella Sarah Kitchin, he became first vicar of Holy Trinity in Richmond and maintained this work for thirty years. A crisis of faith occurred in his life in 1873, when he was led to believe God for full sanctification through faith. Hopkins began to speak at holiness conventions, testifying to the power of God for holy living. From this he was led into the work for which he is best known, that of teaching and expounding God's Word at the Keswick Conventions. He was a leader at the well-known convention, maintaining his strong involvement from Keswick's earliest days in 1875 until a few years before his death.

March 1	*The Law of Liberty in the Spiritual Life*, 121–23
March 3	*The Law of Liberty in the Spiritual Life*, 113, 115

March 4	*The Law of Liberty in the Spiritual Life*, 117
March 7	*The Law of Liberty in the Spiritual Life*, 26–29, 31–32
March 10	*The Law of Liberty in the Spiritual Life*, 115–16
April 1	*The Law of Liberty in the Spiritual Life*, 43–44
April 3	*The Law of Liberty in the Spiritual Life*, 17–18, 20–21
April 5	*The Law of Liberty in the Spiritual Life*, 44–45, 48
April 7	*The Law of Liberty in the Spiritual Life*, 111–12

F. J. Huegel (1889–1971)
Reared in a Christian home, Frederick Julius Huegel's brilliant mind led him to stray in philosophy. At the University of Wisconsin, he was converted while reading F. W. Farrar's *Life of Christ*. Huegel ministered within the Christian Church and then, in World War I, served as chaplain to the American Expeditionary Force in France. Following the war he was a missionary to Mexico; he ministered there for twenty-five years. He taught on the faculty of Union Theological Seminary in Mexico City and had a remarkable evangelistic ministry in the prisons of Mexico. In the anguish of a great trial, the Lord showed him the centrality of the cross as the means of victory. He also acknowledged a great debt to the teaching of Jessie Penn-Lewis. A prolific writer and well-traveled speaker, Huegel was known on both sides of the Atlantic for his preaching on the cross and the victorious life.

February 1	*Bone of His Bone*, 23–24
February 6	*Bone of His Bone*, 11–14, 16–17
February 8	*Bone of His Bone*, 29–30
February 9	*Bone of His Bone*, 59–60
April testimony	*Bone of His Bone*, 99–103
December 8	*Bone of His Bone*, 7–8

J. H. Jowett (1864–1923)
John Henry Jowett was born in 1864 in Halifax, England. Raised by Christian parents, he loved to read from an early age. He intended to study law, but his Sunday school teacher influenced him toward the ministry. After receiving training in Edinburgh and Oxford, Jowett became pastor of St. James Congregational Church in Newcastle-upon-Tyne and later pastored

Carr's Lane Congregational Church in Birmingham, where he published several books and founded the Digbeth Institute to minister to the poor. In 1909 he spoke at D. L. Moody's Northfield Conference in America; while there, he was invited to pastor the Fifth Presbyterian Church in New York City. He declined, but after a third invitation from the church, he accepted and assumed the pastorate in 1911. A lover of words and precise expression, Jowett brought his fully written sermons with him when he preached, yet due to his clarity and depth of knowledge, people lined up around the block to hear him speak. His preaching touched hearts, for he focused on the grace and beauty of the gospel, which he called the "wooing note." Jowett returned to England in 1917 to succeed G. Campbell Morgan as pastor of Westminster Chapel in London. Upon his death at the age of sixty, Jowett's friend and fellow preacher J. D. Jones said, "The mightiest preacher of us all has been taken."

September 17	In Jessie Penn-Lewis, *The Story of Job*, 228

Guy King (?–1956)
A lifelong bachelor, Canon Guy H. King was a clergyman of the Church of England, greatly beloved in the parishes he served and by a much wider circle of evangelical Christians of all denominations. He had engaged in secular business for a short while before studying for ordination, and this gave him understanding of the workday life of ordinary people. For many years he was a leader of the Crusaders Christian Youth Movement (now Urban Saints) and editor of its magazine. A diligent Bible student, his gift of opening the Word to the person in the pew was greatly appreciated by adults and children at the renowned Keswick Convention. His weekly Bible studies at Christ Church in Beckenham, London, where he served as vicar for twenty-one years until his death, enjoyed a large attendance, including many from other churches. His several books are based on these expositions.

January 5	*Philippians: Joy Way*, 14
February 17	*Colossians: True Life in Christ*, 73–74
April 23	*Colossians: True Life in Christ*, 80–81
May 7	*II Timothy: To My Son*, 34–36
July 21	*James: A Belief That Behaves*, 87
September 28	*Philippians: Joy Way*, 61
October 6	*I John: The Fellowship*, 117–18

October 14	*I John: The Fellowship*, 16–17
October 15	*II Timothy: To My Son*, 27–28
October 16	*I Timothy: A Leader Led*, 51–52, 54
October 29	*I Timothy: A Leader Led*, 55–56
November 1	*II Timothy: To My Son*, 133–35
November 13	*I Timothy: A Leader Led*, 44
November 25	*Colossians: True Life in Christ*, 48–49
December 11	*Philippians: Joy Way*, 26–27
December 19	*Philippians: Joy Way*, 55–56

Angus Kinnear (1912–2002)

Angus Ian Kinnear was born in Woolwich, London. After qualifying as a medical doctor from St. Bartholomew's Hospital in London, he went to India, where he served first for ten years with Amy Carmichael at the Dohnavur Hospital. He then worked as medical superintendent of the Christian Medical College Hospital in Vellore. After returning to England, in 1961 Kinnear started as a general practitioner at Herne Hill in south London. He was concerned about contemporary social issues and sought to help others through continuing education and through writing. From London he also carried on publishing work, primarily translating the works of Watchman Nee into English as well as writing Nee's biography. Kinnear, at the request of his patients, worked far beyond retirement age. Even during his final battle with leukemia, he continued to exhibit concern for others. He was known for his gentleness, his sense of fun, and his deep Christian faith.

February 11	*Against the Tide: The Story of Watchman Nee*, 126–27
March testimony	*Against the Tide: The Story of Watchman Nee*, 99–100

William Law (1686–1761)

William Law was an influential eighteenth-century author of devotional works and controversial essays. Ordained and elected fellow of Emmanuel College, Cambridge, in 1711, he forfeited his fellowship and all prospects of advancement in the Church of England because of his refusal to take oaths of allegiance to the English king. Denied the opportunity to preach,

Law did his preaching through his writings, becoming one of the most eminent English writers on practical divinity in the eighteenth century. He was a genuine mystic in a worldly and rationalistic age and is best known for the book *A Serious Call to a Devout and Holy Life.* Although he did not agree with all Law's teachings, Andrew Murray was so impressed by Law's works that he republished many of them. In his preface to *The Power of the Spirit*, a compilation of Law's writings, Murray wrote, "I do not know where to find anywhere else the same clear and powerful statement of the truth which the Church needs at the present day. . . . I ask the help of all who learn to value the book to bring it to the notice of those who preach the gospel" (London: James Nisbet, 1896). *The Power of the Spirit* has been recompiled and contemporized by Dave Hunt.

February 26	*The Power of the Spirit*, 17–18
May 26	*The Power of the Spirit*, 22–24
July 29	*The Power of the Spirit*, 67–68
November 20	*The Power of the Spirit*, 28–29

J. C. Metcalfe (1896–1997)

John Christian Metcalfe was born in the village of Newbottle near Banbury, Northamptonshire. Brought up in the Church of England, he planned to enter the Anglican ministry, but because of World War I, he instead became an officer, earning the Military Cross in the Battle of the Somme. Injured and sent home, one night he gave his heart and life to the Lord Jesus at a gospel hall. Metcalfe became a newspaper journalist but soon left newspaper work to enter evangelical ministry. He pastored several small churches and ran a small but successful Bible school in outer London. During this time he met Jessie Penn-Lewis and wrote articles for the *Overcomer* magazine, a publication of the Overcomer Trust. (The trust was started in 1909 by Penn-Lewis to provide Christian workers with material on the centrality of the cross of Christ; its magazine is still sent worldwide three times yearly.) During World War II, Metcalfe rejoined the army and served in England; after the war he returned to the Overcomer Trust, this time as leader and editor. He served in this way for forty years, traveling extensively in England and abroad and writing many books. He died shortly before his 101st birthday.

November 17	*Molded by the Cross*, 31–33, 39–40, 42

F. B. Meyer (1847–1929)
Frederick Brotherton Meyer was a contemporary and friend of D. L. Moody. He was a greatly loved Baptist pastor and evangelist in England whose pastorates included Victoria Road Church and Melbourne Hall in Leicester and Regent's Park Chapel and Christ Church in London. Born in London and raised in a Christian home, he attended Brighton College and graduated from the University of London in 1869. He studied theology at Regent's Park College. Meyer was involved in ministry and inner-city mission work on both sides of the Atlantic. He is said to have brought about the closing of hundreds of saloons and brothels. He was also a regular preacher at the Keswick Convention. Meyer wrote more than forty books, including Christian biographies and devotional commentaries on the Bible, many of which remain in print today. Besides pastoring, writing, doing social work, and speaking at conventions, Meyer made evangelistic tours to South Africa, Asia, the United States, and Canada. He had great influence upon such giants of the faith as Charles H. Spurgeon and J. Wilbur Chapman. It was Spurgeon who said, "Meyer preaches as a man who has seen God *Face to Face*."

May 18	*Moses*, 74
May 19	*Tried by Fire: Exposition of 1 Peter*, 38–39
May 24	*Paul*, 80
May 25	*Jeremiah*, 124
May 27	*Abraham*, 30–31
May 28	*Abraham*, 42–43
May 31	*Joshua*, 155
June 1	*Tried by Fire: Exposition of 1 Peter*, 49
June 3	*Joseph*, 137–39
June 15	*Joshua*, 149–51
June 26	*Tried by Fire: Exposition of 1 Peter*, 27–28
June 30	*Paul*, 81–82
July 10	*Peter*, 203–4
July 11	*Elijah*, 43–44
July 12	*Joshua*, 25–26
July 31	*Joshua*, 156
August 1	*Jeremiah*, 82–83
August 2	*Jeremiah*, 82–83
August 6	*Moses*, 120–21
August 7	*Elijah*, 46–47
August 23	*Jeremiah*, 83–84
August 24	*Elijah*, 31–33
August 25	*David*, 107–8
August 26	*Joseph*, 149
September 1	*Joshua*, 127–28
September 9	*Israel*, 124–25
September 11	*Jeremiah*, 67–68
September 13	*Tried by Fire: Exposition of 1 Peter*, 33–34
September 14	*Israel*, 124–26
September 21	*Tried by Fire: Exposition of 1 Peter*, 199, 203
September 27	*David*, 50–52
October 3	*Christ in Isaiah*, 84–86
October 4	*Elijah*, 94–95
November 2	*Joseph*, 135–36
November 4	*Joseph*, 60–61
November 10	*Abraham*, 15–16
November 14	*Jeremiah*, 101–2
November 19	*Elijah*, 185, 187–88

November 27	*John the Baptist*, 201-2
December 9	*Paul*, 169-71
December 26	*John the Baptist*, 187-89
December 30	*Paul*, 163-64

H. C. G. Moule (1841-1920)

Handley Carr Glyn Moule was the youngest of eight sons of the vicar of Fordington, Dorchester, in England. He was educated at home with his brothers prior to attending university at Cambridge, where he excelled in his studies and graduated in 1864. After a series of church and academic posts, he became the first principal of Ridley Hall, Cambridge, filling this position from 1881 to 1899. He then held the post of Norrisian Professor of Divinity at the University of Cambridge until his appointment as Bishop of Durham in 1901. Moule was active in the higher-life movement and was closely associated with the Keswick Convention. Although he was a profound scholar, he could speak and write for ordinary people. He wrote many hymns and poems; his works include expositions and commentaries on nearly all the epistles as well as books on devotion and a down-to-earth work on theology, *Outlines of Christian Doctrine*. He is buried in St. Cuthbert's Cemetery, Durham.

January 3	*Colossian and Philemon Studies*, 17, 105-6, 108
January 21	*The Second Epistle to the Corinthians*, 69-70
April 2	*The Epistle to the Romans*, 133
April 8	*Colossian and Philemon Studies*, 68-69
April 18	*Ephesian Studies*, 115
April 19	*Colossian and Philemon Studies*, 122-23
April 22	*The Epistle to the Romans*, 35-37
April 24	*Ephesian Studies*, 113-14
May 2	*Ephesian Studies*, 97
May 29	*Ephesian Studies*, 98
June 11	*Colossian and Philemon Studies*, 113-14
June 13	*Philippian Studies*, 78
June 27	*The Epistle to the Romans*, 180-81
June 28	*The Epistle to the Romans*, 157-58
August 17	*Philippian Studies*, 148, 150

September 2	*The Second Epistle to the Corinthians*, 73-74
September 12	*The Second Epistle to the Corinthians*, 182-83
September 29	*Ephesian Studies*, 224-26
December 28	*The Epistle to the Romans*, 219-21

Andrew Murray (1828-1917)
Andrew Murray went from being a discouraged young minister to becoming one of the best-loved writers on the deeper Christian life. One of four children born to a Dutch Reformed minister, Murray was raised in Graaff-Reinet, South Africa. At the age of nine, he was sent with his older brother to Aberdeen, Scotland, to receive a formal education. In 1845 both received their master's degrees from Aberdeen University and went on to Utrecht University in Holland to pursue theological training, where in 1848 they were ordained. After three years of study in Holland, Andrew returned to South Africa as a minister and missionary. His first appointment was to Bloemfontein, and in 1860 he accepted a call to Cape Colony and began writing numerous devotional books, many of which continue to transform lives today. Murray laid great emphasis on a theme to which many of his books are devoted: the deeper Christian life. He defined this simply as God's desire and commitment to reveal Himself more fully to those who would seek Him. The last twelve years of his life were devoted to speaking at conventions and evangelistic meetings in the U.S., Canada, England, Ireland, Scotland, Holland, and South Africa.

January 1	*The Lord's Table*, 111-12
January 7	*The Lord's Table*, 116-17
January 12	*The Spiritual Life*, 16-17
January 18	*Divine Healing*, 133-34
January 20	*Absolute Surrender*, 141-42
January 23	*Secrets of Intercession and Prayer* (*The Secret of the Abiding Presence*, Day 10)
January 27	*Let Us Draw Near*, 42-44, 46
January 28	*The Two Covenants*, 15-16
January 30	*Let Us Draw Near*, 12, 15-17
January 31	*The Two Covenants*, 31
February 16	*Divine Healing*, 131-32

February 23	*Waiting on God*, 16–17
February 24	*The State of the Church*, 46–47
February 25	*The Inner Chamber*, 74–75
March 15	*Divine Healing*, 134–35
March 19	*The Lord's Table*, 29–31
March 23	*The Lord's Table*, 31–32
April 9	*Abide in Christ*, 29–31
April 17	*Abide in Christ*, 111–12
April 20	*Abide in Christ*, 35–36
April 26	*Abide in Christ*, 79–80
April 28	*Secrets of Intercession and Prayer* (*The Secret of the Abiding Presence*, Day 5)
April 29	*Humility*, 19–21
May 3	*The Power of the Blood of the Cross* (*The Blood of the Cross*, 27–28)
May 4	*The Power of the Blood of the Cross* (*The Blood of the Cross*, 66–67)
May 21	*The Key to the Missionary Problem*, 58–59
May 30	*The Power of the Blood of the Cross* (*The Blood of the Cross*, 22–24)
June 2	*The Spiritual Life*, 169
June 18	*Divine Healing*, 129–30
June 22	*The Lord's Table*, 116
June 23	*The Power of the Blood of the Cross* (*The Blood of the Cross*, 62)
June 25	*Absolute Surrender*, 109–11
July 2	*The Full Blessing of Pentecost*, 14, 18–19
July 3	*Absolute Surrender*, 119–22
July 9	*Absolute Surrender*, 55–56
July 13	*Secrets of Intercession and Prayer* (*The Secret of the Abiding Presence*, Day 25)
July 19	*Absolute Surrender*, 126–27
July 20	*The Full Blessing of Pentecost*, 24–25
July 22	*The Full Blessing of Pentecost*, 26–27
July 25	*Absolute Surrender*, 97–98
July 26	*Let Us Draw Near*, 87–91
August 3	*The Inner Chamber*, 10
August 5	*The Inner Chamber*, 14–15

August 8	*The Lord's Table*, 7-8
August 12	*The Spiritual Life*, 89, 92
August 19	*Waiting on God*, 32-33
August 22	*Waiting on God*, 44
August 27	*Waiting on God*, 56-57
August 28	*Waiting on God*, 91-92
August 31	*The Lord's Table*, 20-22
October 31	*The State of the Church*, 67-68
November 26	*The State of the Church*, 85-86
November 30	*Divine Healing*, 137-39
December 1	*The State of the Church*, 49-52
December 2	*The State of the Church*, 52-53
December 3	*The State of the Church*, 75-76
December 13	*The Key to the Missionary Problem*, 33-34
December 14	*The Key to the Missionary Problem*, 46-47
December 18	*The Key to the Missionary Problem*, 90-91
December 27	*The Key to the Missionary Problem*, 60, 62, 64
December 29	*The Key to the Missionary Problem*, 100-101

Watchman Nee (1903-1972)
Watchman Nee was a noted Chinese Bible teacher and Christian leader. He began his preaching ministry while still a university student. From 1923 to 1950, Nee founded two hundred churches. Starting as small groups meeting in rented houses, these self-supporting congregations became strong spiritually and grew rapidly, continuing to develop after China's Cultural Revolution. As a teacher, Nee concentrated on deepening spiritual life through intensive training in the Word of God. His rich spoken ministry influenced many lives, and his literature ministry was created from a large number of his sermons, resulting in the publication of more than fifty books in English alone. Through these printed pages, Nee's impact continues to be felt today. Nee was arrested in 1952 and found guilty of false charges; he was imprisoned until his death twenty years later.

January 2	*A Table in the Wilderness*, 8
January 4	*A Table in the Wilderness*, 20-21
January 10	*A Table in the Wilderness*, 36
January 11	*What Shall This Man Do?* 26-27

Jessie Penn-Lewis (1861–1927)

Mrs. Jessie Penn-Lewis was a Welsh evangelical speaker and author whose ministry took her to Russia, Scandinavia, Canada, the U.S., and India. Physically frail but spiritually robust, she had a dynamic message that stressed the centrality of the cross of Christ in the life and experience of the Christian. Her own spiritual journey was influenced by the works of Andrew Murray, and she frequently quoted him in her own writings. Penn-Lewis was present during the Welsh revival of 1904–1905, and later in her ministry she spoke on the platform of the Keswick Convention. Her writings include more than twenty books, which have blessed readers for decades.

March 11	*The Cross of Calvary*, 60–62
March 12	*Dying to Live*, 44–45, 48–49
March 20	*Communion with God*, 16–17
March 21	*Fruitful Living (Much Fruit)*, 70–71
April 6	*Power for Service*, 42, 45–46, 49
April 10	*The Cross: The Touchstone of Faith*, 28–29
April 14	*The Centrality of the Cross*, 80–82
April 16	*The Cross of Calvary*, 42–45
April 21	*The Cross of Calvary*, 67–70
May 10	*The Conquest of Canaan*, 12–13
May 13	*The Story of Job*, 234–35
May 15	*Face to Face*, 20–21
June 4	*The Centrality of the Cross*, 109–10
June 7	*The Centrality of the Cross*, 53, 58–59
June 19	*The Story of Job*, 20–21
July 1	*The Work of the Holy Spirit*, 8–11, 13
July 8	*Communion with God*, 37–38, 43–44
July 15	*The Cross of Calvary*, 86–87
August 10	*Prayer and Evangelism*, 28–29
August 15	*Face to Face*, 7–9
September 4	*The Story of Job*, 32–34
September 10	*Prayer and Evangelism*, 15
September 17	*The Story of Job*, 228
September 25	*Life in the Spirit*, 17, 19–20
October 24	*The Awakening in Wales*, 31–34, 39
November 3	*Face to Face*, 26–27, 29
November 5	*Fruitful Living (Much Fruit)*, 83–87
November 6	*Fruitful Living (Much Fruit)*, 89–90
November 8	*Fruitful Living (Abandonment to the Spirit)*, 50–51
November 11	*Face to Face*, 32–33
November 12	*Fruitful Living (Abandonment to the Spirit)*, 18–20
November 29	*Prayer and Evangelism*, 7, 9–10

Hannah Whitall Smith (1832–1911)

Hannah Whitall Smith, born in Philadelphia, came from a long line of Quakers. After her marriage, she and her husband, Robert Pearsall Smith, also a Quaker, came to know Christ as Savior. Hungry to grow spiritually, they were influenced by the Plymouth Brethren, Methodist revivalists, and particularly William Boardman, who wrote *The Higher Christian Life*. In the 1870s Hannah and Robert became conference speakers in the holiness movement and were well received at the burgeoning Broadlands Conference in England. Sadly, their ministry was cut short in 1875 due to questionable moral behavior by Robert. Although their early years in ministry were marked by a sound biblical focus on life in Christ, both Hannah and Robert later wandered into theological error. Nonetheless, Smith's well-known classic *The Christian's Secret of a Happy Life*, written during her early years of ministry and loved by many still today, speaks powerfully of the abundant life in Christ through faith in the promises of God.

John Charles Pollock (1923–2012)

Reverend Dr. John Charles Pollock was a Cambridge-educated clergyman who became Billy Graham's authorized biographer early in the evangelist's career. He wrote many other Christian biographies over the ensuing decades, including the life stories of John Wesley, George Whitefield, Hudson Taylor, William Wilberforce, and John Newton. Dr. Pollock, along with the Reverend John Stott, sat on the board of the John Newton Project, which is dedicated to "the transformation of society through faith in Jesus Christ, using the life and works of John Newton as one great example." He lived with his wife, Anne, in Devonshire, England.

Corrie ten Boom (1892–1983)

It is hard to overestimate the impact of the life of Corrie ten Boom. She and her family risked their lives by hiding Jews in occupied Holland during World War II. Arrested by the Gestapo and sent to Ravensbrück, the notorious Nazi concentration camp, she found for herself the victory that overcomes the world. After being miraculously released, Corrie began an international ministry of writing and speaking. Her extensive traveling to share Christ and counsel the hurting made her a worldwide witness, or, as she put it, a "tramp for the Lord." In her later years Corrie settled in California, continuing her ministry through writing, speaking, and hospitality. She suffered a series of strokes beginning in 1978; she was eventually left unable to speak, but her vibrant love for Christ continued to bless many. Corrie died on her ninety-first birthday.

January 17	*Plenty for Everyone*, 87–88
March 26	*Amazing Love*, 31
March 29	*Amazing Love*, 28–30
April 11	*Plenty for Everyone*, 132–33
June 17	*Plenty for Everyone*, 131
June 20	*Plenty for Everyone*, 129–30
June 24	*Amazing Love*, 54–55
July 6	*Plenty for Everyone*, 128–29
July 28	*Not Good If Detached*, 53–54
September 24	*Marching Orders for the End Battle*, 9–10
December 4	*Plenty for Everyone*, 13–14, 17
December 10	*Not Good If Detached*, 38–39

Charles Trumbull (1872–1941)

Charles G. Trumbull, a protégé of American theologian C. I. Scofield, was editor of the *Sunday School Times*, a respected Christian journal based in Philadelphia with a weekly circulation of more than 100,000 worldwide in the early 1900s. In his early ministry, he often struggled with his sense of failure to maintain a holy life. When he came to a new conception of Christ as one with the believer, his life and ministry were transformed. His testimony, found in his classic book *Victory in Christ* and published as a pamphlet entitled "The Life That Wins," was used to bring missionary Rosalind Goforth into an understanding of rest in Christ. Trumbull was one of the foremost promoters of the Keswick holiness movement and in 1913 helped found America's Keswick Conference Center in southern New Jersey. He is the uncle of Elisabeth Elliot, who wrote a number of books now considered classics, including *Through Gates of Splendor* and *Shadow of the Almighty*.

Arthur Wallis (1922–1988)
Arthur Wallis was an internationally known author and leader in what became known as the house-church movement in Great Britain. Born in Dublin, he was the younger son of Reginald Wallis, a well-known convention speaker and author of several Christian books. His father's death in 1940 precipitated a spiritual crisis for Arthur, and he sensed a call to full-time service, although it was not to be realized until after World War II. He served in the British Army in North Africa, Italy, and Macedonia, narrowly escaping death in a particular battle as one of only twenty survivors in a battalion of four hundred. After the war Arthur went into ministry, and in later life he served on a leadership team overseeing a family of more than thirty churches. He also devoted himself to a worldwide speaking and writing ministry. In 1956 CLC London published his first book, *In the Day of Thy Power*, a significant historical study of revivals and their purposes, distinctive features, and dynamics. He went on to author nine other books, including the classic bestseller *God's Chosen Fast*.

NOTES

Preface to the 2022 Edition

1. Vance Havner, *Playing Marbles with Diamonds and Other Messages for America* (Ada, MI: Baker, 1985).
2. Jim Cymbala, *Storm: Hearing Jesus for the Times We Live In* (Grand Rapids: Zondervan, 2014), 178.

Introduction

1. John Van Gelderen, "Keswick: A Good Word or a Bad One?" *Revival* magazine 5 (2006), posted on Grace Notebook, accessed August 9, 2022, https://gracenotebook.com/keswick-a-good-word-or-a-bad-one/. This article contains an excellent discussion on the biblically unfounded attacks against the Keswick movement, which does not teach sinless perfection, as some assert, but rather teaches a repudiation of self and a dependence on Christ for the holiness that Hebrews 12:14 teaches us to pursue. (See, for example, the entries in this book for February 14 and April 19, by Charles Trumbull and H. C. G. Moule, respectively.) As John Van Gelderen writes, "The heart of Keswick theology is accessing this Holy Life of Jesus by faith—nothing less, nothing more." See an updated and expanded three-part version of this article at Revival Focus, https://www.revivalfocus.org keswick-a-good-word-or-a-bad-one-part-one-historical-background-and-theology/.

Made in the USA
Las Vegas, NV
14 December 2022

62387969R00247